1980

BANGLADESH
THE TEST CASE OF DEVELOPMENT

BANGLADESH
THE TEST CASE
OF DEVELOPMENT

BY

JUST FAALAND

AND

J. R. PARKINSON

WESTVIEW PRESS · BOULDER · COLORADO

Copyright © 1976 in London, England
by Just Faaland and J. R. Parkinson

Published 1976 in London, England by C. Hurst & Co. (Publishers) Ltd.
Published 1976 in the United States of America by Westview Press, Inc.
  1898 Flatiron Court
  Boulder, Colorado 80301
  Frederick A. Praeger, Publisher and Editorial Director

Printed in Great Britain

Library of Congress Cataloging in Publication Data

Faaland, Just.
    Bangladesh : the test case of development.

    Includes index.
    1. Bangladesh--Economic conditions. I. Parkin-
son, John Richard, joint author. II. Title.
HC440.8.F3   330.9'549'205   76-851
ISBN 0-89158-546-X

CONTENTS

TABLES

UNITS AND MEASURES

In the text we have used a number of measures commonly employed in Bangladesh, but which may not be familiar to all foreign readers:

1 crore = 10 million
1 lakh = 100,000
1 maund = 82·2 lb
1 seer = 2·1 lb
1 bale = 400 lb
1 bigha = approximately one-third of an acre

The Taka replaced the Rupee as the name of the currency after Bangladesh was created. Its rate of exchange was fixed at approximately Taka 19 = £1 sterling until May 1975, when it was devalued to Taka 30 = £1.

PREFACE

It is over fifteen years since we were first concerned with the economy of Bangladesh (East Pakistan as it was then) in a professional capacity, that of advisers to the Pakistan Planning Commission located in Karachi. After that we visited Bangladesh from time to time and recently we spent about two years there from mid-1972 to mid-1974, returning again in December 1974 and in November 1975 for short visits to see how things were going. Over the years we have made many friends in Bangladesh and inevitably we feel personally involved in its problems. It is because of this that we have written this book. We refuse to accept the view of Mr. Kevin Rafferty, published in the *Financial Times* (6 June 1975), that Bangladesh is the end of the great development dream. A way must be found to improve the lot of those who live in Bangladesh and of the many more who will succeed them as one generation follows the next. We think that this can be done and that this belief is not just the result of our hearts leading our heads. We should be the first to admit, however, that it will be a very difficult task to mobilise the efforts needed in a constructive way.

We approach the task of developing Bangladesh as economists, reflecting our basic training, although we are well aware of the great complexities of the development process and that the transformations needed are even more social and political than economic in their nature. The problem is not so much discerning what needs to be done but knowing how to put things into effect and how to harness the activities of millions of people for their mutual benefit.

We hope that what we have written will throw some light on the very difficult problems facing the country and explain to those who do not know it well why it is difficult to see solutions to its plight. Only some aspects of development are examined; it is not our intention to give a comprehensive account of everything that could have a bearing on the economy but to concentrate on those aspects that we find of interest or importance. One of our central theses is that we do not think that Bangladesh will be able to progress at a satisfactory rate unless a concerted international effort is made to assist her and to provide large amounts of aid over a long period. The assistance that outsiders can give can be only of a limited nature but, for an economy as poor as that of Bangladesh, substantial aid is vital.

We make no claim to originality in what we say in this book, and inevitably we have drawn extensively on the common pool of knowledge and thought assembled by the many people who have studied the economy of Bangladesh. Our thinking and writing about Bangladesh has been influenced most of all by our Bangalee colleagues and friends over many years, particularly those first extraordinarily able members of the Bangladesh Planning Commission, Professors Mosharaff Hossain, Rehman Sobhan and Anisur Rahman and their brilliant Deputy Chairman Professor Nurul Islam; but our intellectual debt and appreciation of insights gained extends to many others within the Planning Commission and outside, Bangalees and foreigners. To everyone, whether mentioned by name or not, we should like to make our acknowledgements. The subject of Bangladesh is one of controversy and dispute; inevitably also one of emotion and attitude of mind to the unpredictable future. It is particularly pertinent to stress that we take full responsibility for the analysis and balance of argument and judgement presented in this book. For this reason we have abstained from discussing the text with our Bangalee and foreign colleagues in the Bangladesh Government and the World Bank with whom we had official working relationships during our stay in Bangladesh in 1972 to 1974.

Various chapters of the book were typed and retyped in Bergen and Nottingham by our able and patient secretaries Britt Pettersen, Yvonne Rogers and Sandra Coultan; to them and others who have assisted us in the production of the manuscript we wish to express our thanks.

The manuscript was sent to the publishers in February 1975. Since then much has happened. As the book has gone through the press we have been able to take some account of events during the year and to modify the text in some detail, but this has not been possible in all respects.

The prospects for aid to Bangladesh have improved during the year and now appear to be roughly in line with what we have suggested as necessary. In May 1975 the Taka was devalued by about 50 per cent (from Taka 19 to Taka 30 = £1); the section in the original manuscript in which we presented a strongly argued plea for devaluation has therefore been re-cast. International prices of some import commodities of importance to Bangladesh have fallen, the internal price inflation has been halted and by the summer the price of rice in the domestic market had come down from the very high level early in the year. Finally, and most important, the *aman* harvest at the end of the year will, from all reports, be very good compared to previous years.

These improvements give reason to hope that at long last the economy may have reached a stage at which real progress can begin. This prospect, however, may be threatened by continued political instability and turmoil following the assassination of Sheikh Mujibur

Rahman in mid-August and the week of the *coups* in early November 1975. On this we have nothing to say except to hope that stable and effective government, so much needed for development, can speedily be established.

CHAPTER I

FROM POVERTY TO PROGRESS?

With a population of only 10 million people life in Bangladesh could be very pleasant. Incomes could be high and most people could live out of the reach of flood and natural disaster. But the population is now 80 million and rising rapidly. Already for its size of population Bangladesh is the most densely populated country in the world and its position will almost certainly get worse, terribly worse, unless something is done or happens to check the natural increase in population.

It must be the fond hope of most educated people that man can control events and his own future. There is little to give credence to that view in the situation of Bangladesh. There can be little prospect of a spontaneous movement to reduce the increase in population and it is impossible to see how a much larger population can be given any prospect of attaining the type of living standards to which the Western world has become accustomed. Nature, not man, is in charge of the situation in Bangladesh.

The starting-point from which economic development must be attempted is unpromising. Income per head in 1972 was estimated at US$70. In terms of consumption this means a diet mainly of rice with very little to supplement it. In the famine of 1943, when $1\frac{1}{2}$ million died in Bengal, it was necessary to consider what tonnage of ships could be diverted from the transport of munitions to the carriage of food to India. The calculations of need were based on consumption of cereals of 1 lb. per head per day. The same basic calculations are made today, but the calculations are more often based on 15 oz. than 16 oz. a day; fractions of an ounce make a great deal of difference to the amount of imported food required by 80 million people—such fractions also make a great deal of difference to the daily lives of the population. A diet largely based on minimal amounts of rice, besides providing insufficient calories, is deficient in other ways. Rice contains less protein than wheat and there is inadequate consumption of pulses and animal products to supplement it. The most important source of protein is fish, but even so consumption amounts to only about 4 lb. per head per year and consumption of milk, another source of protein, to about 20 lb. per head per year. Over half the households in Bangladesh get too little protein. Fats are also scarce, average consumption of cooking oil amounts to about 5 lb. per year. A diet of rice is deficient in various vitamins which are not supplemented sufficiently by consumption of other foods; shortage of vitamin A in the diet is particularly serious. Inadequate nutrition leaves the way open for disease and combines to reduce the expectation of life. Child mortality is particularly high: about one-quarter of all children die before their fifth birthday; those that survive are smaller and lighter than they would be with better food.

With too little money available for food it is not surprising that few other consumption goods are available to remove the monotony of life. In 1969–70 the consumption of textiles was estimated at $7\frac{1}{2}$ yards per head; in the circumstances of 1972–3 this had dropped to 5 yards per head, and apparently has remained at that level since, well below the 9 yards that might be regarded as reasonably satisfactory in the circumstances of life in Bangladesh. For the men solace is traditionally given by tobacco. Consumption of cigarettes in 1969–70 was estimated to be about 265 *per capita* per year. This at least must have given the adult male some respite.

Other indications of the standard of living of the population tell the same story: about 300 petrol pumps, less than 20,000 private motor-cars, about 5,000 buses, about 70,000 motor vehicles in all, including motorcycles, less than 2,000 miles of railway, 50,000 telephones, 300,000 radio sets and 10,000 television sets. All the indices reveal a standard of living bearing little resemblance to that of Western countries and yet at the same time they show the anachronisms of the development process: the modern businesses with telephones, the favoured few with electric light and radio and television sets, the highly privileged with cars, contrasting as much with the impoverished landless labourer as the maharajahs of not so long ago.

Deprivation of the world's goods is not perhaps the most important aspect of the impoverishment of the people; in the long run the deprivation of access to the world's knowledge may be far more serious. Development will not proceed without a massive education effort. If anything, educational statistics overstate the educational effort that is being made. Some 80 per cent of the population is illiterate; it is said that 60 per cent of the primary age group of the population is enrolled in the schools but it is evident that the drop-out rate is such as to leave little permanent impact on the adult population.

Life in Bangladesh is, of course, very different from that of industrialised countries. There are a few large towns, and most people live in 65,000 small scattered villages of a few hundred to 1,000 people, in houses constructed mainly out of mud and bamboo. There may be a tube-well for the provision of drinking water but this is much more likely to be drawn from a tank or pond. Most of the villagers rely on cultivation for their subsistence but some have no land or too little to do this and earn what living they can by casual labour, while others follow subsidiary occupations such as weaving, handicraft, and fishing if they live near to rivers or the sea. Possessions are few; it is exceptional to have tables, chairs or cupboards, though half the households might have a bed, and earthenware cooking utensils abound. The village family is a very strong influence and arranged marriages are the custom. Few people travel much outside their village except to market; the women observe purdah and seldom leave their homes. New ideas have little influence and percolate only slowly; it is hard for all to see how life can be improved.

In the *World Bank Atlas*[1] only Rwanda was tentatively estimated to have a smaller *per capita* income than Bangladesh; another two countries were bracketed with it, but none of these has anything like the population of Bangladesh. Only Indonesia has a population larger than that of Bangladesh, and a *per capita* income not much greater; but Indonesia increased its *per capita* income by over 4 per cent per annum in the period 1965 to 1972 while *per capita* income in Bangladesh declined. Since then Indonesia has gained significantly from its new oil wealth and from improved terms of trade, while Bangladesh's relative position deteriorated markedly; war and its aftermath held back any increase in real income; population has continued to increase and real income to fall.

All this would not matter if Bangladesh were rich in natural resources and underpopulated, if it were effectively governed and if its social order and economic system were geared to growth, but none of these things obtain. The terrain, in relation to the number of people that inhabit it, is inhospitable and often hostile. It is dominated by mighty rivers which in depositing silt both form and flood the territory over which they flow; in the monsoon the rainfall is intense and unpredictable; the one certainty is that much of the land will be covered with water, and loss of life and interruption to production from flooding may be considerable. Even more dangerous are the cyclones which unpredictably can inundate vast areas of land and cause great damage and loss of life. The cyclone of 1970 killed 200,000 people and their animals, and devastated much agricultural land.

The years since 1971 have been a period of experiment with different styles of government. To begin with there was no con-

[1] Published in 1974.

stitution, and Sheikh Mujibur Rahman, who had led resistance to West Pakistani influence, assumed government with the backing of his Awami League supporters. When a new constitution was established, elections were held and the Sheikh was returned to power in a parliament that included only very few members of opposing parties. The imposition of a presidential system of government and dissolution of parliament (with its own consent) followed in January 1975. Overwhelming support and little in the way of effective opposition did not give rise to strong government, rather the reverse; little was done to come to grips with the administrative, economic and development problems facing the country.

The brutal assassination of Sheikh Mujibur Rahman in August 1975 and the subsequent *coups* and turmoil are evidence of political instability which may have unpredictable effects on the economy. The basic problems remain the same, as does the need for effective government to deal with them. Until a clear lead can be given by government, there is not much hope of improving the lot of the inhabitants of Bangladesh. In the last resort it is the efforts of Bangalees that will determine their economic and political future but a large amount of external assistance will be needed if Bangladesh is to succeed. In the future, as in the past, the outside world cannot fail to be affected by the misery of Bangladesh.

In the face of the devastation of the cyclone of 1970 the world showed its readiness to come to the aid of those suffering cataclysmic disaster. In the civil war of 1971, when refugees poured over the Indian border, the need to intervene in her affairs was manifest. During and after the War of Independence the United Nations through its Relief Operations, Dacca, and later through its Relief Office in Bangladesh, mobilised assistance on a large scale for Bangladesh. Once again the international community supplied substantial support to alleviate suffering caused by the 1974 floods. The long-drawn-out inability to improve the lot of the people and the need to remove the constant threat of starvation is not, however, a problem that the world feels compelled to solve. For Bangladesh, growing dependence on the rest of the world for food is a dangerous position and one which is bound to make it increasingly difficult to find the resources needed for development. A positive approach to the development of Bangladesh on the part of the international community is necessary. Trade *and* aid is still a valid slogan and the world has a responsibility for providing export opportunities for Bangladesh's jute; but this alone will not go very far in dealing with Bangladesh's problem, which is basically one of insufficient capacity to generate resources for development while maintaining minimum consumption levels.

Nothing short of a continuing massive injection of aid is likely in present circumstances to get the economy off the ground sufficiently quickly to give real impetus to the development effort. It is not easy to see how donor-countries can be persuaded to maintain an effort on the scale needed. Bangladesh is not a country of strategic importance to any but her immediate neighbours. Perhaps its only importance politically, lies in its availability as a possible test-bench of two opposing systems of development, collective and compulsive methods on the one hand, and a less fettered working of the private enterprise system on the other. It might be considered worthwhile by some countries to give aid to demonstrate the power of one or the other system, but it can scarcely be felt that large gains are likely to result from such an exercise, to Bangladesh or to potential contestants. If aid is to come for the development of Bangladesh it is more likely to be for economic reasons or on general humanitarian grounds. In the long run it is the latter that is important. Assistance from other countries must be seen as an endeavour to solve the world's most difficult problem of economic development. If the problem of Bangladesh can be solved, there can be reasonable confidence that less difficult problems of development can also be solved. It is in this sense that Bangladesh is to be regarded as the test case.

In what follows we try to assess what are the prospects for Bangladesh and what can be done to improve them. In Chapters III and IV we discuss what needs to be done to improve the management of the economy and to establish a basis from which development can take place. In Chapter V (on the assumption that the preconditions for development can be met) we try to form a judgement about the pace at which development may proceed and to examine the implications of it for investment, domestic resource mobilisation, aid, employment and consumption. The all-important question of population is examined in Chapter VI, and the remaining chapters of the book consider the prospects for growth in the agricultural and rural economy and in industrial production, and some of their implications for trade. But first, in Chapter II, we review the course of events up to the present time in the area that is now Bangladesh.

CHAPTER II

INDEPENDENCE: BEFORE AND AFTER

1. *A Quarter-century of Union with Pakistan*

The territory that is now called Bangladesh was established in 1947 when the British left India, and Pakistan was created as an independent country composed of two wings, West Pakistan, then centred on Karachi, and East Pakistan centred on Dacca. In most other ways there was no new beginning or sudden change for the mass of the inhabitants of East Pakistan. Their way of life is still much as it was a century or even two ago; village life has been little touched by the passage of events, and things have scarcely changed for the better since East Pakistan was first established more than a quarter of a century ago.

The union with West Pakistan was unhappy politically and economically; it might have been better to go it alone from the very beginning. Bangalee economists see the association with West Pakistan as a time of economic exploitation, in fact as a second colonial era. In this respect it is better documented than most. There can be little doubt that in the early years of Pakistan the financial resources of East Pakistan were diverted to the development of West Pakistan. This was possible because of the integrated nature of the two economies. The Central Government operated overall economic control, and the Regional Governments had very little say in the formation of economic policy; there was virtually no room for independent action by the East Pakistan Government. There was a common external tariff on imports from other countries but trade between the wings of the country was regarded as internal trade and no fiscal restraints were imposed upon it, although the quantity of goods that could be moved depended on the availability of transport and to some extent on government regulation. The use of a common currency was combined with freedom to move money from one wing to another. Earnings of West Pakistani business men in East Pakistan could be reinvested in West Pakistan and the proceeds of the export of jute and jute manufactures diverted to the development of other parts of Pakistan.

The devices by which the transfer of resources was accomplished were subtle and powerful.[1] They were possible because of the integrated nature of the economic system but how far they were deliberately contrived for the purpose is another matter on which judgement must be as much political as economic. Since the rupee was overvalued,[2] the rupee earnings of East Pakistan farmers from the export of jute were less than they would have been at an equilibrium rate; on the other hand, overvaluation favoured users of imported consumer goods and raw materials needed in manufacture, who were preponderantly located in West Pakistan.

The instruments of transfer of resources worked through the balance of payments. Up to 1962-3 East Pakistan had a surplus on its external balance of trade and although it imported more goods from West Pakistan than it exported to it, it often had an overall export surplus which went to benefit West Pakistan. West Pakistan had an overall deficit on foreign account which was partly financed by East Pakistan's export surplus and partly through aid. In those years when East Pakistan had an overall surplus on her foreign and domestic balance of payments (roughly until the end of the 1950s), West Pakistan not only effectively secured all the aid but used resources from East Pakistan as well. Subsequently, as East Pakistan's total trade moved into deficit, the transfer of resources was reduced, but East Pakistan continued to be deprived, if account is taken of the fact that it did not receive its fair share of the foreign aid that was given. The extent of the deprivation is difficult to measure with any precision. It depends, among other things, on the view taken of the rate of exchange that should be used for calculations of the transfer of resources, given that the rupee was overvalued, and also on what is regarded as a fair share of the foreign assistance that was forthcoming. The magnitude of the transfer of resources from 1947 to 1968/9 has been estimated by a panel of economists[3] on certain, possibly extreme, assumptions as approximating to a transfer of resources from East to West of Rupees 3,000 crores. This figure almost certainly represents the upper limit that can be assigned to this transfer. It is calculated in terms of effective exchange rates, which

[1] The way in which resources were transferred is described in detail in *Growth and Inequality*, edited by Keith Griffin and A. R. Khan, Macmillan, 1972.

[2] Estimates by A. I. Aminul Islam given in, "An Estimation of the Extent of Over-valuation of the Domestic Currency in Pakistan at the Official Rate of Exchange", *The Pakistan Development Review*, Spring 1970, p. 58, suggest that the over-valuation was considerable and often of the order of 100 per cent or more.

[3] *Reports of the Advisory Panels for the Fourth Five Year Plan*, Volume I, Planning Commission, Government of Pakistan, July 1970.

count foreign exchange transactions at about twice the number of rupees per dollar given by the official exchange rate. There is reason to doubt the analytical treatment of inter-wing trade in respect of exchange rates, and the assumption that aid should have been allocated on the basis of population is contestable, as the economists recognized. Nevertheless, there was a transfer of resources of considerable magnitude which arguably may be put between the limits of Rupees 1,500 to 3,000 crores. In terms of dollars the figure might range from 1,500 to 3,000 million.[4]

There is probably little point in attempting any more precise quantification; it suffices to say in general terms that if resources of the magnitude implied by the economists' calculations could have been used for development in East Pakistan it would have enabled the development effort to be stepped up quite considerably and to accelerate.

The movement of resources to West Pakistan was undoubtedly a factor in the break-away of East Pakistan from the West. It would be wrong to think that it was the only cause. By the end of the 1960s the flow of resources had been much reduced and the longer-term prospects might have been for a transfer of resources the other way. Pakistan has escaped the responsibility for the welfare of East Pakistan that it might have been expected to have assumed at a later stage. In certain respects, the transfer of resources that took place illustrates a perpetual problem of regional development by no means confined to Bangladesh and West Pakistan. The prospects for rapid economic development in the 1950s and 1960s were certainly vastly better for West than for East Pakistan. In some measure this could provide justification for concentrating on the former, but in terms of equity and even political wisdom it should have been accompanied by effective arrangements to ensure that the fruits of development were shared more equally between the wings. The injustice of failing to do so was all the more evident, because a substantial part of the scarce foreign exchange needed for the development effort came from the export of jute grown in East Pakistan. Even if adequate compensation had been arranged, the case for concentrating a high percentage of the combined development effort in West Pakistan is weak because what countries look for is not just an increase in income but a share in the productive investment and activities that bring the increase about. No country will willingly be left in the Stone Age so far as development is concerned, even if the resources for investment provided by it can be invested more profitably in

---

[4] The official exchange rate was about Rupees 4·76 to the dollar. The economists' calculations imply a rate more like Rupees 10.

terms of output elsewhere. These considerations aside, extreme dependence on others is hazardous, as Bangladesh has come to appreciate.

The transfer of resources from East to West has to be seen in the context of the very different standards of living enjoyed in the East and the West. This was a major theme of Mahbub-ul Haq[5] when he pointed out that regional incomes, which had been about 20 per cent higher in West than in East Pakistan at the beginning of the 1950s, were more like 30 per cent greater at the end of the decade. It was in the light of this that he sought to devise a strategy for increasing the rate of development of East Pakistan relative to that of the West. In fact the reverse occurred. By the end of the 1960s *per capita* income in West Pakistan was estimated to be up to twice that of East Pakistan. Such calculations can be regarded only as indicative of the margins involved, but there can be little doubt that development in West Pakistan completely outpaced that of East Pakistan.

To aggravate the situation further, much of the development effort carried out in the private industrial sector in East Pakistan was undertaken by West Pakistani businessmen. So development there enriched non-Bengalis, and this gave rise to considerable resentment. In a modern economy an influx of foreign capital may be welcomed together with the expertise that it brings. The rewards to capital may be low compared with the wages paid out in respect of the employment created. But in a poor undeveloped country the share of wages is often much smaller than in countries with a large supply of capital, and in conditions of near monopoly and protection, much of the advantage of development may go to capitalists and with it the opportunity further to expand their empire by reinvestment, or to salt capital away abroad. These effects are important both because they caused resentment and because they have a bearing on the unsettled question of the claims that Bangladesh is making on Pakistan in compensation for losses and in effect to secure some of the assets that previously were owned in common but now are in the hands of Pakistan.

In 1972, for the second time in twenty-five years, the people of East Bengal were faced with the necessity of adjusting their economy to a new economic order. The partition of India in 1947 severed the traditional ties with surrounding districts; it left the country with a structure of man-made communications unsuited to its new position and it forced structural adjustments to meet new patterns of trade. A quarter of a century later, severance of ties with Pakistan had

[5] *The Strategy of Economic Planning: a Case Study of Pakistan*, Oxford University Press, 1966.

similar effects for Bangladesh. New markets had to be found for products previously sent to Pakistan, new sources of supply had to be developed at a time when the machinery of government had to be established and new institutions built up. The gap left when the Pakistani owners of industrial and commercial establishments fled or were dispossessed had to be filled. This was a factor leading to the takeover and nationalisation of a large part of industry in Bangladesh, which might not have been attempted in the name of socialism if the structure of ownership had remained intact.

History written as a critique of economic exploitation of countries by colonialists (and that is how the association with Pakistan is frequently described by those engaged in the shaping of historical accounts) is far from the whole story. Bangladesh is a country presenting great natural obstacles to development. However much of the stagnation of the country may be blamed on the machinations of politicians or aspiring businessmen, there was evidence in the 1960s that absorptive capacity was severely limited. The Fourth Five Year Plan for the development of Pakistan (East and West) for the period 1970–5 estimated that investment in East Pakistan in the public sector would be only 70 per cent of the money value planned; in the private sector the shortfall was expected to be 50 per cent.[6] There were, of course, some special reasons, although implementation of plans in East Pakistan had always left much to be desired. Nevertheless performance was improving absolutely. By the end of the 1960s about 12–13 per cent of the GNP was being invested and as the development effort increased so did production, though not by enough materially to improve the situation.

In agriculture the output of rice (the all-important crop) showed an upward trend. In the 1950s it had been about $7\frac{1}{2}$ million tons a year, in the second half of the 1960s it was up to $10\frac{3}{4}$ million tons, more by double cropping than by an increase in yield. But it did not keep pace with the growth in population. Imports of foodgrains, partly from Pakistan and partly from abroad, increased from about $\frac{1}{2}$ million tons in the 1950s to about $1\frac{1}{4}$ million tons at the end of the 1960s.

Industrial development also proceeded. It centred mainly on jute textiles, but other ventures were undertaken with varying success. Inevitably some of them were not well conceived. The Chittagong steel plant has seldom produced at anywhere near its rated capacity; the oil refinery appears to have been designed to use types of crude oil not always easy to obtain and with an oil terminal that has

---

[6] *The Fourth Five Year Plan, 1970–75*, Planning Commission, Government of Pakistan, July 1970, p. 535.

TABLE II.1
PRODUCTION OF RICE

	Crop[7]			Annual averages in million tons
	Aus	*Aman*	*Boro*	*Total*
1960/1–1964/5	2·4	6·8	0·5	9·7
1965/6–1969/70	2·8	6·7	1·2	10·7
1970/1–1974/5	2·6	6·0	2·1	10·7

Sources: Statistical Digest of Bangladesh No, 8, 1972, Annual Plans and official estimates.

functioned badly; the assembly of motor-cars, while most efficiently managed, is very small by modern standards and must be regarded mainly as a training ground at present. Nevertheless, a foundation for industrial development was laid.

In a number of other respects the structure of industry was vulnerable. Many of the products made were sold in West Pakistan and enjoyed considerable protection as well as being tailored specifically for that market. One of the worst examples is that of the match industry which produced a poor product sold only on the Pakistan market. Protected markets are not always the advantage that they seem. The tea industry made large profits on the sale of tea mainly in West Pakistan at prices well above those ruling internationally, but soft living did not make for the most efficient cultivation of tea, and now that the tea gardens are facing international competition they find the going hard.

There was thus something to show for the years of independence after British rule, but not much. *Per capita* output is estimated to have risen in the early 1960s but to have fallen again between 1965 and 1971. The foundations for growth have still to be laid and it is still a matter for speculation whether new impetus can be given to development in the next few years after the major setback of war and all the difficulties of making a new-found independence really work.

[7] The *aman* crop is the main crop. Broadcast *aman* may be sown in March–May and grows more rapidly than the rise of the monsoon water, surviving drowning by floating on the surface. It is harvested in October–December. Transplanted *aman* is set in the field after the floodwater has receded. It is harvested in November–December. The *boro* crop is cultivated mainly during the dry season, November–May, and has to be irrigated. The *aus* crop is sown in March–April and harvested in June–August. Various combinations of the rice crops are possible and they can be combined with the cultivation of other crops and periods of fallow. The *aus* crop, in particular, uses land which can be often put down to jute, and the two are competitive in this respect.

2. *1971 War Damage*

The material damage caused by the war in 1971 was estimated to be of the order of $1,200 million.[8] Clearly such a figure cannot be regarded as a precise estimate; neither can it take account of many intangible costs, nor the effects of the war in delaying the recovery of production to normal levels. Included in the cost was the loss of agricultural output caused by the war, estimated at some $300 million, and while this had to be made good out of the contributions made in conjunction with the United Nations Relief Operations, it could be more quickly remedied than the damage to physical structures. Food apart, the damage to agricultural potential was rather small; the major effects were the loss of animals and damage to fishing equipment. Industrial damage was comparatively light as was that to postal services and telecommunications. The most critical form of damage affecting the recovery of the economy was that to transport facilities. Although the total cost of such damage was estimated at no more than $130 million and much of it was speedily repaired by army engineers, it was not until the end of 1973 that a fully functioning transport system could be said to have been restored, and there were still gaps to be filled even at that time.

Damage to housing was estimated to have amounted to about $200 million; this was mainly damage to bamboo huts, which in any case require frequent repair, and the effects on productive capacity were probably small though the costs of repair were real enough. Another major item, the effects of the war on education, included an important element for the rehabilitation of students and teaching staff; again the immediate effects of this on the ability of the country to produce were probably small.

The general impression given by a survey of the calculations of damage is that about half of it was to fixed physical investment likely to affect productive capacity. The rest took mainly the form of loss of food production, destruction of housing and rehabilitation requirements which could be put right fairly readily.

The situation could not have been righted at all speedily if it had not been for the efforts of the United Nations, which distributed food and mobilised assistance from many sources. Sheer organisational ability was an important and costly ingredient of this assistance and it was matched by financial assistance commensurate with the magnitude of the problem. Up to the end of August 1972, nearly $900 million had been committed, and by the end of the year this

[8] *A Survey of Damages and Repairs*, United Nations Relief Operation, Dacca, 1972.

had grown to $1,200 million, corresponding to the estimated amount of damage sustained. Thus the means were made available fully to make good wartime damage. Food aid, much of it coming from India, was speedily mobilised and in other respects the economy was operating with a semblance of normalcy by the middle of 1972, although transport facilities were still very inadequate, in spite of the United Nations efforts. A serious impediment to recovery was the slow resumption of the flow of imported goods needed to replenish the pipelines and get the economy going. In retrospect it seems that there was a failure to grasp either the need to provide immediately for current imports or even more the difficulties that would be experienced in establishing institutional arrangements to purchase imported goods and arrange for their delivery. Financial aid has to be utilised if it is to help.

By the end of 1973 it could be said that the problems of repair and reconstruction and rehabilitation were over in a considerable measure. The problems of learning to run the economy were beginning to override those stemming from the immediate aftermath of the war.

3. After Independence

Production and Prices. In the first year of Bangladesh's independence production of food was well below that of 1969-70 as may be seen in Table II.2. There was a succession of bad harvests in 1972-3 following an unsatisfactory monsoon. Conditions in 1973-4 and 1974-5 were much more favourable, although there was heavy flooding in the latter year. Good harvests notwithstanding, imports of foodgrains remained high, averaging 2 million tons a year. Even so, famine was not entirely averted.

While the initial imports of foodgrains in 1972 were almost entirely in the form of gifts, Bangladesh has had to move progressively to financing more of her requirements herself. In 1973-4 it appears that only about one-third of the imports of foodgrains were foreign financed. This drain on Bangladesh's resources is likely to continue. Agricultural output has been no more than maintained in recent years, and while there may be some reason to hope that a new advance is beginning, it cannot be expected to reduce dependence on grain imports at all rapidly. So long as this continues, Bangladesh will remain heavily dependent on foreign aid to sustain the economy and the development effort.

Industrial production contributes only 8 per cent to the gross domestic product. But the significance of the sector is much greater than this: it is a major export earner and producer of import

TABLE II.2

GROSS DOMESTIC PRODUCT OF BANGLADESH
(Values in $ million at 1972–3 prices)

	1969–70	1972–3	1973–4	1974–5 Preliminary estimates
Agriculture	3,980	3,403	3,788	3,713
Industry	535	412	473	467
Construction	297	215	93	220
Power and gas	15	18	32	33
Transport	300	300	327	327
Trade	483	439	490	491
Housing	287	295	303	312
Public administration	158	174	243	308
Banking and insurance	32	41	42	44
Professional and miscellaneous services	392	404	408	412
Total	6,479	5,702	6,200	6,325

Source: Official estimates.

substitutes, it has linkages with agricultural output and with trade and commerce, it provides employment and the opportunity for some of the population to gain experience in the use of modern techniques.

Table II.3 shows the progress that had been made by the fiscal year 1974–5 for certain key products. It will be seen from the table that by comparison with 1969–70, production has varied greatly from industry to industry. The performance of the jute manufacturing industry is critical and disappointing. High hopes were placed on the export of jute and its manufactures when the First Five Year Plan was drawn up, but the record to date provides very little encouragement for optimism about the prospects of the industry, and the position deteriorated in 1974–5. The output of cotton yarn is back to 1969–70 and that of cloth has exceeded it. The production of urea in 1972 to 1974 was much higher than before independence, because the plant at Ghorasal, based on natural gas, came on stream in 1972 with a capacity for the production of some 340,000 tons of urea per year. The subsequent destruction of the control room of the plant in September 1974 was a disaster causing considerable loss of output until production was restored in 1975. The engineering performance (not shown in the table) has varied, but there are encouraging signs in the growth of production of diesel engines and pumps; this is an area in which Bangladesh badly needs to develop her own production in support of agricultural operations.

TABLE II.3

PRODUCTION BY CERTAIN KEY INDUSTRIES

Industrial product	Unit	Annual Production				Capacity utilisation 1974-5 (estimated)
		1969-70	1972-3	1973-4	1974-5 (estimated)	
Jute textiles	Thousand tons	561	446	500	450	62
Cotton yarn	Million lb.	106	81	91	105	78
Cotton cloth	Million yards	60	58	79	94	70
Steel	Thousand tons	54	68	74	77	31
Newsprint	Thousand tons	35	27	27	33	66
Paper	Thousand tons	42	23	24	29	50
Sugar	Thousand tons	93	19	88	98	58
Cement	Thousand tons	53	31	51	135	35
Cigarettes	Million	17,786	10,879	11,895	14,900	23
Fertiliser urea	Thousand tons	94	207	274	n.a.	61[9]

Source: Based mainly on *Annual Plan for 1974-5*, Dacca, 1974 and *White Paper on Economic situation in Bangladesh*, Dacca, September 1975.

[9] Utilisation in 1973-4.

As Table II.3 shows, recovery of industrial production has some way to go. There is much unused capacity according to the official figures. To some extent this is the result of the previous establishment of units with capacity far beyond the ability of Bangladesh to pay for the imported inputs needed to keep them going, to some extent it is the direct result of continuing import stringency. The lesson for the future is that it is clearly undesirable to add to industrial capacity in general unless import of intermediate goods can be increased.

In total, the GDP in 1974–5 was still short of the 1969–70 level. The difference would have been greater if it had not been for the expansion of government services and banking and insurance: one may well question how valuable such contributions are at a time when the major need is for the increased output of commodities. In real terms the value of output of both agriculture and industry was at least 5 per cent lower in 1974–5 than in 1969–70; yet the population was nearly 15 per cent higher.

The short harvests of 1972–3, the shortage of imports and its effects on industrial production, the near doubling of import prices in two years from 1972/3 to 1974/5, and of course budgetary deficits, all combined to increase prices. Only the price of exports increased by relatively little on balance, which gave Bangladesh the worst of all worlds.

The price of rice, which in 1967–71 had been Taka 1·2 per seer, was double this by the middle of 1973. By the middle of 1974 it was Taka 4·2 and by the end of the year, as the effect of floods on the supply of rice made itself fully felt, the price of medium rice in Dacca rose to Takas 7·8 per seer. Other prices rose less but the increase was severe; by the end of 1974 consumer prices were about four times what they had been in 1969–70. Early in 1975 it became increasingly clear that the inflationary peak was past. Continued imports and better prospects for foodgrain production brought food prices down. By the summer of 1975 the price of medium rice in Dacca was back to about Taka 4·0 per seer.

Foreign Exchange Balance.   It is not only in natural calamity that Bangladesh has been unfortunate since Independence. The production of jute manufactures was resumed at an adequate level by the beginning of the fiscal year 1972/3; in that year exports, excluding invisibles, reached about $380 million and with a strong inflow of aid it was possible to import about $750 million[10] of goods while providing for net invisible payments and continuing to build up

---

[10] No reliable figures for imports are available; the estimate given is based on balance of payment figures and is somewhat lower than provisional estimates given in the Annual Plan for 1973–4.

reserves. In 1969–70 imports had amounted to about £380 million (when valued at exchange rates which take account of the value at international prices of goods received from Pakistan). In the intervening period, dollar prices of imports had probably increased by something of the order of one-third so that the volume of goods that could be afforded in 1972/3 was probably well above that which had sufficed to run the economy prewar. In fact, the volume of imports was totally inadequate in relation to the need to restock the economy, make good war damage and provide for a level of food imports that was nearly double that which had been customary on the average during the second half of the 1960s. In 1972 supplies of consumer goods, raw materials and spare parts were very short. The position might have been eased if it had been possible to utilise more of the aid that had been committed and which was in the pipeline, but there were both difficulties in getting agreement on the use of some kinds of aid and of arranging for the purchase of goods. A build-up of project aid was bound to occur simply because projects take time to prepare and to execute, but the delays in the use of commodity aid were also considerable, and in spite of all the difficulties should have been shortened.

Given time these difficulties might have been straightened out. But time was not on the side of Bangladesh. In the last quarter of 1972 import prices began to rise rapidly and to hit Bangladesh severely. The price of wheat in the United States rose from about $60 per ton to over $100 per ton in January of 1973 and to about $200 per ton by the end of that year. The price of other imports also increased markedly, culminating in the rise in oil prices in October and December 1973 which alone would have added about $100 million to the import bill if cuts in the quantities imported had not been made.

The First Five Year Plan of Bangladesh had been drawn up in an optimistic vein and with the intention of convincing the politicians of what might be accomplished if determined efforts were made to get on with the job of development. The scale of the effort intended was not out of line with the scale of the accelerating development that had been taking place towards the end of the 1960s. However, the economy was still severely disrupted at the time the plan was prepared and was not in a state to resume development where it had been left off. If things had gone smoothly the economy might have recovered within two or three years to a state where something on the scale of the plan could have been put into operation with some chance of success. The rise in import prices completely destroyed any such hopes, and went much further in making it almost impossible to continue to manage the economy and prevent the disruption of production that was bound to follow from the severe reduction in import potential.

Little could be done to counteract the balance of payments crisis in 1973–4 except to economise in imports. Bangladesh reacted to the adverse movement in the price of imports by increasing export prices. The general world inflation of 1973–4 certainly gave scope for some increase in the price of jute without impairing its competitive position against synthetics, but the scope for this is limited. At first sight the decision to raise export prices of jute to roughly £140 per ton, which was taken in July 1974, and again to about £200 later in the year,[11] might have been expected to recoup some of the loss resulting from the deterioration in the terms of trade, but the jute crop in 1974 was almost certainly well below normal levels. Official estimates put the amount of jute produced at about two-thirds of normal. With jute, what is gained on the swings is often lost on the roundabouts and there is really rather little scope in the short run to increase receipts from jute to any marked degree by price manipulations. So far there has also been little respite from the sharp rise in import prices, particularly of foodgrains, but in the longer run lower import prices might relieve the situation.

The whole import programme for 1973–4 was in fact thrown completely off balance by the rise in prices. To make matters worse neither export performance nor the inflow of aid lived up to expectations. Imports had to be severely cut in spite of short-term borrowing and drawing down reserves to an extent that left Bangladesh with an empty kitty. Arrivals of foodgrains attained 1·6 million tons, but this was possible only by dint of postponing payment for half a million tons;[12] non-food imports were cut to varying degrees to give an average of 60 per cent of the amount planned.

Table II.4, based on various estimates for 1973–4, vividly illustrates how the position changed and how severe the cuts in imports were. The price of foodgrains, estimated as likely to be about $100 per ton, worked out in the event at nearly twice this figure. Edible oil imports had to be halved. Petroleum imports, crude or refined, were only about 1 million tons against the 1½ million tons intended. Imports of fertiliser and cement were roughly halved. The value of capital goods was much less than intended and the volume may well have been little more than one-third of that planned. The value of miscellaneous raw materials was up but the volume was only about two-thirds of that originally regarded as essential. Only the quantity of cotton textile imports exceeded its planned level; it might have

[11] Subsequently reduced.
[12] Annual Plan for 1974–5, p. 12.

been better to have cut it and use the savings to buy yarn and raw cotton to keep the mills and handloom workers going.

TABLE II.4

PLANNED AND ACTUAL MERCHANDISE IMPORTS 1973–4
(Value in million dollars)

Commodity	Unit	Annual Plan target for 1973–4 at 1972–3 prices		Estimated actual imports in 1973–4	
		Quantity	Value	Quantity	Value
Foodgrains	million tons	2·2	213	1·6	296
Edible oil	thousand tons	100	48	49	34
Cotton textiles	million yards	50	12	59	18
Petroleum products	thousand tons	360	16	510	49
Crude petroleum	thousand tons	1,300	28	500	39
Raw cotton	thousand bales	360	63	260	34
Cotton yarn	thousand bales	100	32	60	33
Fertilizer	thousand tons	220	25	125	24
Cement	thousand tons	750	16	400	18
Capital goods			224		155
Miscellaneous raw materials, inter-mediate goods and consumer goods			161		217
Total			838		917

Import stringency continued into 1974–5. Aid and the value of imports increased, but the prices were on average much higher; higher imports of foodgrains and of fertilisers to replace the lost output at Ghorasal meant that other imports continued at low levels. Nevertheless, by mid-1975 there were signs that the position was improving. Aid and the promise of future commitments remained high, better financial control was being exercised, output at Ghorasal was restored and production prospects were better.

The consequences of import stringency are severe. The modern sector of the Bangladesh economy is heavily linked to foreign trade in all its aspects. Without sufficient imports to keep the economy going nearly everything else goes wrong. Government revenue is heavily dependent on customs and excise duties so that a low level of imports has a large effect on government revenues. Since development expenditure is also dependent on imports, a restricted import programme limits development activity severely.

Fortunately the direct consequences for rural life are less damaging. The countryside has great resilience and is less dependent on imports. Cuts in fertilisers reduce food production to some extent and cuts in cement and raw materials affect construction in the villages and the activities of artisans. But the bulk of rural activity in Bangladesh today proceeds in a timeless fashion and while imports of food are necessary to help support some of those living in villages, shortages of food imports fall firstly on the towns.

Finance and Money. Although most taxation had previously been raised by the centre and regional taxation powers were minimal, it was not necessary to develop a new taxation system from scratch; it did, however, require radical improvement. Moreover, its administration is defective. It is seldom possible to get definitive figures, particularly of expenditure, at all speedily; besides impairing preparation of the budget, this renders the task of financial control much more difficult.

Table II.5 compares the budget estimates prepared at the beginning of the fiscal year with the revised estimates prepared one year later. Even the revised estimates were not themselves final but subject to subsequent reassessment. It is possible therefore that the observations made below may need to be modified in the light of further information.

TABLE II.5

OVERALL BUDGET ESTIMATES 1972–3, 1973–4, 1974–5 and
1975–6

(Taka crores)

	1972–3		1973–4		1974–5		1975–6
	Budget estim.	Revised estim.	Budget estim.	Revised estim.	Budget estim.	Revised estim.	Budget estim.
Revenue receipts*	292	224	411	347	524	554	711
Non-development (current) expenditure*	218	213	295	331	395	399	455
Development and reconstruction expenditure	501	398	525	464	525	525	950

* Food subsidies and railway receipts and expenditure have been excluded throughout.

The table shows that revenue exceeded estimates in 1974–5 for the first time. In the main this was because imports in earlier years were less than expected, while in 1974–5 a boost to revenues was given by continued high import prices which raised the yield of *ad valorem* duties. Higher rates of duties on imports have had the same effect.

In the budget for 1974–5, new tax proposals were introduced which were expected to raise Taka 89 crores. This was a massive increase in the incidence of taxation of the order of twenty per cent.

The costs of the repatriation of Bangalees to Bangladesh from Pakistan in 1973–4 was one factor increasing expenditure above the estimates, as was the partial implementation of the pay proposals for public service employees made by the Pay Commission.[13] The figures in Table II.5 do not include expenditure on food subsidies which have only recently been brought into the budgetary accounts proper. These have been very large, running at about Taka 100 crores in recent years. The need to finance this by non-inflationary means now seems to be recognised.

Difficulties in implementing planned development expenditure stands out strongly in Table II.5. Expenditure on development and reconstruction scheduled for 1974–5 was scarcely greater in money terms than that originally proposed for 1972–3. In the meantime prices had risen greatly. The expenditure budgeted for 1974–5 was probably only about half, in real terms, of that planned for 1972–3. The future outlook is better. Some of the earlier obstacles to development are receding. Aid is being mobilised more effectively; project preparation is more advanced and there are hopes that implementation capacity will move in line with it. The prospect of generating savings through the government budget has been improved by devaluation and the growing amounts of aid that have been received. The sharp increase in development expenditure proposed for 1975–6 will, if it is implemented, represent no more than a return to the real level originally planned for 1972–3. When development expenditure is at a low ebb, much of it in fact consists of expenditure on overheads—in keeping development institutions in being, paying the salaries of headquarters' staff—rather than on financing projects themselves. The increase proposed for 1975–6 will, therefore, have a more than proportional effect on development.

The government is making increasing efforts to limit demands on the banking system. In the budget for 1975–6 the intention was to avoid deficit financing, though reliance on foreign loans and grants for the development programme was very large. The general impression is that a decided movement to sound finance is taking place.

One effect of this is that the rate of increase in the money supply has been slowing down. Between June 1972 and June 1973 the money supply increased by Takas 210 crores or roughly 40 per cent. Between the corresponding months of 1973 and 1974 the increase was less than 20 per cent. However, the increase in the fiscal year

[13] *Report of the National Pay Commission*, Bangladesh, May 1973.

1973–4 would have been much greater than this if there had not been a number of off-setting factors such as a movement to time deposits and a considerable drawing down of foreign exchange reserves. In 1973–4 the private sector made rather small demands on the banking system, the main activating forces were the public sector enterprises and the Government's financial needs. Table II.6 shows what occurred.

TABLE II.6

MONEY SUPPLY

(Taka crores)

	Currency held outside banks	Demand deposits	Money supply (M₁)	Time deposits	Money supply (M₂)
	(1)	(2)	(1) + (2) (3)	(4)	(3) + (4) (5)
17 December 1971	207	181	388	158	546
30 June 1972	176	310	486	214	699
29 June 1973	286	410	696	293	989
28 June 1974	331	485	817	400	1217
27 June 1975	293	521	814	473	1287

Source: Bangladesh Bank Bulletin.

The first day for which figures were compiled for Bangladesh was 17 December 1971. In two-and-a-half years the money supply has roughly doubled and time deposits have increased two-and-a-half times. There is some reason to believe that time deposits in Bangladesh are genuine savings deposits as it does not appear that their velocity of circulation is large or that they are used as a substitute for demand deposits on a substantial scale. It may therefore be reasonable to attach most importance to column 3 of Table II.6, the sum of currency held outside the banks and demand deposits, as representing the money supply. An important factor in slowing the expansion of the money supply in 1974–5 was the demonetisation of 100 taka notes in April 1975. These were deposited in blocked accounts and the effect was to reduce the money supply immediately by about 20 per cent.

It is easy to ascribe undue significance to the movements of money supply in a country such as Bangladesh. The increase in money supply was much more the consequence of changes in real factors, including the effects of government decisions, than a factor itself setting in train movements in the economy. In real terms there has been a decline since mid-1973 in the value of banking balances held.

Financial measures helped to restrain the increase in money supply, but underlying all that happened was the sluggishness of domestic production and the world shortage of foodgrains. A reversal of these movements could be even more significant for prices in Bangladesh than monetary restraint.

4. *Looking to the Future*

It was not to be expected that a fully functioning economic system could be established in as short a period as three or four years, after the disruptions of war and in the face of the deteriorating world economic situation, which fell particularly heavily on Bangladesh. The economy of Bangladesh was in a very bad state as it entered the second half of the 1970s. The most serious weakness was the continuing increase in the population and the uncertain outlook for the production of food which was failing to keep pace with it. The large rise in the price of imports that had taken place had practically reduced Bangladesh to international bankruptcy. All these factors and the limited prospects for increasing exports made it impossible to raise the resources needed for economic development on the scale necessary.

There could be no doubt by 1975 of the need of Bangladesh for large-scale financial assistance from abroad. Prospects for this were improved by the establishment in October 1974 of a consortium of countries who provide aid to Bangladesh. The subsequent response, including aid from oil-producing countries, is helping to change the situation. At times there has been a feeling in some quarters that Bangladesh might do better to go it alone and do without aid. We do not share this view. There is something in the argument that foreign assistance may lead to a relaxation of domestic effort and to the postponement of hard political decisions. No aid at all might in the end force the issue of mobilisation of resources on those whose responsibility it really is. It is not, however, an answer to Bangladesh's problems; neither would some compromise proposal for limited amounts of aid suffice to carry the economy through. It might only make matters worse. The only solution for Bangladesh is a combination of firm domestic measures and large-scale international support. Without such a combination, efforts to develop Bangladesh will fail. The contention that "Aid merely allows the Awami League to live off the fat of the land. It would be far better to let the country fend for itself, let the people suffer and kick the rulers out",[14] is not the right answer.

[14] Kevin Rafferty, in the *Financial Times*, 6 January 1974.

Such are the uncertainties and dilemmas of analysis, prognosis and prescription in the face of the poverty of Bangladesh as they present themselves to Bangladesh herself and the international community. Our own considered conclusion is that major support by the international community in attacking the poverty of Bangladesh is not only a *conditio sine qua non* of development but also something that could be made to work. This conclusion is conditional on a whole set of changes in policy being genuinely accepted and implemented by government; it is also conditional on foreign assistance of major proportions being made available.

In the next two chapters we discuss the needs for early changes in the structure and content of economic policies and in economic administration and institutions, in an effort to cope with the tremendous current problems of scarcities and imbalances, and in order to prepare for structural change and growth. In Chapter V we seek to draw a picture of the longer-term future, of the extent and balance of change and growth to the end of the century and of major potentials and options of policy strategies. The discussion in Chapter V can have an air of reality only on the assumption that the changes in politics and administration as discussed in Chapters III and IV are actually implemented. In fact, it is one of our own main criticisms of the government's First Five Year Plan that it does not distinguish clearly enough in its analysis and prescription between, on the one hand, the requirements and policies to rehabilitate the economy and put it on a forward course and, on the other, the plans and policies for medium-term development; in the language of the Plan, the changes and policies required to regain "benchmark" levels of production and trade as opposed to the measures required for further growth and to reach the full Plan targets. What we present in Chapters III and IV is, of course, no substitute for a full government review of policies and institutions, but our analysis and description may give a fair view of the nature and extent of the current problems facing Bangladesh and of the inadequacy of Bangladesh's resources to deal with them.

CHAPTER III

MANAGEMENT OF THE ECONOMY: GOVERNMENT AND CONTROLS

1. *Effective Government*

The few years of Bangladesh's existence have thrown up quite serious weaknesses of economic organisation and of political determination to put matters right. Even in 1975 Bangladesh was still far from being in a position to launch the massive and sustained development effort that will be needed. It would be fruitless to attempt to do so without first overcoming some of the major problems of current economic policy and economic management that remain unsolved. The most conspicuous consequences of these are low levels of production and efficiency in agriculture and industry, and—perhaps most serious—inequities in distribution of output and of economic assets and opportunities.

It is tempting to press on with development and to hope that current difficulties can gradually be resolved. We do not think that this is the right answer. If the present functioning of the economy cannot be improved, much of the development effort will be wasted. There is very little point in creating new capacity if existing capacity cannot be fully used due to shortage of raw materials, spares or fuels; better use of existing facilities will do much to provide the output and resources needed for development. This is not to say that all development effort should immediately cease (even with the acceleration now proposed, it remains small) but that the pace of development should be restrained until the immediate difficulties are on their way to solution, until institutions for management of the economy have been made to work, and until the economy is in better shape to withstand the strains that an increased development effort will cause. What is needed first is a period of consolidation, of rethinking policies and trying to get the economy to function more efficiently, largely with the physical and institutional infrastructure already at hand. Some of the ways in which this can be initiated are discussed below.

The high hopes and expectations for a better life aroused by independence and liberation have faded away and disenchantment with government has set in. There have been many weaknesses in government and its administration, and in the face of unusually severe economic difficulties these deficiencies of government have been made to look worse, in some respects, than has been warranted by the facts. The result is that the morale of those in positions of political and administrative authority has been at a very low ebb. At the end of 1974 there was a general attitude of despondency and indeed almost despair among many key people in government and its administration, and many of the most able men in the country were considering with more than usual attention whether they could get jobs abroad—in this instance not solely in the hope of personal aggrandisement but because there seemed to be so little hope for the future, or opportunity to do a good and fruitful job at home.

The machinery of government itself was under attack; there were persistent reports that there were areas of the country in which control had been lost and growing violence was both a threat to the government and a sign that opposition forces were gradually being guided to oppose it. Many of these problems are essentially political but there can be no doubt that they have been multiplied by maladministration, by the failure to recognise and adhere to priorities for action and by overcentralisation of the administration of the country to an extent which has made it difficult or impossible to get things done. In this process it has been all too easy for unscrupulous people in power to profit from the disorganisation. This brought government into disrepute.

Violence, sabotage and destruction have been a continuing feature of the Bangladesh scene, and this has adversely affected both the current operation and the development of the economy. In December 1974 and subsequently emergency powers were used to deal with this problem and to stabilise the situation. At the best this can be only a short-run solution. The long-term need is for the improvement of the administrative machinery, not necessarily through the centralisation of power as has occurred in the past. In the next few years attention must be concentrated on motivation, training, organisation and institution building. This applies quite generally, but it has particular bearing on the machinery of government. The system of government is still heavily steeped in British traditions and there are, of course, the usual departmental rivalries and special, and sometimes conflicting, interests which impede the progress of administration and development. There is too much emphasis on seniority, and the concept of the élite of the erstwhile civil service of Pakistan, outstanding men though many of the members of that service were, is not likely to be the best answer to getting the country moving. It is more important to recognise that civil servants must be deployed where they are needed, allowed personal responsibility to get on with the jobs entrusted to them and rewarded according to the responsibilities that they bear and the results that they achieve. This entails creating positions of special responsibility with suitable financial incentives for those outstanding civil servants who can be relied upon to put policies into effect for such essential things as family planning and agricultural production and to ensure their success.

The extent and seriousness of the present disorganisation of the administrative system must not be underplayed. Effective government must be fully re-established whatever ideologies and priorities activate the Government. This is not something that can be speedily attained; persistent efforts to improve the situation will have to be made by the relatively few people who have the capacity and flair to organise the work of others and to introduce order and discipline into the government of the country. There can be no clean-cut blueprint for such improvement; it is not the kind of thing that can be attained simply by constitutional changes, though these may be necessary and helpful. It is something that has to be worked for constantly while responding to the needs of the situation, and changing the emphasis in the light of new circumstances or insights; in general this is a plea for pragmatism.

Corruption has been rife. It is never easy to document the evidence for such a statement, but there cannot be much doubt as to the prevalence of smuggling and capital flight when it is referred to openly, if guardedly, in official publications.[1] In some countries corruption may be a way of circumventing obstructive bureaucratic activities. In Bangladesh it has hardly had even this saving grace; rather it has paved the way for capital accumulation by a corrupt and favoured few. It is no excuse to hide behind the defence that corruption is present everywhere or to criticise the innocence of observers.[2] The presence of corruption on a destructive scale is also a powerful influence making donors reluctant to contemplate the scale of effort that is really needed on their part in support of the Bangladesh economy.

2. Economic Systems and Control

Economic Systems. In some respects Bangladesh is getting the worst of all forms of economic organisation. It is neither a fully

---

[1] *Economic Development in 1973–74 and Annual Plan for 1974–75*, Planning Commission, Bangladesh, July 1974, p. 173.

[2] See the *Financial Times*, 10 September 1974, for an account of an interview given by the Prime Minister of Bangladesh to Mr. Kevin Rafferty.

fledged socialistic and centrally planned country really given to directing economic affairs, nor a country fully dedicated to the unfettered pursuit of private enterprise and capitalism, although it combines some of the features of both these opposite worlds.

There are a number of often conflicting considerations that have to be weighed in Bangladesh, as in any other country, in considering the role to be given to public and private activities. It is tempting to sidestep these issues by saying that what can clearly be done best by the public sector of the economy should be left to it, and those things that can be done best by the private sector should be carried out by it; activities for which such judgements could not be made with certainty could be put in one sector or the other. But what is best cannot be determined in the abstract and without knowledge of the objectives which it is desired to attain. There are people in Bangladesh as anywhere else who wish to curtail private sector activities for political reasons, firmly believing that economic activity should be organised on a socialist basis. Whether the economy would function better or worse from the point of view of efficiency or growth under private control is a secondary issue in such cases. Some take the view that development will not give satisfactory results or proceed at a rapid pace unless the key items of wealth are redistributed or nationalised as a prelude to maintaining an egalitarian distribution of resources in later years. Still others see co-operative activity as a means to transform the rural scene, again through communal action. Participation in such activities is regarded as an instrument of social change. Others are against communal action and ownership on the grounds that it is wasteful, that it is conducive to the assembly of an army of bureaucrats managing industries and other activities without adequate regard to efficiency. Still others see private endeavour as a major instrument of social and economic advancement which should not be impeded by excessive government intervention.

In Bangladesh the resolution of such matters is largely pragmatic. In many respects it is a conservative country inclined to maintain the *status quo* except when the pressure of events forces change. Thus sudden switches of activity from the public to the private sector are not to be expected. Economic life is dominated by the government and public sectors of the economy, and the probability seems to us to be that this domination will grow.

If the division of labour between the public and private sectors of the economy is to be decided on the virtues of increasing output (even though this may be—at least in theory—an old-fashioned view of what development is about, now that so much emphasis is laid on other objectives such as employment or the distribution of income) a case could be made for laying more stress on development in the private sector than seems to have been the case so far. The Bangladesh First Five Year Plan put as much as four-fifths of total planned development expenditure into the public sector, leaving very little room for private activities.[3] Nationalisation of industry has naturally reduced the scope for investment in the private sector. Of total investment 17 per cent was scheduled for public sector industry; if this had been destined for the private sector of the economy the distribution between public and private development expenditure would have been vastly different.

In some respects the allocation made to the private sector was probably too low. There is a need to tap every scrap of private initiative that can enhance production without harmful effects on equity and social welfare. Also the private sector—at whatever level of operation can be contemplated in Bangladesh today— is likely to generate a considerable volume of savings which, if it cannot be used productively within the planned allocation of investment, will be used in less productive ways, including capital flight. Finally, the composition of the development programme is itself something that determines how much of it should be executed in the public sector and how much of it in the private sector. The programme devised for the First Five Year Plan was tilted towards the kind of projects that could best be executed in the public sector by central and powerful agencies and formed part of the basic strategy of development which is discussed later.

The economic control system permeates economic life in Bangladesh, in spite of recent measures to reduce its impact. We deal below specifically with control of industry and trade. Although in the vast sector of agriculture, government seeks to influence decisions of millions of farmers and tens of thousands of traders in order to get them to respond to the priorities and needs of the country as seen by the government, the rural economy remains largely a private sector operation, subject only to rather distant government intervention. This affects supplies of important inputs for production, in particular fertilisers and water, and marketing arrangements for some outputs, notably jute and to some extent rice. The government also decides on policies for land reform, controls of land ownership and tenure. We have something to say about these matters in other parts of the book. Much of what we say in the following sections on

[3] Of total development outlay of Taka 5,000 crores about Taka 500 crores were expected to be undertaken in the subsistence (private) sector while in the monetised sector only another Taka 500 crores were to be in the private sector.

control of industry and trade also applies to agriculture and the rural economy.

Control of Industry. The development of industry must be seen against a background of government control. The basic philosophy has been that the industrial sector must conform to the planned development of the country and that private enterprise must work within the confines of the framework laid down by government. When Bangladesh formed part of Pakistan, such planning did not prevent great accumulation of wealth; indeed it almost certainly facilitated it, and in some respects produced an inefficient use of investment and other resources. The danger is that the present system operating in Bangladesh, which is not vastly different from the previous one, in spite of nationalisation measures, will prove equally inefficient.

The effects of controls on the working of the economy of Pakistan have been described as follows:

By 1958 the government made nearly all the important and many un-important decisions. The system had a substantial cost. The scope of control was too great in relation to the manpower, information, and administrative machinery available. The results were individual decisions that were incorrect, delays, excessive stocks, errors in the direction of investment and in composition of imports. The inefficiencies introduced in the economy were substantial and significant; moreover the goal of equity was inadequately met.[4]

The economic rationale of excessive direct controls was the scarcity of resources, a condition that exists in Bangladesh to an even greater extent today than it did in the whole of Pakistan during the period covered by the strictures quoted above. As yet there is nothing to suggest that the Government of Bangladesh is any more capable of directing industrial affairs effectively than its predecessors. It is tempting to argue that control should be abandoned rather than improved and rationalised, but the proposition does not really stand up to examination.

Investment decisions cannot be left entirely to the free-for-all of the market place. Our reasons for this are not wholly ideological. Many of the profitable fields of industrial endeavour require more money than can be raised by local business men; many require large amounts of foreign exchange; and while a partnership between private enterprise and foreign industrialists which is now politically acceptable, might seem to be the answer, it might be rejected by

[4] Gustav F. Papanek, *Pakistan's Development: Social Goals and Private Incentives*, Cambridge, Mass., Harvard University Press, 1967, p. 142.

foreign investors who could find better uses for their money and expertise. Proposals to establish petrochemical complexes, for example, will not be undertaken by foreign interests without government involvement in the financial arrangements, and not perhaps even then. The total size of the investment programme is also something that the government must be highly instrumental in deciding and by implication this is likely to involve some attempt to determine the magnitude of the share of the different sectors of the economy. In principle, this could be done without the government getting involved in the details of the various investment projects under consideration; in practice it may be difficult to avoid some involvement, for instance for projects requiring foreign finance; and apart from this, those responsible for deciding what amounts should be allotted to various sectors are unlikely to do so without examining and comparing in some detail the individual projects competing for inclusion in the development and foreign exchange programmes, so long as the total investment programme and imports are not large enough for all to be included.

This applies to private as well as nationalised industries and some intervention in determining what they will be allowed to carry out is likely to follow. Most schemes put up for consideration will, of course, be framed in terms that meet the known minimum requirements of government for projects that are considered as soundly based and acceptable in terms of returns on capital, employment, import content, etc. Since there will generally be far more projects requiring approval than funds available for the purpose, decisions will have to be taken as to which schemes are allowed to go ahead. In practice this will necessitate a fairly detailed review by government of the major individual schemes and the final pattern will be decided in relation to the predilections of civil servants as much as in conformity with the views of managers and cost accountants preparing the projects for submission to the government.

Altogether in present circumstances it is difficult to think that government will, or indeed should, refrain from playing a major part in deciding which projects are to be included in the industrial programmes. Only in a distant future—and an unlikely one at that—when the financial situation may be easier and the development programmes less dependent on foreign aid, could government contemplate leaving private sector investment decisions altogether alone, and for individual nationalised corporations, perhaps, agree only on the total amount to be invested over a period of years without seeking to examine their specific proposals, project by project.

There has been a very marked change in the attitude of the government towards private industry. Originally only a small place seemed to have been left for it. Private firms were restricted first to those employing no more fixed capital, including land, than Taka 1·5 million; later this was raised to Taka 2·5 million, but in 1974 the decision was taken to increase the limit radically to Taka 30 million. This is a remarkable departure from the previous approach. Taka 30 million is not a large amount of capital to employ, and it will continue to be impossible for the private sector to establish such costly projects as steel mills, oil refineries or deep mining operations. Nevertheless, the increase in the limit was a clear signal that the government was ready to accept private industry as a force for the development of the country. In certain other respects the restrictions on private sector operations were also eased. Foreign participation was allowed in private as well as in public enterprises, contrary to previous regulations, and a Bangladesh controlling interest in such mixed endeavours might not be insisted upon. In 1975 steps were taken to dispose of a number of "abandoned enterprises" to their previous owners, private bidders or workers' co-operatives.

So long as resources are severely strained, it will not be possible greatly to relax controls over the private sector. Indigenous resources are limited, and while there are some forms of manufacture that could make better use of what is available and some that make small demands on imports, often an expansion of the private sector depends on being able to increase the volume of imports allocated to it. There is no question but that private industrialists will have to toe the line in restricting their use of imports; nevertheless it matters a great deal how this is brought about.

The decision to raise the size of firms permitted in the private sector does not really confer much additional freedom for the time being. It may mean that some projects that would otherwise have been in the public sector will now be allowed to be privately owned, but it will not enable private industrialists to establish enterprises which would not have been included in investment programmes for either the public or the private sector previously. Enterprises cannot be established at will in the private sector; they must be included within the investment schedule prepared for private enterprise operation. Apart from this, if they need to raise capital (and most certainly they will do) they will fall within the scrutiny of institutions established for that purpose. The institutional arrangements for providing capital to private (and for that matter public) enterprise have not yet been tested out in the circumstances of Bangladesh on any scale. There are considerable doubts about whether they will aid rather than impede the establishment of private industry.

Managing Nationalised Industries. The question of the control of nationalised industries is a general one not confined to any one country. The tendency seems to be to subject them to increasing surveillance. The problems faced by the Bangladesh nationalised sector are more than usually severe. There is no ready-made system of management; there is labour unrest; corruption is a constant danger; in some cases there are legacies of debt taken over from previous owners; in many enterprises equipment is run down; throughout there is a shortage of raw materials needed to operate plants at full efficiency, and there are many other difficulties stemming from the severe economic position that the country is facing.

There is a distinct difference between the operations of industrial concerns and the policy-making role of governments. The two types of operation need to be separated and provided with their own type of organization suited to their particular tasks. This will not be enough to protect the industry from government interference but it may help to keep it within bounds. Certain powers will need to be exercised wholly by the minister responsible for the nationalised industry in question. As a minimum the minister will expect to have the right to make key appointments to the boards of the industries, approve the annual draft budget of the industry (in effect its annual plan, prepared for purposes of budgetary control),[5] approve the main lines of the investment programme in relation to that of the country as a whole and regulate the raising of new capital. In practice much greater intervention than this is certain to be practised and it is difficult to say that it should not be so. Not all the problems experienced in industry can be resolved by those in the industry themselves. It needed the personal intervention of the prime minister to deal with the difficulties experienced in one jute factory and some of the labour difficulties experienced are not so much related to conditions of work as to political considerations. There are also economic problems that transcend the responsibilities of one industry alone, such as leapfrogging wage claims which could destroy attempts to restrain wage increases.

A number of nationalised enterprises inherited debts run up by their former owners immediately prior to liberation as a counterpart to building up financial assets in West Pakistan. This created management problems for the enterprises concerned and for the relations between government and enterprises although it clearly should not have been allowed to do so. A debt from a nationalised corporation to the government or to a nationalised bank also owned by the government is not a matter which should give rise to difficulties, at least not compared to those that arise in the case of private

[5] The first steps were taken in this direction when budgets for public sector organisations were submitted at the time of the 1975–6 budget.

enterprises whose position would be governed wholly by their financial position. The accumulation of current debt, if it reflects inefficient management, is a more serious matter and this may also be true if the debt is accumulated not as a result of mismanagement of the enterprise itself but because of directives issued by the government; the accumulation of debt may be the government's fault but this may be no protection to the corporation.

In fully socialistic economies the surpluses (profits) generated by enterprises may not have significance provided that the enterprise is doing what is expected of it. The same view seemed to be taken about the public sector industries in Bangladesh. If it was necessary to pay a price for raw jute that at current prices for jute manufactures on the international market did not allow the jute mills to make a profit, the government appeared to be ready to accept the philosophy that losses must be incurred. They might be provided for out of the government's budget (though in fact this has not been done so far) or, as at present, from advances made by the banking system; in effect by deficit financing incurred not by the government itself but by the industries themselves. There are considerable objections to this procedure, extending far beyond the ordinary canons of sound finance. To begin with, extending finance to the nationalised industries by the banking system has repercussions on the general financial position. The sums involved are not trivial; under present financial arrangements (or the lack of them) losses could easily amount to Taka 50 crores a year. Jute mills hemmed in by the price at which they can buy jute (government determined) and the price at which manufactures may be sold, may be powerless to produce satisfactory results. The feeling of impotence that this generates destroys any incentive to increase efficiency and attain profitability. A well-run jute mill might have made profits even under the adverse financial rules laid down by government, although delivery delays, shipping delays, technical trouble and shortage of inputs made this very difficult.

Enterprises are faced with continually rising costs. Prices once fixed by government are slow to change, but need to be adjusted at fairly frequent intervals. This has led to the recommendation that the nationalised industries should be told to fix prices high enough to make a profit.[6] For some companies this might be impossible in practice, while for others producing goods in short supply the issue might be much more how much profit to make. With the decision to allow the nationalised textile corporations to fix their own prices,

[6] This point was particularly strongly argued to us by Professor W. B. Reddaway.

a start seems to have been made in the direction of introducing greater market freedom.

In present circumstances, extensive government intervention in the affairs of the nationalised industries (and for that matter in other public bodies) appears inevitable. Yet government cannot take the decisions the chairmen, boards of directors and managers of enterprises habitually take. The aim must be to create efficiently functioning enterprises that can manage their own affairs and avoid outside interference. Of course things will go wrong from time to time, price increases may be used to mask inefficiency or managers prove to be incapable. When this happens the government will have to intervene, but the form of the intervention should not consist of the government's attempting to run the enterprises, but of changes in management, the introduction of consultants or general measures to create conditions in which the enterprises will function well.

Monetary Controls. After the formation of Bangladesh the domestic banks were nationalised. The branch of the Pakistan State Bank established in Dacca became the Bangladesh Bank, the central bank of Bangladesh. Other non-specialised banks and bank branches were grouped into six commercial banks, and three specialised banks, the Krishi Bank with special responsibility for agriculture and the Bangladesh Shilpa Bank and the Bangladesh Shilpa Rin Sangsta Bank concerned mainly with finance for development in other sectors. There is also the cooperative apex bank, the Bangladesh Sanabaya Bank. Foreign banks were not nationalised and include American Express, the Chartered Bank, and National and Grindlay's Bank. The foreign banks finance internal as well as overseas transactions and so form part of the domestic financial system.

The effects of nationalising virtually all the internal banking operations of the country do not seem to have been grasped. In private enterprise economies, banks, operating through the supply of credit that they make available and the forms and direction in which they lend, are regarded as having considerable influence on the working of the economy. There is no reason in principle why nationalised banks should not work in the same way as private banks, subject to the same type of controls and the use of monetary and administrative instruments to guide their operations. In some respects the banks are regarded as competitors, as would be commercial banks in other economic systems. The instruments of control which are used by Bangladesh might find a place in any non-socialist country. They include the regulation of interest rates, cash and liquidity rates, rediscounting facilities, the operation of selective credit controls and the use of directives and moral suasion.

The opportunity for the banks to play a part in the management of the economy arise because half the deposits of the banks are held by the private sector and two-fifths of bank credit goes to this sector. The remainder of the deposits and the credits advanced relate to the public sector of the economy and it is uncertain here what role the banks might be expected to play. The annual projected budgets of the public sector enterprises are subject to the scrutiny of the government departments responsible for them. If these are approved, it might seem reasonable to suppose that the credit facilities needed to put them into effect should be forthcoming almost automatically, provided they adhered to their plans. When plans for public sector enterprises in Bangladesh go wrong—as they occasionally do anywhere—the banks as instruments of financial control could in principle come into the picture in the guise of a public watchdog. In practice, however, when such cases occur in Bangladesh the final decisions are not likely to be reached by a bank. There have been many occasions when the borrowings of nationalised corporations have reached the limits that have been set on their banking facilities; but nationalised undertakings cannot really be made bankrupt or forced to revise their policies, plans or prices through the decisions of another nationalised body, a bank; in the end the government will decide what it is proper to do.

In the case of the private sector, the position appears somewhat different; sound commercial finance may be expected to operate here and the normal canons of good banking procedure applied. If, however, the question is not one of the solvency of an individual firm but of the total amount of credit to be given to the private sector, does it really make sense to govern this by some adjustment of reserve ratios or control of rediscounting facilities? Might it not be better to rely on fiat by fixing the total limits of the credit that the banks can advance in one direction or another? Many of the historical methods of monetary administration seem to be archaic in relation to the operation of a largely nationalised banking sector.

The main controls over banking operations in Bangladesh are likely to be direct in nature. The planning mechanism underlying them is familiar. The government needs for finance are worked out at the time of the budget; the total increase in credit which is acceptable is worked out and the difference between these figures is then regarded as available for expansion in credit elsewhere. The amount of additional finance for non-government use can then be allocated provisionally between banks and purposes. In fact financial planning will not be so tidy or so easy to operate as the foregoing might show. Too little credit may be made available for the non-government sector so that limits get exceeded, or the demands for credit from individual industries or agriculture may turn out differently from those originally supposed. We do not believe that such aberrations from credit programmes can be controlled by the subtleties of traditional monetary management in an economy such as Bangladesh. Either direct action will be resorted to and new limits established by directive or the position will be allowed to develop unchecked.

The fact that Western monetary measures of banking management are not likely to have much effect in Bangladesh does not mean that interest rates are unimportant. In the main, it is desirable that interest rates should move with changes in the volume of credit that it is thought can be made available and that they should be related to changing circumstances. So far, this principle has not been effectively exploited in Bangladesh.[7]

To some extent ·the rise in internal prices has been a monetary phenomenon. This is not meant to imply that it is something that the banking system could or even should have controlled. The activating forces were not primarily of a monetary nature; they found their expression in this way, but really as a reflection of the failure of the government and the nationalised industries to meet their expenditure out of current revenues. Monetary inflation stemmed from the policies laid down by government.

Control of Trade. No one can doubt the severity of the balance of payments problem or fail to see the effect it is having on the Bangladesh economy. Nothing much can be done to change this situation in the short run. Even with generous balance of payments assistance, imports fall short of the level needed for the economy to operate efficiently, while exports show little resilience. In the longer run the situation may change; in the shorter run there can only be palliatives to help Bangladesh to live with the foreign exchange shortages, avoid economic and financial collapse and provide a basis for gradual if slow improvement.

The prime need is to try to ensure that the amount of imports that can be afforded is used to the best advantage. Import requirements are worked out in total and in detail by committees representing such government bodies as the Planning Commission, the Ministry of

[7] In 1973–4, when the world was experiencing one of the largest increases in prices that had ever occurred in peacetime, it was possible to borrow from banking institutions in Bangladesh at 9–10 per cent; the rate for advances from moneylenders at the time was 30 per cent and often much higher. However, an indication that the government was ready to act on interest rates was evidenced by the decision in the summer of 1974 to raise the bank rate from 5 to 8 per cent. Long-term deposits then earned 10 per cent and lending rates were as high as 13 per cent. This was definitely a step in the right direction.

Finance and the Ministry of Commerce. Anybody with experience of allocation systems working in conditions of extreme scarcity knows what difficult decisions are involved in deciding how much can be imported in total. There is very little margin for error. Bangladesh is already heavily in debt, and at times it has been a problem to find the cash to meet current obligations. Planning ahead is difficult because the value of export receipts and of emigrants remittances is uncertain and the amount of aid that can be utilised is far from precisely known. Countries lay conditions on the use of aid, whether it is used for project or for commodity purchases. Certain goods may be purchased but not others; the list may be altered at short notice; delivery may or may not be available at some particular time. The resources that will be available for an importing period for which plans are being prepared can at best only be estimated; often elements within the total are no more than guesses.

The total of goods that can be purchased largely determines the composition of imports. If the total is large there is much greater flexibility and the range of imports can be extended; but generally it is small and must be used with maximum discernment. Certain requirements can be listed in order of priority, but decisions are seldom simple; it requires fine judgement to determine what should be included and what left out and to balance political and economic requirements—e.g. the need for powdered milk against the need to give employment in the factories, and the vital need to maintain oil supplies against the need for cement for construction. These are not solutions that can be seen entirely in relation to temporary needs; the composition of imports must also have regard to changing requirements over time.

There is certainly room for improvement in the process of planning the list of imported goods to be licensed. In 1972–3 little was known about the actual value and composition of imports entering the country. The position is now somewhat better but the figures are far from reliable. Goods may be cleared without customs declaration, in other cases clearance may be delayed for long periods; not all types of entrances by sea, or land or air are equally well-recorded. Statistics and the procedures behind them must be improved to give a better basis for decisions about import needs.

There is also very little information about needs themselves. Statistics of stocks do not exist for the most part; spares may not be listed or accounted for although available; the movement of commodities is not checked. In consequence there may be losses and diversions of goods as well as difficulty in reaching decisions in the face of lack of information. All this is capable of improvement, but behind attempts to get at needs in the absence of statistics lies fundamental ignorance about the state of the economy and what is really required. Any list of imports is bound to be an imperfect representation of real needs; it is a wonder that the right commodities are ever imported. When they are it is likely to be the result of pressures exerted by users who are short of supplies, as much as any analytical assessment of real needs. When unexpected changes occur in international prices, further adjustments become necessary and the whole system may be knocked from pillar to post under the pressure of changing needs and scarcities and varying costs of meeting them. It is scarcely surprising that, in the face of such difficulties, the government-controlled system of importing goods (which leaves very little scope for private enterprise) has not worked well. At first, import procedures operated by bodies unaccustomed to them were slow, unwieldy and inefficient; imports arrived only with great delay and often were not of the type needed. Great difficulty was experienced in using international commodity credits and getting orders placed for goods available under them. Improvements have been made in the light of experience, but fundamental difficulties still remain and the system is open to abuse so long as imports are scarce and market prices are in excess of landed costs.

One effect of the scarcity of imports is to encourage smuggling. The priorities imposed by planners tend to emphasise the importation of essentials; other goods are correspondingly scarce and the incentive to smuggle supplies all the greater. There is little real knowledge about the intensity of the smuggling operations, but measures to reduce them by the use of border patrols are thought to have had some effect. They will be helped by any measures to affect the profitability of illegal border traffic. One such example is special concessions related to emigrants' remittances. A decision to allow such remittances to come in the form of goods was an added incentive but it obviously runs counter to the government's desire to establish its own priorities.

Imposing Priorities. In the present situation of extreme shortages, combined with the dislocation and disorganisation of economic life which threaten the very fabric of national and social organisation, the first priority for economic policy must be to get the economy working effectively. It is not possible to import goods for development instead of food when harvests fail; it does not make sense to increase productive capacity when what exists cannot be operated for lack of imports; it is scarcely possible to insist on raising domestic savings at a time when production of food and manufactures is low and prices rising at a rate which could exacerbate political unrest or produce revolution. Yet the economy cannot continue indefinitely to postpone development expenditure, or there will be no end to poverty. Moreover, at low levels of development expenditures it becomes both more critical and more difficult to set and adhere to efficient allocations.

National policy-makers are never wholly free to impose economic priorities, to concentrate wholly on current economic management or to determine the structure of the development programme completely. Projects with short gestation periods are to be preferred in the present situation but it is not possible in practice to abandon all projects with long gestation periods or one that seem of low priority. Donors also exert considerable influence in all these respects. Was it really right in 1973 to consider constructing a bridge across the Jamuna River with Japanese aid?

Nevertheless, it is necessary to seek to maintain essential priorities, first to lay the foundation for a build-up in effort and then to ensure that it is directed to essential areas. The necessity and opportunity to develop food production is beyond question; it is here that resources for development must be concentrated. Efforts to reduce the rate of increase in population will produce relatively little effect until 1990 or by the end of the century, but current efforts will be critical for the years thereafter. The fact that there is a long lag does not mean that family planning programmes should be postponed, but rather that they should be accelerated; every year lost will tell so heavily later that delay must be avoided. Then there are development projects not formally in the agricultural or population control sectors which nevertheless are related to them: fertiliser production and provision of doctors and of para-medicals. Such programmes cannot be cut off. Nevertheless the general nature of the short-term priorities is clear: agriculture and population control; it is efforts in these areas that must be put first, cuts must be imposed on other sectors and the need to preseve a diminished but effective core of development activity respected if there is to be hope for the future.

None of these priorities will impose themselves automatically or without the assistance of government. Individuals want motor-cars if they are rich enough, not family planning; those without food can do relatively little to increase the supply of it; aid donors often want markets rather than the development of Bangladesh, and they want visibly successful projects. The extreme scarcity of resources for current operation of the economy and for development must somehow be made to convince all concerned that any deviation from essential priorities can be only slight.

3. *Conclusions*

There is still a long way to go to get the economy functioning in such a way that the development programme can be accelerated. Law and order is frequently decried as a condition of development but there can be no doubt about the need to establish it in Bangladesh. Good administration does not come so much from changes in constitutions as from painstaking efforts over a number of years to improve performance in many detailed ways.

Issues of control, both in form and content, are determined in part pragmatically and by the exigencies of the economic and political situation. In the Bangladesh situation today it seems to us that the dominant ideological commitment, or the characteristics of the choices made in terms of social and economic system, is less important for the efficiency of economic management than are consistency, rationality and determination in the implementation of policies within the system chosen. We expect that Bangladesh will move neither to a clear-cut capitalist system nor to a fully socialist system in the foreseeable future. What we urge is that the balance be explicitly formulated and consistently adhered to in government decision making.

CHAPTER IV

MANAGEMENT OF THE ECONOMY:
PUBLIC FINANCE AND PRICES

1. *Public Finance*

Overall Budget. The government exercises a dominant influence on both the public and private sectors of the economy through its management of public finance. Government is responsible for nearly 90 per cent of all development expenditure and this combined with current expenditure amounts to at least 15 per cent of the gross domestic product. The ways in which resources are used and raised, therefore, profoundly affect the rest of the economy, as do the ways in which budgetary deficits are financed.

Bangladesh has experienced great difficulty in raising resources to cover current budgetary expenditures and to provide for that part of the small development programme which is internally financed. The budget for 1975–6 was the first to show a comfortable surplus on current account; even after allowing for a subsidy on the sale of foodgrains purchased by Bangladesh, it was estimated that a revenue surplus of Taka 156 crore would be produced. This is not, however, a large sum in absolute terms; it amounts only to $100 million at current exchange rates.[1] After allowing for extra-budgetary receipts it appears that about three-quarters of the development programme in the public sector is intended to be financed by foreign loans and grants.[2]

The public sector development programme, while as large as can be financed with present resources, is in no sense adequate to ensure development in the longer term. It probably amounts to only 6 per

---

[1] Here the current official rate may be a pretty good yardstick, since development expenditures in Bangladesh have a very high import content.

[2] The proportion would appear to be even higher if different systems of accounting were adopted. The loss made on the sale of foodgrains provided under aid programmes is not recorded as a subsidy in the budgetary estimates; if it were so (and the contribution of foreign loans and grants to the finance of development were increased correspondingly), it would become even more evident that the development programme is almost entirely dependent for its financing on foreign assistance.

cent of the gross domestic product and it is hardly big enough to provide for the increase in population.[3]

Foreign assistance has been maintained at a high level in recent years and must be increased still further, but as time goes on Bangladesh will have to finance a greater proportion of the development programme from internal resources. Improvement in the operation of the economy will increase production and with it government revenues; some part of this will come automatically as existing taxes are applied to a higher level of gross domestic product. More than this automatic revenue increase will be needed, however; every effort will have to be made to increase revenue by imposing additional taxes and making existing ones more effective. In the budget for 1974-5 taxation was increased substantially, but the improved budgetary position estimated for 1975-6 reduced the pressure to increase the incidence of taxation and only minor changes were introduced.

There is, of course, no object in attempting to increase government saving beyond the point where it contributes effectively to improving the functioning of the economy either by providing current services or by increasing development expenditure; it may have been judged by the Minister of Finance that this point had been reached temporarily in 1975, but it will certainly not obtain in later years. There is every reason, therefore, to examine the management of public finance from the point of view of the government's ability to raise money for its activities by the imposition of taxes and the raising of other revenues. In a Note we also make some comments on the use made in Bangladesh of the distinction between development and non-development expenditures as a central element of public finance management.

Structure of Current Receipts. The taxation base is weak. Much of the money that is raised by government depends on direct or indirect levies on imports, either on the imports themselves or on commodities manufactured from them. The structure of revenues estimated in the budget for 1975-6 is shown in Table IV.1.

The importance of customs duties, excise duties and sales tax is evident from the table. Other sources of revenue can be increased but are of lesser significance in the short term. Some items of revenue essentially balance outgoings, for example the item for the railways. For the short run, improving government revenue really comes down to increasing indirect taxes such as customs and excise and making

---

[3] Some development will also be financed in the private sector from private resources, but this will be small and will not change the position materially.

TABLE IV.1
CURRENT GOVERNMENT REVENUE BUDGET 1975–6
BY MAJOR ITEMS

	Taka Crores
Custom duties	240
Excise duties	155
Sales tax	105
Nationalised sector	21
Income and corporation taxes	65
Land revenue	6
Interest receipts	64
Railways	44
All other	55
Total receipts	755

Source: Annual Budget for 1975–6.

them more effective, while recognising that there is scope to increase the yield also of some other taxes. It is always possible to obtain some increase in the efficiency of taxation systems. Tax evasion is a common feature of life in Bangladesh and further measures to tighten up tax administration could have the effect of increasing revenue considerably. This applies also to the operations of local government authorities and to statutory bodies concerned with the provision of utilities.

The scope for raising money for the government is limited in the short run. To increase revenues by about Taka 250 crores at the prices ruling in 1975 is likely to be as much as can be done in the next three or four years, even if things go much better than they have during the difficult years since Independence.

In the long run the agricultural sector can be and must be made to pay taxes to the government. At the present time this sector accounts for 60 per cent of the national product; major increases in income of many agriculturalists can be expected as development gets going. Similarly, in the long run the nationalised industries may contribute significantly to government revenue, but at the moment their real contribution is a matter for conjecture; what they contribute to the government may well be offset by the losses they make and now cover by direct borrowing from the banking system. While an early beginning is called for in terms of tax or other payments to the public exchequer from the sectors of agriculture and nationalised industry, we see little prospect of significant contributions from these sectors in the next few years.

Customs Duties. Rates of duty vary greatly. Some goods enter duty free, in other cases duties exceed 100 per cent, but the average incidence is moderate, and excluding foodgrains (which are duty free) amounts to only about 20–25 per cent. For a long time imported goods were so scarce on the Bangladesh market that it was possible to sell them at a considerable premium. Cigarettes made from imported tobacco were selling in 1973 at 1 Taka per packet above the controlled prices. This alone amounted to Taka 60 crores on the output then being produced by the factories. Cotton cloth and yarn were also selling at prices over 100 per cent higher than those fixed ex-mill and in quantities which could have netted Taka 70–80 crores.

There were still opportunities to make excessive profits from imported goods in 1975 but they were much less than formerly as a result of changes in policy. Devaluation in May 1975 raised internal prices of imports while the supply had been augmented by an increased flow of aid; in the case of the textile corporations, permission had been given for them to fix their own prices so that any premium that could be obtained from the sale of manufactured imports accrued to the corporations (and hence to the government) and not necessarily to merchants or consumers. Nevertheless, there is still scope to increase import duties and this is likely to be increasingly evident as development proceeds and demand rises.

There would be much to be said for increasing duties on types of goods previously lightly taxed. In the past, in the interests of giving greater protection to industries engaged in the early stages of manufacture, raw materials tended to be lightly taxed; in spite of some revisions to the tariff structure since Bangladesh was established, this continues to be the case. There is really no good reason why raw materials, semi-finished manufactures and imports of capital goods should not be submitted to much the same rates of duty, and distortions in the structure of effective protection thereby removed. In particular, there is no case for exempting capital goods from duties. When such goods are used in government-financed projects an increase in tax revenue confers no net advantage to the government because investment costs rise correspondingly. For the private sector of the economy this is different. The reason for advocating the imposition of import duties on capital goods in both cases lies in the need to economise on these, as on any other purchase, and to make sure that appropriate price relativities are maintained between capital and other types of goods. It need not be feared that this will have the effect of holding up development because of the high cost of capital goods. It is not lack of demand that is holding up investment so much as a shortage of imports, financial resources and implementation capacity. The imposition of a tariff on capital goods in line with that on other goods would help to cure this.

While there is a strong case for simplifying the tariff structure, high rates of taxation (whether in the form of tariffs or sales taxes) should continue to be applied to luxury goods. The purpose of this is to discourage luxury consumption as strongly as possible whether domestic or imported resources are involved; this means that domestic production in this case should also bear high rates of taxation. High import duties are always liable to encourage smuggling; this is another reason for spreading duties as widely as possible so as to prevent duties on some commodities from being so high as to make smuggling very profitable. So far as luxury goods are concerned much higher than average duties will have this effect but this is something that will have to be borne with. Altogether it might be possible to increase government revenues by as much as Taka 150 crores by rearranging and increasing the incidence of tariffs.[4]

Excise Duties. Excise duties in 1975–6 were expected to raise Taka 155 crore. There is scope for further increases. Over sixty items are dutiable, but in practice 85 per cent of the revenue comes from tobacco and petroleum and 95 per cent from these and six other items—tea, sugar, cement, soap, matches and man-made fibres and yarn. The two main revenue raisers, petroleum and tobacco, depend largely on imported raw materials; they could just as well be taxed through the operation of a tariff, but it is convenient to single them out and subject them to excise duties in the interests of raising revenue in a flexible way. Tea and sugar depend much more on domestically produced products and the excise duty may have the effect of taxing agricultural incomes to some extent. No reliable estimates exist of the value of manufacturing output on which excise duties might have been levied in 1975. The net output of large-scale manufacturing industry on which excise duties are easiest to levy has been estimated to be about Taka 300 crores in 1974–5 at 1972–3 prices. The corresponding figure in 1974–5 prices must have been much greater but no figures are available. The gross value of output is, of course, much higher still. A large part of industrial output consists of jute manufactures for export and this may be considered as largely ineligible for the imposition of an excise duty. It is also convenient to exclude tobacco and petroleum because they are very highly taxed.

[4] If the composition of non-food imports was such that one-quarter of the total consisted of goods used for development purposes, increasing the average incidence of customs duties from about 20 per cent to 40 per cent of their cost would increase revenues by Taka 200 crores in total but by only Taka 150 crores on balance, after allowing for the increased cost of development.

The remainder of the industries on which excise duties could be imposed may have produced a gross output of the order of Taka 400 crores on which excise duties of about Taka 30 crores would be levied. The incidence of the duties on this section is clearly small and even allowing for the uncertainties of the figures can scarcely be more than 10 per cent; even so the scope for further increase is limited. There are always some goods which governments do not wish to tax and there are problems in levying excise duties on a large number of minor commodities which are produced by considerable numbers of establishments. In fact, to spread the excise net much wider than it was in 1974 might involve bringing a further 1,500 establishments into the taxation net. In a country where every endeavour is made to avoid taxation—very often successfully—this is a much more difficult assignment than it may seem. Thus it is unrealistic to think that more than perhaps Taka 20 crores could be raised additionally in the near future without raising the incidence of excise tax to quite high levels in a large number of cases.

Although the opportunities to raise revenue through increases in excise tax are limited at the present time, longer term prospects remain quite strong.[5] Basically the excise tax is a flexible means of raising revenues. Provided that development really gets under way, excise taxes will form an increasingly valuable source of revenue.

Local Taxes and Water Rates. The opportunities for local government to raise revenue are not great. The most important of these are taxes on immovable property, and the octroi. There is the usual conflict between the needs of central and local revenues, particularly in relation to property taxes. The national budget of 1974–5 introduced a betterment levy as well as taxes on rents that could have been raised just as well by the local authorities. It is disappointing that both these taxes were abandoned in the budget for 1975–6 without any indication being given that they would be transferred to local authorities.

[5] It is difficult to estimate what part of the revenue raised by Pakistan from excise duties in the 1960s can properly be regarded as resulting from activity in Bangladesh but Alamgir's estimates in *Bangladesh National Income and Expenditure, 1949/50–1969/70,* Bangladesh Institute of Development Studies, June 1974, p. 200, for the period 1959/60 to 1969/70 appear to demonstrate that it is a flexible means of raising revenue. In 1960, 10 per cent of Pakistan's revenue receipts, which could reasonably be attributed to Bangladesh, were raised from excise duties equivalent to only about $\frac{1}{2}$ per cent of the gross domestic product; ten years later this had risen to about 20 per cent of taxation revenue and 2 per cent of the GDP.

Very considerable difficulty can be met in attempting to get consumers to pay for their use of gas, electricity and water. In order to make people pay their bills and wipe out their arrears even curfews have been imposed in which all the houses in areas selected from day to day were checked for payment of bills and for the unauthorised tapping of supplies without payment. Use of water has traditionally been assessed in relation to the rental value of houses and other buildings. As a condition of a World Bank loan for the provision of water in Dacca and Chittagong, a move has been made to the use of metering as a basis for assessing charges. In economic terms such an arrangement has much to commend it, but in practice it may give rise to abuse as it is associated with higher charges for water, and illegal connection to the water mains may be encouraged too. It is almost impossible to effect charges for communal supplies of water, such as those supplied by street taps. It is also nearly impossible to ensure that such taps are ever turned off. Devices fitted to turn the water off automatically when it was not being used were frequently broken off and water continued to be a free good for many.

Nationalised Industries. The government's immediate financial position would be helped if the nationalised industries were making a reasonable return on the capital invested in them. As we have seen, their failure to do so is not always their fault and in some respects government policy has been such that they have been forced into an unprofitable condition. The railways and the post office are included in the government's accounts and their financial performance is thus subject to scrutiny. The nationalised industries are only beginning to get the same attention, and the need for all of them to make profits related to their capital and turnover remains. In the First Five Year Plan their potentiality as a source of finance was well understood. It was suggested that by 1977–8 they would be able to make a contribution to the government amounting to 12 per cent of their assets (in addition to making provision for depreciation). In the long run this is really too small; industry in Bangladesh should be able to get a greater return than this on its capital; the same applies to banks and other nationalised institutions whose financial performance (in easier circumstances) has been much better. The sector as a whole could reasonably be expected to provide the government with taxes or profits (excluding depreciation) of Taka 100 crores or more. The prospects for reaching such a sum even in five years' time will not, however, be at all good unless all the nationalised industries are allowed to charge higher prices in addition to being able to improve their real performance.

Agricultural Taxation. The most striking change that has been made in the taxation structure since Independence has been the relaxation of taxation on agriculture. The reason for this is largely political, but it is also a reflection of the difficulties that are experienced in taxing agriculture when many small and impoverished farmers are involved. Traditionally, agriculture has been subjected to a land tax. This was how the Mughals prospered and no less how the British strove to raise taxes from the agricultural sector. Land tax was once an important source of revenue in Bangladesh but its contribution to central revenues declined severely after the end of British rule. The Awami League, in which large landowners are prominent, was committed to the abolition of land tax before Bangladesh was established, and when it came to power this was carried into effect on holdings less than 25 bighas. In fact the net loss of revenue was not great, but as a tax there is potential for the future. Land tax in its most sophisticated form is capable of adaptation to varying conditions of fertility and to changing profitability. It is not an easy tax to collect, however, and it has to be remitted when crops fail. The current yield from taxing holdings of 25 bighas and above is about Taka 5 crores, compared with about Taka 15 crores before Independence when the tax was much more widely spread. There is an agricultural income tax in force, but its effects are largely confined to the tea estates and it has little immediate potential for the collection of increased revenue.

Agriculture provides almost 60 per cent of the gross domestic product; there are very considerable opportunities for increasing output in this sector, and if total revenue is to be buoyant as total output increases, means will have to be found to bring a much increased weight of taxation to bear upon it. In principle taxation can be levied on the inputs used by agriculture, on the output produced by the sector and on the income generated and on the expenditure made out of those incomes.

The scope for taxing land must be judged in relation to the output that can be obtained from it. One acre of land cultivated by traditional methods can yield 15 maunds of paddy[6] per crop. At a price of Taka 50 per maund,[7] the value of the crop is Taka 750. Part of the output will be needed to pay for outgoings but the actual cash outflow is likely to be small and, calculated in terms of money, the return should not be less than Taka 500. Farmers with 2–3 acres, a typical holding, could expect an income of Taka 1,000 to 1,500 per year from a single crop. This is, of course, a very small sum of money, but a family of say five equivalent adults requires about 30

[6] Paddy is rice in the husk.
[7] The procurement price fixed by the government for 1974–5 was Taka 74 per maund.

maunds of paddy to live on, and the larger holding would yield a substantial surplus with which to buy other things. Two acres of rice cultivated by traditional methods and yielding only one crop a year provides for subsistence. If it is possible to get two crops a year, if more than two acres are owned, and the use of more advanced technologies increases yields, the picture can change dramatically. A farmer with 5 acres obtaining yields of 30 maunds of paddy for two crops a year would in fact be far above the starvation line. It is true that his outgoings would rise more than in proportion to the increase in output because the better strains of rice require fertilizer, and two crops a year would probably require expenditure on irrigation and hired labour; nevertheless, he might net something like Taka 10,000. Thus, for favourably placed farms, and as new technologies are deployed, there is clearly scope for agricultural taxation.

A start can be made in relation to this by applying a progressive land (or income) tax to agricultural holdings in excess of 25 bighas, which apparently has always been politically permissible. A tax of Taka 25 per acre on holdings of 25 to 30 bighas rising to Taka 75 per acre for holdings of over 75 acres would yield additional net revenue of over Taka 20 crores if it could be collected economically and if evasion could be thwarted. In a later chapter we discuss the need and scope for elimination of existing subsidies on agricultural inputs, including water, in the interest of improving the use of such inputs; this also would have the effect of increasing the contribution that agriculture makes to central revenues. In the main, however, it is clear that the contribution that agriculture can be expected to make to public revenue depends on the extent to which output can be increased. It was hoped in the First Five Year Plan to increase the output of foodgrains from a level of about 11 million tons of available rice to $15\frac{1}{2}$ million tons within five years. This may be too optimistic, but if it came to pass, the increase in the annual value of output would be about Taka 1,000 crores if the price were Taka 75 per maund. A tax of 20 per cent on the additional income produced by such an increase in rice output alone would raise Taka 200 crores.

There are thus many ways and means of taxing agriculture and much scope for realising significant resources for the public sector if introduction of the new technologies is successful and if production increases on the scale presupposed in the Plan. Of course, if government fails to provide the support needed or mismanages its agricultural policies, the scope for increased revenue will be very much reduced.

Borrowing Private Savings. The problem of government finance could be readily managed if there were any real prospect that private sector savings would be larger than the amount required to finance private investment, and if such net savings would in fact be lent to the government, in particular through the purchase of government bonds. Since in the case of Bangladesh today and in the near future this is most unlikely to occur on any scale, the government is reduced to relying on the banking system for substantial amounts of finance to meet its requirements. Again, provided the government's drawings on the banking system are balanced by net savings made by the private sector and deposited there, this would not be inflationary, but it would require skilful government control of the banks.

Private savings need to be increased if investment is to be financed. When there are famine conditions not many people can save but some individuals are not on the poverty line and some have made large windfall profits. The first aim must be to stop people getting money for nothing simply because they are a merchant for something in scarce supply. This was not done in the first years of the existence of Bangladesh. Much of what was made in this way was, no doubt, not put into bank accounts but part presumably was. In addition, there were savings of less wealthy people and of profitable enterprises to ensure, among other reasons, that they had enough money in the bank to conduct their day-to-day transactions. Private savings may in fact have been quite considerable.

The decision to allow the private sector greater opportunity for industrial investment will help to channel some savings into development directly but only if enough inputs are available. Without some opportunity to use savings profitably, either they will decline or they will produce unpleasant financial effects: soaring land values, pressures to send money out of the country or to buy any other available asset. The move to higher interest rates will help, but it needs to go much further if it is to have the desired effect both of encouraging savings and of enabling the government to borrow such savings directly by the issue of bonds, savings certificates and other fixed interest securities.

Unfortunately there is no apparent readiness to invest such savings in government bonds, and private sector savings fall short of the demands on the banks for finance for the private sector itself and the nationalised industries. As a result the financial resources that the government could lay its hands on without drawing on new money created by the central bank were much too low.

2. Price Inflation and Policy

The world is getting reconciled to price inflation. It is no strange experience for inhabitants of the Indian sub-continent to be submitted to very large increases in prices when food is short and famine among them, but the sustained increase in prices in Bangladesh has transcended previous experience in its severity and longevity. By the middle of 1974 retail price indices were three to three-and-a-half times their level in 1969–70 and were rising further under the pressures of famine conditions, so that by the end of 1974 prices were roughly four to four-and-a-half times the 1969–70 level. There is a general feeling that government has failed disastrously in handling the problems of inflation and thereby has brought suffering to millions and ill repute to itself. Much of this is exaggerated, but price rises of the size and nature experienced in Bangladesh are proof of serious and persistent imbalances in the economy, the causes and consequences of which are critical matters for government concern as well as indicators of the government's ability to govern the economic life of the nation effectively.

Short-term fluctuation in the cost of living in response to variations in the supply of rice are not difficult to explain. The demand for rice in such a poor economy is very inelastic; when rice is short, consumers divert most of their current income to purchasing it; the near-destitute sell the little they have to get the money to buy food, parting with land if necessary; the destitute starve. Moreover, the market is very narrow, so that those suffer who habitually buy the rice that they consume rather than grow it. Many face difficulties not only over payment but also in securing the rice itself, as producers and traders hoard it as an asset of value and as a speculation in the hope of still further price increase.

General inflation, spread over all commodities, affects most classes of the community alike; but increases in the price of rice (and reductions when they occur) relative to other commodities, fall unevenly in their impact, and affect different classes of the population in different ways. Farmers with large amounts of productive land benefit. They get much higher prices for the amounts they sell. Those with small holdings are protected by the amount they grow, but if they have to buy rice because the amount of land they own is too little to support a family, they also suffer from the rise in price; even if they have supplementary employment they will not get wage increases sufficient to compensate for the full increase in price. It is these small-holders who may be forced to sell their one asset, land.

Government employees whose incomes do not follow the price of rice are also subject to strain. They can for a time curtail their purchases of other things or draw on savings if they have any, but they too are not in a good position to resist a general rice shortage, particularly if, as is likely to be the case, the price of other foods has risen in sympathy, or because production of these foods has also been reduced by adverse growing conditions. They may be insulated to some extent from the worst effects of famine conditions by the issue of rations at controlled prices in the towns (the rationing system provides much less well for those outside the urban areas), always assuming that the government has enough grain in hand to continue to operate the rationing scheme on a significant scale. Other sections of the community suffer or benefit according to the extent that they have an interest in food production, or have savings to draw on or others assets to sell. Those with surplus income over and above that needed for bare necessities can manage and draw their rations. Food scarcity falls very unevenly.

There are no easy solutions to the rise in prices engendered by a fall in production, or by its failure to grow in line with population. The lines on which the problem should be attacked are well-known. If Bangladesh could increase the output of food sufficiently to generate an export surplus, a bad crop could be accommodated by reducing exports and the problem moved to other people who ought to be able to buy elsewhere. If Bangladesh were rich enough, temporary food shortages could be met by imports as they now are to some extent; the consequences of doing this at present are, of course, that other imports cannot be purchased for lack of resources. In practice, international assistance will help to secure food but only some of what is needed. In any case shipment of grain takes time and the famine may have taken its toll by the time imports arrive.

Emergency relief might not be necessary if it were possible to establish a reserve of grain within Bangladesh. This has been recognised for very many years. The difficulty is to accumulate the 1–2 million tons that would be needed. Increased production must be the ultimate answer to all the problems of food shortage but it will be some years before the increase will be big enough to leave a sufficient margin for stock-building; accummulating a reserve from imports depends in the last resort on what other countries are prepared to give Bangladesh. There is, however, one well-recognised way of trying to even out the availability of rice and that is by procurement. This is not a popular measure. If food is bought openly in the market by the government, the ruling price will rise rapidly, probably out of all proportion to the government's purchases; government intervention is always likely to affect prices more than purchases of private individuals who buy in small lots, over a wide area and who can respond speedily to market fluctuations. The government is believed to have an unlimited purse and there will be considerable publicity, including adverse comment, if it is falling behind on its planned purchases. In short, government purchases are likely to affect expectations more than those carried out by the private sector. The solution is not to get the government to purchase through private hands; that would not change the matter, it might even make it worse.

Difficult though it may be, the government may have to procure the rice from farmers at less than the market price. Rice must be procured from those with a surplus to sell. Certain rules governing the amounts that farmers can be made to provide have been developed. Two-thirds of a maund of paddy per month (to the next harvest) per member of the family over three years of age, can be retained in addition to seed. Under the policy the government would procure 50 per cent of the surplus up to 200 maunds and 100 per cent of the balance in excess of this figure. It is these rules and the effectiveness with which they are implemented which govern both the total of rice purchases and the equity with which they are made. Attempts to evade them are certain to be made, and with increasing vigour, the lower the purchase price. The experience of government procurement has not so far been encouraging. In 1973–4, a year of excellent harvests, only 70,000 tons of foodgrains were bought by the government; in 1974–5, 127,000 tons are said to have been procured, but it was far short of expectations.

Until it is possible to establish a reserve of rice there is very little that the government can do directly to control prices. It is not just a question of the price of rice. In an economy as open as that of Bangladesh it is almost impossible to insulate the price level from movements in international prices. No country importing on a considerable scale was able to protect itself from the rise in prices of imported commodities that took place in 1973 and in 1974, and Bangladesh was particularly badly affected. The fact of the matter is that price movements are very difficult to regulate by government action though they can, of course, be aggravated by it. It must also be recognised that price control by government action is not an easy thing to enforce in any country and is even more difficult in Bangladesh.

Imported foodgrains have been issued under the rationing schemes at prices below cost. It is not hard to find a justification for this procedure in the desire to protect those with inadequate access to food, but there is not really much scope in a country as poor as Bangladesh to subsidise consumption. Subsidies designed to improve living standards might be better made in the form of payments for work, for it is lack of remunerative work that leads to the most abject forms of poverty. A further disadvantage of the subsidy is that it is indiscriminate in its operation; in the towns all individuals are given ration cards not just those who are desperately impoverished. In the modified statutory rationing areas only low income earners are entitled to a limited number of rationed commodities and this seems to be preferable. Another problem is that it does not appear that the rationing system can be administered very efficiently. In 1973 a determined drive was made to eliminate the use of fake ration cards, but the problem was still with the government in 1974.[8]

Efforts to establish fair price shops are also subject to similar and rather worse difficulties. After liberation about 4,700 fair price shops were established with the intention of distributing consumer supplies at prices related to production costs. Many of the shops were originally run by "freedom fighters",[9] but the arrangement proved to be unsatisfactory. The difference between controlled and market prices has often been very great, and the opportunities to make windfall profits were bound to give rise to abuse. Politically the sale of goods at controlled prices in conditions of scarcity has much to commend it, and although the policy may not produce the results that were intended from it, to abandon it would be particularly awkward. But if in practice there is not much chance of enforcing price control, it is not only pointless to continue it, but also positively harmful when it results in a number of individuals becoming rich because they exploit the profitable opportunities that it presents. This has been one of the scourges of Bangladesh's economic organisation so far.

3. The Exchange Rate

Balance of Payments Pressures. By 1974 there could be no doubt about the severity of the balance of payments problem or about the effect that it was having on the Bangladesh economy. Imports of foodgrains, which seem bound to continue on a substantial scale for many years (say 1 million tons even in 1980), are likely to cost $300 million in a year of good harvests and $400 or more in one of bad, unless there is a big fall in prices. Consumption of oil ($1\frac{1}{2}$ million tons) may cost $150 million, cement and fertilizers another $100 million, cotton and yarn $100 million, and edible oil $75. Other current inputs on a modest scale may come to $300 million and capital goods for very modest development programmes to, say, $300 million. Altogether a total of the order of $1,400 million a year.

---

[8] See the *Bangladesh Observer* for 1 July 1974, for example, reporting 60,000 fake ration cards in Dinajpur.

[9] Those who had fought to establish Bangladesh.

Against this can be set earnings from commodity exports of say $450 million and a net deficit of about $50 million on invisible account. Even with some success in export promotion, the accounts can be balanced with any semblance of ease only if $1,000 million or more can be found each year in the form of foreign assistance. It is against this background of dependence on aid and inadequate export performance that the significance of exchange rate policy needs to be examined.

The system of import controls and export incentives inherited by Bangladesh gave the official rate of exchange a secondary role in regulating the economy. The exchange rate was over-valued; attempts to correct for this by licensing imports and by subsidising exports failed lamentably and did little to prevent the economy from developing in a distorted and inefficient way. At independence a new rate of exchange was fixed of Taka 19 to the pound compared to the previous official rate of about Taka 12. Although this might suggest that the currency was devalued substantially, this was not in fact the case: previously exports had been subsidised by a complicated system of effectively multiple exchange rates, and the new exchange rate represented if anything a marginal revaluation of the currency.[10] Pakistan took the opportunity to devalue her currency after the war and profited from this in being able to increase exports. The position was not the same for Bangladesh; there was little to export that was not already being exported, and little prospect that the position could be speedily improved; it seemed convenient to equate the currency with the Indian rupee, in turn aligned with sterling. Events speedily showed that the new exchange rate was inappropriate and that the economy was suffering from a serious over-valuation of the currency that was having much the same drawbacks as in earlier days.

Any hope that an over-valued currency would have the effect of keeping the price of imports down to the final consumer was speedily shown to be misplaced. The price of imported goods reflects the relative scarcity of such goods; price control was ineffectual, and in

[10] Under the Pakistani regime the industry benefited from a system of bonus voucher licences whereby those exporting goods were given import licences which could be sold on the open market or used outside the allocation system to purchase goods needed for the running of the business. Towards the end of 1971 the bonuses allowed for raw jute, jute goods and other exports were 15, 35, and 45 per cent of the value of exports respectively. Since the premium on the bonus vouchers amounted to almost 200 per cent, the effective exchange rate for the goods in question worked out at about Taka 15 for raw jute, Taka 20 for jute goods and Taka 22 for other export items.

the face of a limited supply of goods from abroad, prices rose to the point at which excess demand was cut off. In the process there were opportunities for those in possession of import licences to make a killing. The demand for imported goods in Bangladesh at present levels is highly inelastic and the consumer was mulcted by those marketing consumer goods. The most severe criticisms of the system were that it led to too easy pickings, to political favouritism, and that it surrounded government with fringe supporters who existed for what they could get out of it. Against these criticisms the economic consequences of the overvalued exchange rate may seem of lesser significance. Imports appeared much cheaper than real costs dictated. The virtues of monopoly as a means to get rich rather than hard endeavour were abundantly demonstrated, while exports were relegated into a backwater of inattention. The misallocation of resources led to waste and abuse.

The defects of the system were most obvious in relation to exports. Hardly any goods could be exported at a profit. At the going exchange rate it was almost impossible to offer the farmer a price that would encourage him to grow jute rather than rice; the jute mills, plagued with a series of difficulties, operated at a loss with little hope of turning it to a profit; losses were made good by borrowing from the banks and this led to inflationary tendencies. The same was true of other exporting industries and, where the banks were not forced to support loss-making operations, the government itself had to come to the rescue of the lesser export industries by offering subsidies to keep them in operation. In so doing the government overtly acknowledged the need to counteract the effects of an over-valued currency. Subsidies offered in 1974 included 30 per cent for some items of so-called slow-moving exports, ranging from betel leaves and animal by-products to bamboo and art products. The reluctance of emigrants to repatriate funds through official channels was recognised by offering a special rate of Taka 30 to the pound; even so the flow was intermittent when the black market rate rose above this figure. For tea, special subsidies were also introduced to stem the losses that were being made by the tea gardens. As with the jute mills, inefficient production methods played a part in making tea production unprofitable, but the over-valued exchange rate was a major factor.

Devaluation in May 1975 was a tardy recognition of the damage that was being done by an over-valued exchange rate. The size of the devaluation was also a recognition of the extent to which the Taka had been over-valued previously—there are few countries that are prepared to devalue their currencies by 50 per cent. Even so the new exchange rate did not remove all the premium obtained from the sale of imported goods, although it was greatly reduced.

In the last resort the appropriateness of the exchange rate will be determined by whether it will make exports sufficiently profitable to offer some long-term prospect that Bangladesh will balance her international receipts and outgoings without recourse to licensing. It is not only the profitability of the traditional exports of Bangladesh that is in question but also the profitability of exporting goods which so far have been sold abroad in small quantities, or which so far have not been thought of as export goods. This, however, is for the future; for the next few years Bangladesh must continue to survive in export markets on the strength of her traditional exports, mainly jute and its manufactures. Jute competes with rice for the use of land and in considering how the exchange rate should be fixed it is necessary to expose the underlying facts which determine the relative profitability of growing these two crops.

Profitability of Exports. The problem for the next few years may not be so much to increase the sale of jute and manufactures from it, as to arrest the decline in jute production that has taken place. This has come about because the severe shortage of rice has pushed up its price relative to jute and led to a reduction in the jute acreage. If Bangladesh is to continue as a producer of jute and jute manufactures for export, supplies of jute have to be safeguarded. Failure to do so will lead to the gradual erosion of overseas markets as synthetics or natural substitute fibres from other countries cut into Bangladesh's markets. Production of jute can to some extent be influenced by the price that the government is prepared to guarantee to growers. At the very least, prices must be offered for jute which will ensure that sufficient is produced to keep the domestic mills in full production; clearly much more than this is needed if export markets for jute are to be preserved. The main varieties of jute are cultivated from March to August. During this period they compete for the use of land, mainly with rice and to some extent with sugar and other crops. The cropping pattern is complicated and affected by soils, rainfall and flooding; planting jute is an alternative to raising an aus crop of rice in most cases, but it may also preclude the sowing of broadcast aman which is harvested in November and December, and in other cases it competes with the *boro* crop, which is harvested about April. It is not surprising that the amount of land put down to jute depends on the relative profitability of growing rice and jute to a considerable degree.

Estimates of the returns from growing jute depend on assumptions about yields and upon estimates of the cost of labour and of ploughing and on the extent to which chemical fertiliser and pesticides are used which may be subsidised by the government. With traditional technology the key standard costs per acre for jute are 110 man-days of labour, 23 bullock-days, 40 maunds of farmyard manure and a small amount of seed. Various prices can be assigned to these inputs and on reasonable assumptions the cost of cultivation may be of the order of Taka 600–800.

The cost per acre of growing rice may be estimated similarly, using standard costs for traditional technology of 65 man-days, 25 bullock-days and 26 maunds of farmyard manure, giving a range of cost on various price assumptions of Taka 500–700, i.e. somewhat less than the per-acre cost of growing jute by traditional methods. There is not, however, a great deal in the cost differences.

The yields of jute and rice per acre (measured as paddy) are very similar for traditional technology, about 15 maunds per acre. This suggests that if jute is to be cultivated in competition with rice, the "farmgate" price of jute must be of the same order of magnitude as that of paddy. These are average relationships. On some land jute does better and on other land paddy; in some cases substitution between them is difficult or resisted. Nevertheless, relative price is a crucial factor in determining the proportion of land used for growing jute (and of course rice). Historically it seems that the acreage put down to jute in a particular year reflects in large measure the relative price of jute and rice the previous year, so that a 10 per cent change in relative prices (jute to rice) increases the acreage put down to jute by 5 per cent. The relationship shows some signs of changing and it is believed that the acreage is less responsive than it was in earlier periods; also the conditions now obtaining are vastly different from those of even ten years ago; jute has shown little price change, but the price of rice has risen markedly. Past relationships may not, in changing circumstances, be much guide to current practice.

To the extent to which such relationships hold, the exchange rate could be used as an instrument to influence the production of jute for export. If investigations of the demand for jute and the competitive pressure of major substitute fibres, particularly polypropylene, the main synthetic competitor, suggested a target figure for the quantity of raw jute to be exported, an "equilibrium" exchange rate could then in principle be selected that would bring forth this quantity. If, for example, for the required quantity a price of Taka 90 per maund[11] would persuade farmers to grow the target quantity, and if Taka 50 per maund would cover the cost of preparing the jute for export and transporting it to the ports, then the rate of exchange would have to be such as to equate Taka 140 per maund to the

[11] The minimum price fixed for purchases from growers in 1975.

appropriate international price, say £150 per ton. Since a maund is 80 pounds approximately, the required rate of exchange works out at just over Taka 26 to £1. Similar reasoning may be advanced in relation to the export of jute manufactures also.

The relevance of this line of reasoning is, however, affected by the fact that the profitability of growing rice is also dependent on the exchange rate. Although at present Bangladesh is an importer of foodgrains, the domestic price of rice is not altogether determined by the world market. The market is fragmented in various ways and in fact rice is exported, or rather smuggled, to India where it commands a price which is dependent on the local Indian market. The issue of the relative prices of jute and rice is clouded by the fact that while much jute is exported at the official exchange rate, both may be exported at black market rates. Looking to the future, Bangladesh may be faced by a situation in which world prices will govern internal prices of both jute and rice. The internal price of jute depends on international prices for synthetics (polypropylene) and general world demand for jute; the internal price of rice depends on the Indian supply position in particular and on the world market in general. If, at some point in the future, Bangladesh becomes a net rice exporter on a large scale, the role of international pricing would become dominant, and cultivation of jute and rice would become competitive and alternative in terms of earning foreign exchange, and therefore, adjustments in the exchange rate would not be an instrument for altering the relative profitability of growing rice and jute.

In the longer term, however, there are many uncertainties, and in the shorter run prices of rice and jute may deviate considerably from world parities. So long as the rice price does not automatically reflect movements in the exchange rate, the rate that is set will in fact affect the relative profitability of growing jute rather than rice.

The relative internal prices of jute and rice are bound to fluctuate from year to year. Steps may be taken to regulate the price of jute; but these may be largely ineffective as regulators of jute production, since farmers' reactions will also depend on the price of rice which it would be much more difficult to control. Market changes in foodgrain prices, such as have occurred in the last few years, affect the acreage put down to jute considerably; alterations in the exchange rate could scarcely be regarded as a device for short-term regulation of production and supply. The use of buffer stocks would be more appropriate for this purpose or possibly the imposition of a tax, at varying rates on the export of jute, which may have been in the mind of the government when it imposed an export tax of Taka 50 per bale in 1975.

The previous calculation suggests that devaluation may have done a good deal to restore the potential profitability of jute for export. Long-term trends, however, may continue to be against jute. The rise in the price of oil has done only a little to subdue competition from synthetics, largely because raw material costs account for a small proportion of total production costs. Where rice can be grown as an alternative to jute, changes in technology will affect relative profitability. In the immediate future it is likely that yields of rice will improve much more quickly than yields of jute. New varieties of rice are getting accepted, and some of the fertiliser needed for their cultivation is being supplied. New technologies can also be used for jute but they are less well known, more uncertain, and unlikely to be adopted on an appreciable scale in the immediate future. It should not be at all unreasonable to expect an increase in the average yield of the *aus* crop, and this might seem to give a long-term advantage to rice. However, quantity and price are related, as we have seen; if yields of rice rise, shortages will be less likely and there will be greater readiness to cultivate jute.

At the new exchange rate the profitability of the jute mills should be considerably enhanced, but devaluation affects not only manufacturing costs. Raw jute is exported for manufacture elsewhere and so commands a world price; devaluation gives the domestic industry no advantage in this respect, and since the cost of raw materials accounts for a large proportion of the cost of jute manufactures, efficiency in manufacturing is an all-important matter. The best insurance of efficiency would be a high level of world demand for jute goods manufactured in Bangladesh and sufficient raw jute to enable the jute mills to manufacture at levels approaching capacity. Incentives to cultivate jute are thus of as much importance to the jute manufacturing industry as they are to ensure a supply of raw jute for export.

Income Transfers and the Exchange Rate. Devaluation is frequently regarded as equivalent to the imposition of a tax on imports combined with a subsidy on exports. In some respects this is true, but there are also differences which are important in Bangladesh's situation. The effect of the devaluation on imports was to reduce the profit previously obtained by those selling imported goods or goods manufactured mainly from imported materials; it did not increase government revenues directly as the imposition of higher import duties would have done. The effect of the devaluation on exports also had very little direct affect on government receipts, although the opportunity was taken to tax exports of jute; indirectly, however, it improved the financial position of the nationalised industries and so the financial position of the government as the owner of the enterprises. In doing so, it augmented the government's cash receipts from taxation levied on the nationalised industries in the same way as it did in relation to private concerns. Since subsidies for "slow-moving" exports should not be necessary in the new situation, revenue expenditure will also be saved. In limiting the adverse effects of devaluation on government revenue, an important aspect was to pass on the increase in the cost of imported foodgrains and sell them at their higher Taka equivalent prices. Issue prices of foodgrain rations were raised.

It is not easy to judge the relative magnitudes of these movements or how they will affect the government financial position on balance. Possibly in the short run the effects may have been adverse to the budgetary position; there is always some trade-off between the need to raise revenue and the selection of the best exchange rate. If so, the time chosen for devaluation was fortunate because it coincided with a strong upward movement in government receipts from imports due to an increase in the volume of imports coming forward as well as from the higher yield received from *ad valorem* import duties. There are signs that the devaluation will benefit the economy quite considerably, and we think it would be a mistake in future not to be ready to adjust the exchange rate if circumstances change. In considering this, a major consideration must continue to be the need to make an increased flow of exports profitable.

Black Markets and the Exchange Rate. Devaluation has helped to diminish one area of grey market activity, that of making profits out of the overvalued Taka by importing goods under licence and selling them at a large mark-up. It was not to be expected, however, that it would eliminate all black market activities. The extent of such activities are always difficult to assess: there are no censuses of black market operations. What is believed about them is largely a matter of judging what truth lies behind rumour. The activities most relevant to the exchange rate are those of the export of capital and the smuggling of goods over the border. One of the best-known ways of exporting capital is through the under-recording of exports or the over-invoicing of imports. Placing import orders through the Trading Corporation of Bangladesh reduces the opportunities for this kind of evasion of the law; it would be naïve, however, to suppose that it eliminates it entirely. There are other ways of engineering capital flight; when distrust in the economic future of a community is rife, it is not too difficult to find ways and means. Quantitatively the most important of these methods is to smuggle tradeable commodities from Bangladesh over the border to India. To some extent, this also was confined by state trading when jute was brought and sold through government corporations, although growers might not sell to them. The freedom given in 1975 for private traders to export jute (although only at controlled prices) represents a loosening up in trading arrangements which might have the effect of increasing smuggling.

Rice also is reported to have been exported illegally to India. The extent to which this occurred in 1974 is difficult to gauge. Newspaper guesses of the quantity of foodgrains exported are not to be relied upon, but figures have varied from 1 to 2 million tons. Similar guesses for the export of jute suggest that 10–20 per cent of the crop was smuggled out. These are very large figures.[12] The higher estimates for the export of grain are equal to the actual flow of foodgrain imports in the same year. The estimated flow of jute would be at least equivalent to the amount that was to have been exported to India under the trade agreement for 1973–4 (the actual amount officially exported was much less). The evidence is very difficult to appraise, but it points strongly to the conclusion that there must have been smuggling of rice and jute on a large scale.[13]

Whether exchange rate adjustments can reduce such flows depends largely on the motives and incentives that lie behind the smuggling operation and unauthorized capital exports. Those determined to leave the country and take their capital with them are not likely to be deterred by measures designed to increase the cost of their operations. Similarly, those bent on smuggling in order to import goods not available under the import licensing system will not be much affected either.[14]

For the smuggler who is not concerned to secure goods or to establish a currency balance abroad, but wishes to acquire Takas directly, devaluation may have the effect of reducing the incentive to

[12] Only a massive expertly organised operation could have made it possible to ship as much as a million or more tons of foodgrains across the border. It took very considerable international initiative and organisation to move this quantity into Bangladesh after liberation.

[13] Is it plausible, for instance, that India had a bumper harvest of jute in 1972–3 at a time when the price of foodgrains had risen very strikingly, tending to tip the balance in the direction of the production of foodgrains, and when the Bangladesh harvest had shown no signs of abnormally high yields? Was it, as was suggested, the case that jute produced in Bangladesh simply moved over the border to reinforce the Indian crop?

[14] Smuggled goods are sold in the foreign market (India) for foreign currency (Indian rupees). This foreign exchange is often left abroad—and represents illegal capital export—or is used to buy goods which are then imported illegally to Bangladesh. In the latter case a barter transaction in fact takes place; that does not really require any financial expression and therefore is independent of the exchange rate. The effect of devaluation on such transactions is likely to be minimal.

export goods illegally. In this case the smuggled goods would be sold in, say, India and the proceeds used to buy Takas on the black market there. It is the difference between the official and the black market rate of exchange that makes such an operation possible. If the effect of devaluation is to narrow this gap the incentive to smuggle will be reduced. Since there are always costs and risks in smuggling, the gap need not be entirely eliminated for this to happen.[15]

Even a very considerable devaluation might not close the gap between the official and the black market rate very appreciably.[16] The pressures to secure foreign currency outside official exchange arrangements are high. Black markets are not so much monetary affairs as a phenomenon associated with real scarcities. It is only when scarcities are eliminated that illegal transactions cease. Until this happens the only real checks to smuggling will be those that are concerned with the enforcement of the law.

NOTE TO CHAPTER IV: *The Concept of Development Expenditure*

The central concept of financial planning in Bangladesh is that of development expenditure. In statistical terms there is not much difference between expenditure on development and investment. Conceptually there are differences; certain types of expenditure are included as development which would not normally be included under investment expenditures. One argument for this procedure is that such expenditure contributes to development as much as investment. This has led to the inclusion in development expenditure of some expenditures that would normally be regarded as current or consumption expenditures, such as the cost of teachers' salaries paid during the first few years of establishing a new school. Subsidies on such things as the use of fertilisers and loans to development bodies by the public sector may also be included on the grounds that they promote development elsewhere.[17] Definitions of development

[15] Periodically the newspapers publish information about the number of persons shot in the process of smuggling. Between March 1972 and April 1974, 162 were claimed to have been disposed of in this way. It remains to be seen what discouragement this will prove!

[16] It appears that the effect of the devaluation in 1975 was to improve the black market value of the Taka in terms of the Indian Rupee, but this may also have reflected increased import availability.

[17] This practice can sometimes give rise to double counting of investment expenditure, for example, when investment in a sector of the economy is directly estimated from physical indicators while part of the finance provided for the investment is included as public sector development expenditure.

expenditure are arbitrary and may be better or worse in varying contexts than the more conventional definition used for the purpose of measuring investment. They may give a measure of activity that is greater than that which would result if investment alone were measured.

The desire to distinguish between development expenditure and non-development expenditure and for that matter between investment and consumption is simply that the one type of activity is expected to lead to advancement in the future and the other essentially to the maintenance of existing scales of activity. Development expenditure, because of its promise for the future, is often regarded as a superior type of expenditure of greater value than other types. This view also tends to be held by countries and agencies providing aid. Assistance with development expenditure is generally the aim, and assistance directed to maintaining current expenditure and consumption tends to be regarded as being in some sense unproductive because it ought to be met out of finances raised by the country itself without the need for assistance. In fact, reflection shows the distinction to be blurred. Current expenditures often constitute as important an element of development as so-called development expenditures themselves.

Administrative classification of development expenditures may be blurred for other reasons. Estimates of future expenditure by government departments probably have a better chance of administrative acceptance if they can be described as developmental in character. Sometimes it is possible to include large planning staffs within the developmental budget. How much such staffs contribute depends on the extent of the development activities of these departments and their activities can be regarded as in the nature of overheads of development. It is because of this that cutting a development programme can often have an effect out of all proportion to the extent of the cut if, as is usual, it falls mainly on activity in the field but not on expenditure on planning staffs and the administrative support organisation.

In Bangladesh the need in post-independence years was to be able to keep the economy operating and the people fed. Non-development expenditure and aid to sustain it was just as important as development expenditure. In the past, Pakistani administrative arrangements tended to pay too much attention to investment and too little to the means to operate the capacity created. Bangladesh must not make the same mistake; whenever capacity cannot be operated fully for the lack of inputs there is a *prima facie* case to cut back the development effort and direct resources to current needs.

CHAPTER V

DEVELOPMENT OF THE ECONOMY

1. *The Outlook for Change*

There is no shortage of econometric models capable of predicting, on certain assumptions, the course of the Bangladesh economy over a period of years. The problem is that there are too few reliable figures to put in them, and the relationships used in the equations are inevitably highly questionable. Nevertheless, some speculation about where the economy may be in twenty-five years' time is necessary, if only to point to key items for immediate decision. It is true that many decisions are likely to affect the course of events for only a few years ahead and can be recast in the light of events. But not all decisions are of this nature. To take but one example: some decisions related to physical planning will affect the character of the countryside for many years and the effects of taking action, or failing to do so, will be intensified as time goes on. Apart from this, we wish to see for our own interest what it might be possible to do to improve the lot of the inhabitants of Bangladesh by the end of the century and to gauge how much assistance from outside would be necessary to support the development of the economy at a realistic rate.

An imaginative solution to the difficulty of the absence of good data for Bangladesh was devised by Professor Robert Dorfman and those associated with him in developing a model[1] based on relationships chosen from the experience of other countries bearing some resemblance to Bangladesh in their stage of evolution and characteristics. The objective of the Dorfman model was to determine the amount of foreign assistance that would be needed by Bangladesh, if a reasonable level of employment were to be maintained. Ingenious and sophisticated as this approach is and in spite of the flexibility with which it can be applied, it is far from clear that it makes proper allowance for the peculiarities of Bangladesh's economy and its institutional problems. To some degree countries do follow similar paths of development, as Simon Kuznets has demonstrated.[2]

[1] This model has not been published, but is summarised in a World Bank study on agriculture and water development issued in 1972.

[2] For example in *Modern Economic Growth, Rate, Structure and Spread*, New Haven, Yale University Press, 1966.

Sectors such as agriculture decline in importance as productivity increases, while industry grows in relative importance, in line with the changing needs of wealthier people. After a time, services also expand in relative importance and eventually the number of people engaged in producing goods may be exceeded by that of people providing services in education, commerce, transport, government and other similar occupations. Something of these changes will become manifest in Bangladesh if development really gets going, but it is not to be expected that there will be any close imitation of the development paths followed by other countries; moreover, there may have to be a conscious effort to direct the pattern of development differently in order to cope better with the extreme poverty that Bangladesh is likely to experience for a considerable time and to make it more bearable.

The perspective we present in this chapter can hardly be dignified with being described as a model; the analysis underlying it is essentially an extremely simple one; we doubt whether the uncertainties involved justify the use of anything much more complicated. The real uncertainties are not so much those related to economic relationships as those inherent in the view that is formed about the prospects of getting the force of political commitment and the reorganisation of systems for development that are indispensable.

The task we have set ourselves in this chapter is to look beyond the next few years to draw an overall picture of Bangladesh's potential for continuous and longer term structural change and development. In this forward look we base our analysis on the assumption that the preconditions for development (as discussed in Chapters III and IV) will be met. As an aid to presentation, rather than as the core of the argument, we have summarised our assumptions, prognostications, judgements and analysis in Table V.I: Development Scenario 1975 to 2000.

For our discussion of potential development to the end of the century we need a base against which to measure change. For the sake of comparison we have chosen to present our best estimates for the current year, 1975.[3] It is a comment on the state of basic information and statistics about the Bangladesh economy that the base figures have to be somewhat arbitrary.

At the time of writing there is still considerable uncertainty with respect to the size of the *population* (and even more the momentum for further growth inherent in current demographic characteristics). Our estimate of 80 million for mid 1975 is roughly consistent with current government estimates and also with the provisional figures

---

[3] Note that estimates in Table V.1 are in approximate 1974 prices.

Table V.1
DEVELOPMENT SCENARIO 1975–2000
(values in approximate 1974 prices in US$ equivalent)

A. Population and Major National Accounts Magnitudes

	1975	1980	1985	1990	1995	2000	Total Growth Index 1975/2000
1 Population (mill.)	80	93	106	121	136	150	187
2 Gross Domestic Product (mill. $)	6400	8170	10930	14630	19610	26140	401
3 Gross Investment ”	550	1225	1965	2635	3530	4710	855
4 Net Capital Import ”	800	980	1310	1465	1570	1570	218
5 Domestic Savings ”	−250	245	655	1170	1960	3140	184
6 Consumption	6650	7925	10275	13460	17650	23000	n.a.
7 Gross Product Per Capita ($)	80	88	103	121	145	174	n.a.
8 Consumption Per Capita ”	83	85	97	111	130	153	n.a.
9 Domestic Savings Per Capita ($)	−3	3	6	10	15	21	
10 Gross Investment as Per Cent of GDP	8	15	18	18	18	18	
11 Capital Import as Per Cent of GDP	12	12	12	10	8	6	
12 Domestic Savings as Per Cent of GDP	−4	3	6	8	10	12	

B. Annual Growth Rates and 25-year growth index

	1975/80	1980/5	1985/90	1990/5	1995/2000	1980/2000
13 Population	3·0	2·8	2·6	2·3	2·0	2·4
14 Gross Domestic Product	5·0	6·0	6·0	6·0	6·0	6·0
15 Gross Investment	17·4	10·0	6·0	6·0	6·0	7·0
16 Gross Product Per Capita	2·0	3·1	3·3	3·6	3·8	3·5
17 Consumption Per Capita	0·6	2·5	2·9	3·2	3·3	3·0

C. Selected Ratios

	1975/80	1980/5	1985/90	1990/5	1995/2000	1980/2000
18 Capital-Output Ratio	(2·0)	2·7	3·0	3·0	3·0	3·0
19 Marginal Overall Savings Rate (per cent)	(28)	15	14	16	14	16
20 Marginal Per Capita Savings Rate (per cent)	(62)	32	24	20	22	21

obtained from the 1974 population census, if the latter as in previous censuses reflects an under-enumeration of 5 to 8 per cent.

The estimate of *gross domestic product* in total or *per capita* is even more uncertain. Available estimates for previous years differ and in any case need to be adjusted for changes in prices and volumes for recent years. For the purposes of these comparisons, we shall use a base year (1975) figure of US$80 equivalents for *per capita* GDP. This is higher than the figure for gross national product of $70 used by the World Bank in its international comparisons (for an earlier year and at different prices and exchange rates),[4] but with the present inflated domestic and international prices of Bangladesh's major crop rice, our estimate of $80 may in fact be on the low side.

Gross investment in our base year (1975) is bound to be low— perhaps roughly as in 1974. Our estimate of $550 million includes both public and private investments.

Net capital imports—or the value of the overall current import surplus—of $800 million in the base year (1975) corresponds to disbursements in 1974–5 as expected following the meeting of the Bangladesh Consortium in October 1974 and subsequent experience with actual aid arrivals.

The four estimates described above determine the structure of the economy in our base year 1975 as shown in Table V.1, including levels of overall and *per capita* consumption and savings. The picture drawn reflects the extremely low level of production, income and productivity in Bangladesh, the relatively very large addition to domestic production represented by foreign assistance (corresponding to more than 10 per cent of total use of resources in Bangladesh), and the dependence of Bangladesh on foreign supplies for investments and for food and other consumption items.

Numerically, our picture of development and change over the period to the end of the century as given in the Table is generated from our assumptions and judgements about the future course of development of population, gross domestic product, gross investment, and the proportion of investment financed from net imports and domestic saving. Each of these major parameters is analysed in the following sections.

2. *Population*

As a matter of practical judgement, it is hard to believe that there is any hope of checking the growth of population at all speedily, so

[4] *World Bank Atlas*, 1974. The difference in concepts used, GDP *versus* GNP, is numerically insignificant for the purpose of our discussion.

long as it can be fed. But every year lost in making progress in this respect makes the problem more difficult. In the first four years after the creation of Bangladesh, virtually nothing has been accomplished to stem the rise in population. How long will it take to mount an ambitious programme? How effective could efforts to check the rise in population be once a large enough programme were put in hand? Realistically it seems unlikely that Bangladesh will mount any effective programme for the control of population within the next five years. The programme so far as it has gone is weak and ineffective. In the Annual Plan for 1974–5 it is said:[5] "The targets for 1973–4 were modest and not achieving these targets would cast doubts about the objective of slowing down the population growth rate." The Plan goes on to put its faith in the effects of the organisational changes that were introduced in 1973–4. With the experience of other countries in mind it may be doubted if the claim to have reduced the number of births in 1973–4 by as much as 40,000 will prove to have been well founded; but even if it were, it would amount to no more than 1 per cent of the total births that in fact occurred in that year. Even if this is regarded only as a start, it will be several years before the programme builds up to a level at which it will have a real effect. There is nothing as yet to suggest either that the actual population growth rate is less than 3 per cent per annum or that it would fall to less than 2 per cent within the next twenty-five years. It may not fall at all and that would mean that the population would more than double by the end of the century. Still less does it seem credible that the reproduction rate would fall by the end of the century so as to reach a level corresponding to an ultimately stationary population. Thus, in reflecting on the future, it is reasonable to assume that the population will increase for a while at something like the present rate of 3 per cent per annum on the average, slowing down it may be hoped as time goes on. However, until there is a very major change in the priority given to family limitation in Bangladesh, the decline can hardly be significant before the end of the century. A simple assumption of 3 per cent annual growth of population to the end of the century might well be unduly pessimistic, but to alter the assumption to one of a gradual decline in the growth rate as time goes on makes uncomfortably little difference to the arithmetic of the population size in the year 2000.[6] It does make a much more

___

[5] *Economic Development in 1973–74 and Annual Plan for 1974–75*, Planning Commission, Government of Bangladesh, July 1974, p. 176.

[6] A 3 per cent rate of growth over twenty-five years gives a population size at the end of the century about 10 per cent larger than a growth rate declining gradually from 3 to 2 per cent during the same period.

significant difference, however, to the momentum for further growth in the next century.

The relationship between the postulated rate of increase of population and the rate at which food output can increase is critical. It is difficult to think that the population could double or more than double if Bangladesh were not able to increase her food output, for if this occurred she would become wholly dependent on foreign charity to feed the additional mouths. Foodgrain imports are already necessary to feed one out of every six of Bangladesh's population. Nothing that happened at the World Food Conference in Rome or since leads us to believe that the world would be ready to sustain on a continuing and cumulative basis an additional 2 to 3 million people per year in Bangladesh for very long.

3. *Food and Agriculture*

In the past Bangladesh has managed to increase her output of rice quite significantly. Between the early 1950s and the late 1960s production of rice increased by 40–50 per cent. The increase did not quite keep pace with the increase in needs but the balance was not too greatly disturbed. The opportunities to continue to increase output of food are still there; in many ways they have been enhanced. How quickly they will be taken advantage of is a matter that is difficult to determine. The scope for an increase in output stems from the basic fact that although the soil and climate favours rice cultivation, yields are low and much lower than is technically possible.

The means to increase yields are well known: the rate at which they can be applied is not. There is very little prospect of being able to increase the acreage of agricultural land in Bangladesh; indeed it will almost certainly be reduced because of the need to increase the use of land for other purposes as population increases. Increased output of foodgrains depends on increasing the productivity of land by using improved types of seeds and fertiliser, by irrigation, by drainage and flood protection and by expanding the acreage under multi-cropping.

There are uncertainties about every aspect of the programmes that will have to be put in hand. Probably the least of these uncertainties lies in the possibility of making enough seed available and persuading farmers to use it. The advantage of using new varieties of rice is now well appreciated, and while government action can help and has helped to supply seed and get it accepted, progress will be made irrespective of any assistance that government may give; the demonstration effect will eventually be sufficient to make farmers wish to take advantage of them. Recent experience suggests that estimates of the speed with which farmers have already adopted the new seeds have been exaggerated, but the change-over to new seeds is sufficiently profitable for there to be confidence in the assumption that farmers will gradually, if not with dramatic speed, wish to acquire and use them.

There can be much less certainty about the prospects of providing the fertiliser that is needed for use with the new varieties of rice. Given time, Bangladesh can provide the nitrogenous fertilisers she requires as well as a surplus for export. Potassic and phosphatic fertilisers have to be imported, and supplies of these may not be readily available. This apart, how much can be bought will depend on foreign aid programmes.

Irrigation will be necessary if much greater use is to be made of the land area during the dry season (December to April). Attempts to install tubewells have gone slowly so far. If, as is currently planned, an additional 250,000 acres could be irrigated per year, this would increase the annual output of rice by $\frac{1}{4}$–$\frac{1}{2}$ million tons or more per year, perhaps enough to provide for the increase in population until such time as irrigation is fully exploited.

The potential for increased production has been studied in great detail by the World Bank. The conclusions reached are both tentative and intricate, but they may be illustrated by a picture of development to the end of the century as follows: by changing the inputs alone—i.e. by introducing new seeds, fertilisers and pesticides—it would be possible to double rice output; if irrigation were also practised to the fullest extent, output could be trebled, while with the further addition of drainage and flood control, it would be possible to quadruple output. Economic constraints were not taken into account in reaching these conclusions. The cost of increasing output rises progressively as additional measures become necessary and the whole of the improvements that could be made economically within the limits of presently known technology would realistically take several decades.

Historically, an increase in rice output of 3 per cent per year would seem quite large, but this has been within the reach of Bangladesh in the past, and it ought to be possible to do better in the future. In this respect the experience of other countries adopting the use of new techniques is of interest. Average output of rice in Pakistan (where major irrigation facilities as well as new techniques were introduced) increased by 73 per cent between 1960–3 and 1970–3. This was not at the expense of output of wheat (the main staple crop of Pakistan), for this increased by 45 per cent over the same period. Increases in other countries were less spectacular over the same period, but Indonesia achieved a 30 per cent increase in yield as did the Philip-

pines. In wheat India increased her average yield by over 50 per cent.[7]
In the case of Bangladesh it should be possible to increase rice
production by as much as say 4–5 per cent per annum provided that
a determined development programme is carried through. Allowing
for opportunities to increase double cropping, it does not seem too
unreasonable to suppose that output of grain might increase at an
accelerated rate compared with the past and that there would be a
good chance of increasing domestic foodgrain supplies more rapidly
—perhaps up to 2 per cent more rapidly—than population. Also for
the agricultural sector generally—i.e. including all crops, livestock,
forestry and fisheries—an average annual rate of growth of value
added of 3–5 per cent ought to be attainable until the end of the
century.

The assumption that it will be possible to increase output of foodgrains *per capita* at the rate of 2 per cent per annum holds out the
prospect of attaining food self-sufficiency and ultimately, possibly, of
exporting food. It also provides some indication of the extent to
which it might be possible to generate savings for the finance of
development from the increase in agricultural incomes, following the
well-worn economic argument that it is out of the surplus over
subsistence that economic growth may be generated.

One of the difficulties in assessing when food self-sufficiency can
be attained is that increased production of food will inevitably give
rise to an increase in the consumption of food by the producers
themselves. Very little is known with certainty about how the
consumption of foodgrains will increase with increased income. It is
not just a question of increased human consumption of grain, but also
of the quite strong probability that farmers would use part of the
foodgrain surplus that they generated to increase the output of
livestock and animal products. Indeed some increase in the livestock
population will be necessary in order to secure the increase in grain
output presupposed. Estimates of the increase in the consumption
of foodgrains as incomes increase have varied greatly for Bangladesh
and similar countries. As a working assumption it might be reasonable to conclude that foodgrain consumption will increase *pari passu*
with the increased population, currently 3 per cent annually, *plus*
1 per cent annually to meet higher levels of consumption by producers
themselves, leaving only 1 out of the assumed maximum of 5 per
cent increase in rice production for increased sales on the market.

If this proved to be a valid assumption, about an additional
100,000 tons of grain would become available year by year for sale

[7] Figures quoted from a draft paper presented by Dana G. Dalrymple
at a conference held in Oxford in 1974.

during years of normal harvests. Such a rate of progression may seem much too slow. It would mean that imports of food would diminish only slowly and would take nearly the whole of the period to the end of the century to be eliminated. If consumption *per capita* could be kept down to its present level, the time to self-sufficiency would be shortened but it might still take ten years. In the First Five Year Plan it was assumed that it would be possible to attain self-sufficiency in the plan period; this was too optimistic but it underlines the need to increase production more rapidly than seems likely to occur without a good deal of stimulation. As Akhter Hameed Khan has pointed out in his fascinating survey of events,[8] in every crisis in Bangladesh agricultural policy is subjected to the concept of a crash programme. That, of course, is what is needed, but crash programmes seldom materialise as effective stimulants.

4. *Overall Growth and Investment*

We need now to make some assumptions about the rate at which output of other sectors of the economy may increase. The output of a number of them will be linked to that of agriculture, particularly because this will determine the amount of resources that can be channelled to them. From historical comparisons and on general grounds we would expect them to increase rather more quickly than agricultural output. In industry, for example, an increase of 10 per cent per annum or more can be attained, and civil works might be increased even more rapidly with the object of increasing employment. We assume that a rate of increase of 7 per cent on the average for non-agricultural output would be a resaonable figure to take. This again is probably at the top end of the scale and it may take some time to realise it.

Put in the simplest terms, what we are saying is that it seems practicable to us for Bangladesh to increase value added in agriculture by 4–5 per cent per annum and in other sectors of the economy by 6–7 per cent per annum, which would mean that overall GDP would grow by about 5–6 per cent per annum in total, roughly doubling GDP *per capita* over the twenty-five year period. This will mean that the share of agriculture in the total product will fall slightly and that from being somewhat more important than all the other sectors combined, it will become somewhat less important.

The expansion of overall output which we have projected for the

[8] *Three Essays by Akhter Hameed Khan: Land Reform, Rural Works and the Food Problem in Pakistan*, Asian Studies Center, Michigan State University, East Lansing, May 1973.

rest of this century depends on Bangladesh's being able to deal successfully with the problems of economic management and then to move into a period of sustained and growing investment. As we have repeatedly stated, unless the government takes effective command of the economy, the state of extreme poverty and deprivation, of recurring deep crises and of further social disorganisation will become all-pervasive and inevitable; growth and development will be a fading dream. If, however, the government gradually comes to grips with the management of the economy, this will in itself stimulate initiative and production and growth in agriculture and industry, construction, transport and services, both in the public and the private sector; it will also provide a basis for subsequent investment and development to strengthen and expand the economic and institutional capital for further growth. None of this will happen with dramatic speed; in Bangladesh only disaster and destruction happen overnight. But over a period of five years much could be changed for the better and the current dislocation and slack in the economy could gradually be overcome. Indeed, for the next few years it is the establishment of control over the economy by the government and improved management of current economic affairs, rather than expanded new investments, which are needed to re-establish the economy and lift it out of its present depression. In fact the 5 per cent annual average growth we have projected during the rest of this decade will come about with comparatively little new investment or development expenditure. By 1980, when in our judgement the period of establishing reasonably efficient management would be completed, further growth and development would depend more directly on commensurate capital investment. In Note A to this chapter we have some comments on the concept and use of capital–output ratios in this kind of analysis.

Between capital investment and production of output there is necessarily a lag, for an economy such as that of Bangladesh, of perhaps two years on the average. We have postulated that development expenditure will remain at the present relatively depressed level for one or two more years, and then roughly double by 1980, and eventually reach 18 per cent of GDP in the early or mid-1980s. At these levels of investment we calculate that a sustained rate of growth of 6 per cent of GDP would be attained and maintained throughout the rest of this century.

5. *Sector Balance and Strategy*

The levels of gross investment described above (reaching 18 per cent of GNP by the early or mid-1980s) are large enough, if sustained, to effect a gradual but definite change in the structure of the economy and to double the standard of living in the span of a generation. If this is to happen, however, the use of investment resources must be carefully and comprehensively planned in order to ensure a sustained increase in output of goods and services of high social as well as market value. This is a major undertaking, but one which is essential if the government is to be able to see what the future could be made to hold and to be in a position to make the choices that will be open to it. It is no less essential in order to adopt policies and priorities for immediate and medium-term action by the government.

The First Five Year Plan of Bangladesh for the period to mid-1978, which was prepared in 1972-3, represents a beginning of such an effort. While subsequent events have radically altered the basic structure on which the details of the Plan were formulated, it still gives an incisive and explicit statement of basic ideology, objectives and general strategy of development for Bangladesh. The First Five Year Plan was drawn up in the expectation that a quick return to immediate pre-Independence levels of development effort was possible and it produced what later turned out to be rather optimistic estimates of what might be accomplished in the first five years; in the present situation we cannot set our sights so high. Among other things, the Plan discussed how development expenditure should be allocated between sectors on the assumption that more resources would be available for development than can be provided in the next few years.

Table V.2 compares the last development plan drawn up for East Pakistan before Independence with that planned in Bangladesh's First Five Year Plan, and with the Annual Development Plan for 1975-6. The various categories of expenditure are almost certainly not entirely comparable, for classifications have changed from one plan to the next, but differences of definition are probably small enough to allow some tentative conclusions to the drawn. In real terms the magnitude of expenditure proposed in the First Five Year Plan drawn up by Bangladesh was of about the same order of magnitude as that intended for East Pakistan during the five-year period 1970-5, but the composition of expenditure was very different. Rather more than 40 per cent of expenditure in the plan for East Pakistan was intended to be spent on agriculture and rural activities; in the Bangladesh Five Year Plan only about 25 per cent of expenditure was expected to be spent in this way. In the annual plans for 1974 and 1975-6[9] the balance has been changed so that about one-

---

[9] The 1975-6 Annual Plan appears to be about the same magnitude in real terms as the development expenditure planned originally for 1972-3. It represents the mid-year of the Five Year Plan.

third of expenditure is intended for agriculture and rural development. How far this is the result of a deliberate attempt to increase the
share of agricultural activity and how far it is the result of financial
stringencies falling unevenly on different activities is a matter for
conjecture. To concentrate development activity on agriculture is
clearly right in conditions of stringency and one in line with the
strategy necessary to get living standards improved over the next
twenty-five years. It is possible that expenditure on agricultural
development was circumscribed in the Bangladesh Five Year Plan by
problems of devising programmes which would be productive, and
by fears that the inputs needed to launch a really large agricultural
campaign would not be forthcoming. However, there is clearly
considerable scope for increasing development efforts in the countryside once the groundwork of organisation is laid; there would be
much to be said for attempting to spend, say, half of development
expenditure in the villages on activities aimed at increasing food
production and improving rural amenities, and on providing
improved health care and fostering family planning.

In contrast to agriculture, the First Five Year Plan of Bangladesh
increased the amount of expenditure intended for industry by
comparison with previous plans. There were some special reasons
for this, notably the need to increase the output of fertilisers and the
desire of Bangladesh to exploit her resources of natural gas in other
ways. The production of urea is needed to support the agricultural
programmes and to increase exports if there is anything to spare.
It is seldom possible to look at sectoral investment plans in isolation
and this is a case in point. Nevertheless, in total, expenditure on
industrial development needs to be held back when it is in danger of
leading to the neglect of agricultural development either because of
the limited amount of money that can be spent on development or
because of a shortage of administrative talent.

In reflecting on the priorities of development, it is helpful to bear
in mind the intended future pattern of consumption. If the emphasis
of development is laid on improving the lot of those living in villages,
investment and production programmes will have to be devised
accordingly. This means, for example, directing production of
consumption goods to those items which can be economically
produced for mass consumption. The handloom industry may not
be economically viable in the long run, but if fed with yarn it can
provide for the clothing needs of the villagers; it will not be able to
do this if the pressure of fashion moves demand in the direction of the
finer cloths and more expensive shirtings and saris manufactured
by modern machinery. The need is not for colour television but for
television as a means of communication, not for radios operating on

four or more bands, which it seems to be everybody's desire to purchase, so much as for simpler sets that can be produced more cheaply and which will make it possible for the bulk of the population to receive the local stations of Bangladesh. What is required is not the provision of running water in every home or modern sewage systems, so much as the establishment of supplies of pure water within easy reach so as to improve health while at the same time cutting down on the labour of transporting water to the home. Bicycles and the tracks over which they can be ridden must take precedence over cars. Neglect of the simpler needs will lead to investment programmes directed too much in the direction of the requirements of rich, sophisticated and materially oriented societies which Bangladesh cannot afford. Basic needs of the many must come first and the resources available for development have to be channelled accordingly. For education the strategy should be directed primarily to the needs of the village population and to educating them to make the best use of the opportunities open to them in their own environment.

All these considerations point to the need to change quite radically the style of the development effort outlined in the First Five Year Plan, and to shift much of its focus to the villages and to local rather than central administration. But it is a shift in the balance that is required, not a change to the total exclusion of other activities. Investment in transport facilities, in the search for oil, in industries with export prospects, in research establishments and in the distribution of electricity is also required. The main consideration (which we share with the authors of the Five Year Plan) is that investments of this kind should be directed largely to the ultimate ends of improving the lot of the rural mass of the people rather than to establishing economic activities directed to the needs of rich urban communities.

6. *Domestic Resources for Development*

The realism of an investment programme aimed at investing the equivalent of 18 per cent of gross domestic product in five or ten years' time requires to be considered in relation to domestic savings and the provision of resources for investment from abroad. We take the view that domestic savings cannot, and should not, be counted on to finance the full investment bill, either in the immediate situation or in the future. Even by the year 2000 we assume that domestic savings levels will reach no more than 12 per cent of the gross domestic product or two-thirds of investment; the rest we assume should be covered by foreign aid and other net capital import.

The immediate effort needed to increase savings is quite considerable. Currently, Bangladesh saves nothing; in fact we judge that the
need to import food has meant that Bangladesh, in a strict accounting
sense, is dissaving quite considerably.[10] To move from this to
positive savings of perhaps 3 per cent of GDP by 1980 will require a
considerable effort. Yet, in striving not to be overambitious, we
recognise that there are strong arguments for increasing domestic
savings as rapidly as possible, provided that this can be done without
causing political or economic unrest of a counterproductive kind,
and that the savings can be used productively and will not go to
waste for lack of complementary inputs, notably imports needed for
development. In Note B to this chapter we present a discussion of the
costs of saving and benefits of development.

Bangladesh's saving record[11] does hold out some hope of mobilising
resources for development. Domestic savings reached 9-10 per cent
of GNP by the end of the 1960s while net capital inflow amounted to
about 3 per cent of GNP. In some respects, however, these figures
are deceptive. The Pakistan Rupee was overvalued, and the value of
foreign aid correspondingly understated. If this were taken account
of, the estimates of domestic savings might have to be reduced and
certainly the proportion of investment financed by an influx of
foreign capital would be raised. Thus it is probably not wise to base
estimates of the potential of Bangladesh to save on the assumption
that she was in fact able to finance investment equivalent to 9-10 per
cent of the GNP in the late 1960s.

Any increased growth of output in excess of growth of population
will raise the potentiality to save. This is particularly important in
terms of the food balance. Even though food self-sufficiency may not
be attained for ten years or more, growth of output in excess of
population will progressively help the balance of payments and
provide the means to increase imports of other goods, including
those needed for the development effort. It could also be the means
of providing domestic resources for development. But if this is to
occur it will be essential to devise policies that will prevent increases in
production of foodgrains from being frittered away. Increased
consumption and smuggling could rapidly devour any incipient
surplus that might be developed. The ways in which this might be
frustrated include taxing farmers to a much greater degree than is

[10] In national income accounting a deficit on the balance of payments
is conventionally regarded as financing investment. In fact it should be
remembered that foreign aid is also intended to finance consumption,
for example, the import of foodgrains.

[11] See Mohiuddin Alamgir and Atiqur Rahman, *Savings in Bangladesh,
1959/60-1969/70*, Bangladesh Institute of Development Studies, 1974.

done at present, the active procurement of grain from the villages and, as an inducement to sell grain, the provision of adequate supplies of consumer goods in the rural areas. It is impossible to judge with confidence what success policies of this kind might have. One factor that may work in their favour will be the likelihood that the increase in agricultural output will be very unequally spread. Although we have postulated an average increase of only 4–5 per cent per annum in the output of grain the increase which will materialise will be dramatic for those farmers who are able to secure new seeds, adequate supplies of fertiliser and access to water supplies for irrigation. With the new techniques it is perfectly possible to double output from one harvest to the next. Thus many farmers will find themselves with much more rice than they have any wish to consume; this will make it easier to procure rice from them and they may be prepared to sell it through official channels or through the open domestic market, provided prices are attractive, and that they can use the sales proceeds to purchase goods they need without having to resort to smuggling.

As indicated above, it is doubtful if even the most vigorous policies will make it possible to capture more than one-fifth of increases in food production for improving savings and the balance of payments. Nevertheless, even this—if it could be secured—would represent a substantial increase in domestic resources for development. It would mean adding cumulatively to savings each year the equivalent of perhaps as much as $\frac{1}{2}$ per cent of the GDP of that year. To many observers of the previous record of Bangladesh this will seem too optimistic; it will be accomplished only if a series of policies such as those discussed elsewhere in this book are put into effect.

The increase in income generated in other sectors of the economy also add to the potential for saving. Only at the end of the period we consider will other sectors combined be as important as that of agriculture in terms of net output, but they will be easier to tax in certain respects. The activities of industry and commerce lend themselves to the imposition of indirect taxes; construction of buildings adds to the rates; expansion of transportation activities gives the opportunity to raise money from taxes on fuel or through appropriate pricing from the profits of the nationalised transport sector. Expansion of some other sectors is less productive of public sector receipts and savings. Education is seldom paid for by the general public, the output of civil servants is often not taxed and, if it is, simply adds to expenditure; but all these activities, while providing additional incomes from which personal savings can be generated, also help to swell indirect revenues to government.

In summary, it ought to be possible over time—and provided

development in fact proceeds as envisaged—to increase domestic savings from its present low (probably negative) rate to 10 per cent or more of GDP towards the end of the century. With population then increasing by perhaps 2 per cent, this would allow a margin for addition to capital from Bangladesh's own resources beyond what is required just to replace old capital and put the additional population on the same level as those already living in Bangladesh in terms of the capital stock with which they work.

The potential of domestic resource mobilisation for investment as discussed above can be realised only if savings are in fact used to build the country's capital stock; those who save must release their savings for real development activities by those who invest. If the mechanism for such transfer does not work or works deficiently, savings will fall short of their potential—or they will find a way of being transferred abroad as capital export.

The First Five Year Plan relied heavily on private savings as a source of finance for the development programme but made very little provision for investment by that sector. Private sector saving was estimated to amount to nearly Taka 1,000 crore during the plan period, while private investment was put at little more than half that figure. It was assumed that the difference would be lent to the public sector, including the banks. This meant that the proportion of private saving taking the form of the accumulation of financial assets amounted to well over 40 per cent in the Plan calculations. Such a proportion was never approached before Independence; in 1969–70, 30 per cent of the savings of the then private sector (including concerns subsequently nationalised) was placed in financial assets but 20 per cent was a more normal pre-independence figure.

The First Five Year Plan gave insufficient attention to this issue. The mechanism of monetary policy and for that matter direct controls are quite unlikely to be strong enough to cope with a transfer problem between private sector savers and public sector investors of the magnitude required by the Plan. In the scenario we have developed in this chapter, however, the problem may be manageable. We have set more modest overall domestic savings targets, relying for finance of development, as we shall see in the next section, relatively more on large and sustained aid flows; we have relied on a strategy of improved management rather than heavy investments for the early years, thus also giving time for financial policies to be sharpened up and for public sector savings to expand, particularly through measures to revise agricultural taxes and receipts from nationalised industries; we have taken account of the wider role now given to the private sector in industry; and we have outlined a strategy of development which gives more weight than in the Plan to the rural economy, to agricultural and related services, to locally initiated and financed development and to construction. All of this would give a better initial balance between savings potential and need for development finance in each sector, public and private. The problem of transfer of resources from savers to investors will of course not disappear, the need for monetary and financial institutions and policies to handle such matters will remain important but the scenario we have outlined, in contrast to the Plan itself, is unlikely to set an impossible task of mobilising adequate domestic resources in the right hands.

7. *Foreign Aid and Capital Import*

No attempt is made in Table V.1 to predict by how much exports and imports will increase in the next twenty-five years although the balance between them, representing a new inflow of resources, is shown. A net import of resources could be consistent with varying levels of trade but we are assuming that a policy of encouraging the flow of trade will be followed. In this case the supply of exports that can be made available will be the determining factor. For the next five years the trend of exports seems unlikely to be a rising one; the prospects for exports of jute and manufactures are rather bad and the supply of other exportable goods, whether new or traditional is also unlikely to increase very much. After that things may change, and in Chapter X we suggest a number of ways in which a more diversified pattern of exports might be developed and earnings increased. One result of this is that the value of imports will not increase very greatly between 1975 and 1980. Nevertheless, what is suggested will represent an appreciable increase over the average of 1973-4, perhaps as much as 20 per cent. The position would be improved further if the fall in prices of imported goods, started in 1974, enabled Bangladesh to secure some continued improvement in her terms of trade and, more important, to the extent that output of foodgrains increased so that money spent on importing them (including foodgrains provided under aid) could be diverted to other purposes. Even so the import position will remain tight in spite of the fact that the value of imports might amount to about 20 per cent of the gross domestic product over the period 1975-80. If imports were to continue to represent the same proportion of gross domestic product as the latter increased over the years, exports would have to increase considerably until in the year 2000 they amounted to about 14 per cent of the gross domestic product, compared with about 8 per cent before 1975. This might be possible in favourable circumstances.

The net capital import shown in Table V.1 will be less than the amount of aid that will be necessary. The reason for this is that Bangladesh already has existing debts to service and, dependent on what proportion of the foreign assistance placed at her disposal is in the form of loans and the terms on which these are made, a considerable burden of debt service could accumulate by the year 2000. Thus at that point of time the total of foreign assistance necessary to provide for the inflow of resources required as well as debt service might be as much as say $2,000 million, compared to the net figure of $1,570 million given in the table. This is a large sum which has to be seen in relation to the need to assist 150 million people who certainly at that date will still be among the poorest in the world. An increasing flow of aid over a period of twenty-five years is contrary to the usual picture of giving assistance which it is presumed will bring the recipient country within a few years to a position where it can progressively be able to do with less help from others. In the context of Bangladesh the standard picture makes little sense. As implementation capacity improves, it will be possible to use increasing amounts of resources effectively and accelerate the measures needed to improve living standards and bring about population control.

In spite of the suggestion that aid should be increased until at least the end of the century the proportion of the net import of capital to gross investment would diminish to only one-third; in 1975 aid will virtually be financing all development expenditures. The present need to help with the maintenance of consumption reflects, of course, the poverty of the country and the amount of foodgrains which have to be imported to prevent starvation.

8. *Employment*

There are vast reservoirs of unemployed and underemployed labour in Bangladesh. It may be surmised that if work were available the number of man-days utilised might increase by rather more than one-third. With the kind of investment opportunities that can effectively be opened up and financed with the resources that are likely to be available, it is quite impossible to think that any real inroads will be made into the problem of unemployment.

A rough analysis of the occupations of the present population of Bangladesh is given in Table V.3, together with illustrative figures for the year 2000.

There is scarcely any possibility that the increase foreseen in agricultural production can give rise to any great increase in employment. New techniques in agriculture do offer increased employment in a number of ways. The application of fertiliser, the use of irrigation facilities, better preparation of the land and the increased effort

TABLE V.3

EMPLOYMENT BY ECONOMIC SECTOR AND TOTAL LABOUR FORCE 1975 AND 2000

Illustrative Calculations of the Incidence of Unemployment

	Million man-years	
	1975	2000
Employment in:		
Agriculture	15	20
Manufacturing	1	4
Commerce	1	2
Services	2	6
All other (including construction)	1	4
Total employment	20	36
Unemployment	8	20
Total labour force	28	56

Note: The figures for 1975 are rough estimates only, based on incomplete information. They must be considered only as indicative of the structure of occupations rather than absolute levels.

needed to sow, plant and harvest a larger crop all add to the labour input. Often, however, the increase in labour needed is not great. For some crops labour requirements double with the full use of modern and productive techniques; but in most cases the increase is no more than 50 per cent and often it is less. It seems extremely doubtful if the amount of employment that the land can offer can be increased by more than one-third on the average, an additional 5 million jobs. When allowance is made for the growth of jobs in other sectors it seems likely that the number of unemployed will increase from something like 8 million to 20 million by the end of the century.

It is necessary to consider this conclusion in relation to agriculture and its implications for development in this sector. The fact that land in some regions of the country will respond much better to the use of modern techniques than in others will itself make for inequality in incomes; so will the fact that individual plots of land will lend themselves better to prior introduction of the new techniques and that some owners will prove more energetic in securing the inputs needed and in applying them. Thus inequality of income among farmers is likely to increase. This effect will be aggravated by the fact that the numbers of people who have no land will increase much more than the amount of additional employment that the land can be expected to offer. The situation may become socially and politically untenable if there is a great increase in the incomes of some at the same time as the number of landless labourers is growing.

It is not at all easy to see how these problems could be dealt with within the existing social order. Families with land will be able to support their relatives through the operation of the extended family system; there will in many cases, at least, be the additional output needed for this, although not in every case. Some families will not increase the yields of their land for some considerable time; in these cases there will be a serious problem.

The difficulties will be at their most acute for the landless. They may seek a solution by moving to other occupations outside agriculture and by migrating to the urban centres, but without much prospect of success unless a vastly greater investment programme can be introduced than appears to have any prospect of feasibility.

Output of manufacturing might possibly increase eight- or even ten-fold over the period we are considering but even if it did, the number employed in manufacturing could hardly be expected to increase more than five-fold. In fact the increase is almost certain to be smaller unless the unions insist on enforcing some massive system of work sharing. This is not so far fetched as it appears, for many of the factories are in fact greatly overmanned at the present time and may remain so for the future. However, it seems unlikely and also undesirable on general grounds that there should be any increase in the relative overmanning of industrial enterprises. Also it is to be expected that the general development of technology will in fact increase labour productivity in spite of policies that may be envisaged for making greater use of intermediate technology, better use of capital through shift working, and by concentrating on industrial sectors in which the labour-capital ratio is greater. The major opportunities for increasing employment outside agriculture and manufacturing lie in building and construction and in the service sectors.

From the point of view of government the important thing may be to try to bring unemployment and underemployment down to a level where it becomes a problem which can in fact be handled, politically and economically, without social disintegration and breakdown of law and order. It is difficult to gauge what such a level might be. With something like 30 per cent unemployment in Bangladesh today there is a good deal of unrest, but the situation today is burdened also by numerous other deficiencies of social organisation and economic management. However, perhaps an unemployment level of 30 per cent of the much greater population in the year 2000 would be even more dangerous from the point of view of social stability.

Even to contain unemployment at 30 per cent to the end of the century would require finding jobs for an additional 3 to 4 million people over and above the employment opportunities foreseen and included in the above calculations. Taxation at the rate of 10 per cent of the gross domestic product would then be required to finance the employment programme alone, which is scarcely practicable in terms of budgetary financing.

The above line of reasoning, insecure as it is, strongly suggests that the present system of ownership of land within a market orientated economy would not function. The essential wealth in Bangladesh is land. It is this that guarantees employment. The average holding of land at the present time is less than three acres; if population continues to increase, as we have supposed, the average holding will be down to less than $1\frac{1}{2}$ acres. This would be enough on average land to feed a family on our suppositions of the increased yields that can be produced. It seems inescapable that there will be great pressure to secure at least this amount of land. In all probability land will have to be allocated to the landless at the expense of those with larger land holdings, if political stability is to be maintained. Such a step will obviously be an extremely difficult one to take. Some measure of expropriation, however, seems quite inescapable. If it were certain that the rise in population would finally have ended by the turn of the century, expropriation and land redistribution might have been a possible solution. But so long as the population continues to increase there will be a continuing need to redistribute land. The alternative of a state takeover of all land of Bangladesh might be a better answer in some respects. Under state or communal management it is possible in principle, although not very readily so in practice, to give employment creation and work sharing explicit and separate weight along with output expansion and financial cost efficiency.

Thus it may seem that if the problems of income distribution and access to work are to be solved, communal cultivation systems will have to be introduced. If this were to be ultimately unavoidable, it would be best to attempt the change gradually. There are not enough trained administrators to take the whole of the land into state or other communal ownership and to ensure that it will be well and effectively cultivated. A pilot scheme, modelled perhaps on that of the Gezira in the Sudan, might offer experience in management. Any such scheme means some form of compulsory transfer of land. The money for purchase on a sufficient scale simply cannot be found by the government, short of creating an inflationary situation which would be totally disruptive. But it would be possible to guarantee former owners of land a share of the amount of product that they have been able to raise from it hitherto, because the opportunities to increase yields are so great. As the increased yields accumulated, it would be possible to use them to provide employment for other workers who were not landowners. Employment might be found on the land for some of them for, as we have argued, the new techniques require some increase in agricultural labour to implement them. But it would also give an opportunity to employ them in other activities within the rural community in which they live, using the increase in the yields of the land to provide the finance needed.

All this is of course straight socialism for which Bangladesh may not be socially and politically ready. But the analysis stems not from any doctrinaire view but from the difficulty of seeing how, given the acute scarcity of land, incomes can be assured for those without it. The only alternative involves the imposition of quite crushing taxation. It would probably have to take the form of imposing a land tax sufficient to ensure that the owner of land was forced to sell a substantial part, perhaps half, of his product in order to pay his taxes. Perhaps a solution along these lines might be attempted. It is possible that it would ensure that owner occupiers attended fully to the cultivation of their land; but it might well retard the application of the most suitable systems of cultivation to other holdings which would be divided into tiny and uneconomic plots little larger than gardens in other countries.

9. *Consumption*

If the rate of increase in output that we think possible is in fact accomplished over the next quarter of a century, what effect will this have on life in Bangladesn? In the first place, it is clear that there will be no great change in the life-style of the country's inhabitants. Consumption will have to rise at a lower rate than the increase in output, otherwise no resources will be available for development; this is particularly so in the first five or ten years. On our calculations, *per capita* consumption would not quite double in one generation of twenty-five years. This would be a very real amelioration of the situation in Bangladesh but no transformation. Income per head at the end of the century would be no higher than roughly the equivalent of that of Pakistan or China at the present day. Bangladesh, almost inevitably, will remain the poorest large country at the end of this century, but it may by then also have become a country in which development has taken hold.

The results of the projected increase in agricultural output on welfare are not easy to predict. The nation will continue to be undernourished for a long time to come. Much of the increase in output which we have argued can be secured will be needed to replace imports of foodgrains. We have also assumed that Bangladesh will be able to increase output of other crops to some extent in line with the increase of rice production. There is hardly any branch of agriculture that does not present considerable opportunities for improvement; yet, to move from a diet of foodgrains supplemented to some extent by fish, animal products, fruit and vegetables to one containing significant amounts of the more attractive and nutritious foods is a costly process. It will also require greater knowledge, and knowledge of a different kind, on the part of the farmers and their families than that needed for adopting new methods of rice cultivation which apparently are now spreading. The diet may be improved in twenty-five years but it will still be deficient in many ways for the majority of the population.

There are severe limits to the extent to which material welfare can be increased. There is no prospect that by the end of the century the inhabitants of Bangladesh will be able to possess many of the things that are so coveted in the developed world. We wonder whether attempts to do so may not only be frustrated by poverty but will also prevent some other improvements in the standard of life that otherwise might come about. To emulate the Joneses without their income may sometimes lead to neglect of alternative patterns of economic expenditure that might, if they were accepted, lead to real improvement in living standards. The essence of the point was made by Professor Sir John Hicks in his article *World Recovery after War*.[12] He argued that market forces could sometimes be unproductive in reacting in conditions of scarcity. The specific situation to which he referred was that of the United Kingdom in conditions of wartime scarcity, in which there were strong pressures of demand for consumer goods. While individuals might be prepared to save up to 15 per cent of full employment income, available capacity for the production of consumer goods might be sufficient only to produce the equivalent of 70 per cent of full employment output. The problem was to ensure that the investment effort was maintained at a level which ensured full output even though consumers, left to themselves, would have been unprepared to save enough to finance the investment needed to fill the gap. The equivalent question for Bangladesh is this: can government action in Bangladesh result in the production of goods and services that otherwise would go undemanded? If so, more employment would be created while greater output would add to the material welfare of the population.

[12] *Economic Journal*, June 1947.

Governments do not hesitate nowadays to intervene actively in deciding the composition of output that it is thought desirable to produce. Some consumers arguing on economic lines may feel that this leads to economic loss, but it is possible that the social gain may compensate for individual deprivation or loss.

Models such as that developed by Dorfman[13] imply that there is some predetermined pattern of production and consumption which economies may be expected to follow. This is far from certain in practice; in principle it is certainly not inevitable. Might it be possible to introduce into Bangladesh a pattern of consumption radically different from that of most countries and still get the same or a higher consumer satisfaction from it? Such a question is almost impossible to answer, but it has to be asked. Consumers' tastes are susceptible to alteration or there would be little point in advertising campaigns; individuals do in fact differ greatly in their tastes and what they wish to consume depends very much on their environment.

In the case of Bangladesh there would be something to be said for attempting to mould the pattern of consumption away from some aspects of the materialistic pattern of Western societies. The shifts that would bring most benefit would concentrate on patterns of consumption of goods over and above minimum needs of basic foods, elementary shelter and clothing, the shift would in general be from goods to services, and from goods that are heavily dependent on imports to those that are more completely domestically produced. It might be possible for instance to concentrate in Bangladesh on having a very high standard of basic education available for all; to develop a village health service of high repute, to direct demand to the provision of housing where this can be done without making heavy demands on imported goods and, perhaps more important, to avoid the wholesale use of the motor-car against which so many countries and towns plagued with traffic-jams and pollution are now revolting. Are the stresses and strains of "modern consumerism" really worth it? Can alternative patterns of living be developed which would give greater satisfaction?

There are a number of ways in which the pattern of demand might be influenced. There is the composition of government expenditure itself which could be directed to the provision of services, the encouragement of the development of cheap housing, the attainment of high standards of culture and sport and other things offering satisfaction which are more readily within the capability of Bangladesh to provide. Taxation could be used to reinforce this process and more generally opinion might be formed to try to influence the

---

[13] Referred to in Section 1 above.

pattern of consumption. It is probably better to face these issues than to leave them to uncontrolled market forces, to demand manipulation by commercial advertising, and to the multinational corporations ready to fashion the pattern of demand in their own interests.

It will not be easy to steer the direction of change in the general pattern of demand. There is every indication in Bangladesh that the wealthy wish nothing better than to follow the patterns of consumption laid down in the West. The tendency on the part of the wealthy to prefer the motor-car, air-conditioners, luxury houses and foreign travel to other things is deeply ingrained, and it will not be easy within the present social and economic system to bring about a transformation in attitudes.

Another aspect of the need to control the pattern of demand is the importance of controlling the environment. At the end of the century the density of population in Bangladesh will be getting on for twice that of the present most densely highly inhabited area; the position will be aggravated by the fact that so much of the country can be pushed under floods as it was in 1974. Land is precious now, and it will be all the more important to use it to the best advantage in the future.

Town and country planning may seem a luxury for a country in Bangladesh's position, but the reverse is really the case. The poorer a country, the more essential it is to use its resources to the best advantage. There are a number of aspects of this that require some discussion. Villages take up agricultural land that might otherwise be used for agriculture. In many countries this is a negligible factor, but the present village population densities of about thirty persons per acre means that the present population requires about $2\frac{1}{2}$ million acres. Doubling the population by the end of the century would require a further $2\frac{1}{2}$ million acres, or 10 per cent of the cultivatable area. The density of housing to be aimed at in villages will have to be much higher than that of many large towns in Europe if land is to be saved. In the towns, in an effort to save land, much higher densities will have to be the norm, perhaps as much as 100 persons per acre.

The second requirement that stems from this disturbing picture is the need to try to prevent the growth of large towns with large numbers of persons living in squalor, often in shacks or unhoused. Movement to towns arises from two causes, the growth in the population itself and the tendency for industrialisation and administration to give rise to large conglomerations of people. The pressures for this to occur in Bangladesh will be very great, particularly if endeavours to find employment in the villages were to fail. An esti-

mate by the Harvard University Population Centre[14] suggested that
the urban population in Bangladesh could increase ten-fold from
its present level of about 5 millions. It is impossible to think that an
increase in urban population of this magnitude could be absorbed
with the resources that are likely to be available for construction,
and it is exceedingly difficult to think that it would be possible to
find employment for such large numbers in urban surroundings;
but even if the resources were there for the construction needed, it
would be best to prevent it.

The enlargement of most towns and the construction of some new
ones will be inevitable as the population grows. It is only in towns of
moderate size that a reasonable range of facilities can be established
economically. But it is seldom necessary to go above 100,000 people
to achieve this, although the key towns of the region such as Dacca,
Chittagong, and Khulna are already above this level and will
continue to grow.

If the population is to be stopped from migrating to the large
towns, very strict control will have to be maintained over the
location of industry to ensure that the development opportunities
it offers are dispersed over much of the country. This policy has been
accepted for some time, and specific encouragements have been
devised to try to give it teeth. What is needed is the co-ordination of
planning efforts on a long-term basis that will ensure that the
infrastructure needed by industry is available. Fiscal and planning
incentives to establish businesses in particular places will not work
unless they are made reasonably attractive also in other ways.

If the broad outlines of trying to maintain the rural character of
Bangladesh could be maintained, life would be much more attractive
than if all the misery of slum dwelling were to be imposed on those
whose standard of living is so low in so many other ways.

10. Conclusions

It is clear from the foregoing that there is little reason for optimism
about the future of Bangladesh. The simple arithmetical processes
that we have gone through offer little reassurance that standards of
living can be greatly raised by the end of the century. We believe
that the assumptions on which we have worked are reasonably
realistic. We hope that things will be better than we envisage; but
fear that they may be worse. Over everything hangs the uncontrollable
increase in population that will make a drastic shortage of land and

[14] Quoted in *Some Social Aspects of Development Planning in
Bangladesh*, United Nations Relief Operation, Dacca, December 1972.

employment opportunities even more severe. We have tried to suggest some ways in which the situation can be ameliorated, but we think that the difficulties of dealing with the economy are bound to create circumstances of great social instability in the future.

The future is always difficult to foresee; it is nevertheless desirable to try to look some distance ahead. In the rest of the book we continue to do this by examining the outlook for change and development, and the strategies and policies needed to influence, control or alter the course of events in some major sectors of the economy.

NOTE A TO CHAPTER V: *Concept and Use of Capital–Output Ratios*

Our analysis of investments required to sustain the long-term growth rate of 5–6 per cent for the economy as a whole makes considerable use of the concept of capital–output ratios. It would be as well to point out some of the limitations of this concept for the purpose for which we use it. In the first place sectoral capital–output ratios can be extremely misleading unless carefully interpreted. This may be illustrated by reference to the construction sector where the ratio is rather low for the construction phase and very high for the subsequent period of actual use of constructed facilities.

Considerable difficulties are also caused by changes in relative prices. Capital–output ratios assume certain sets of prices; if these prices change, the ratios will change also. This is of special significance in relation to the output of agricultural products, the prices of which can change very markedly in a short period of time. With the rapid changes in world prices that have taken place in the last few years, it becomes even more difficult to make reasonable estimates of capital–output ratios, for the inputs needed to increase output will often be bought on world markets and the outputs sold domestically, and different rates of changes in internal and external prices can change the assumed ratios quite considerably. One other consequence of fluctuations in relative prices is that it is very difficult to translate investment requirements as revealed by capital–output ratios into requirements for international aid, all the more as exchange rates may not be fixed in relation to market conditions. Inherent complications such as these mean that there is unavoidably a good deal of uncertainty about the results of the arithmetical exercises we carry out.

Agricultural development drawing on improved techniques has the advantage of being comparatively light on capital. It is not, however, as light as is commonly supposed. New seed can be generated within the sector itself without the need for new investment; it simply replaces the old varieties which can then be consumed. Many other inputs, however, can be produced only if additional investment is provided. Draught animals are conventionally treated as not being part of the capital stock used in agriculture. This is a most peculiar practice, for in most respects they are substitutes for mechanical devices which are unquestionably regarded as part of the capital stock. The kind of expansion programme we envisage would require the number of animals used in agriculture to be doubled by the end of the century (or tractors and other mechanical devices to be introduced). It is also necessary to have some regard to the consequential demands on capital in other parts of the economy which will be needed to support the increase in an agricultural output that it is hoped to produce. The provision of fertiliser will require heavy investment. The consumption of urea alone might increase by as much as 100,000 tons a year. A plant producing 500,000 tons would now cost about $250 millions. Again, as the increase in output becomes more dependent on the provision of irrigation facilities, considerable capital investment will be involved and there will also be attendant investment in other inputs closely associated with agriculture. Since in Bangladesh the associated or indirect capital costs of agricultural development are most definitely going to be of increasing absolute and relative importance, it is very important to take this into account in the assessment of investment needs in support of that development. It is a matter of convenience as well as convention whether such associated or indirect capital needs should be accounted for within the sector of agriculture or in other economic sectors. Combining the sector of agriculture and water resource development, however, the capital–output ratio can hardly be less than one and a half to one; moreover this ratio must be expected to increase as major water resource development projects gain importance in the second half of the period considered. However, the case for investment in agriculture is really made much more directly by the need to increase the output of food to maintain the population than by consideration of the capital–output ratio involved.

Investment in other sectors of the economy must be seen in the light of the support that they give to the agricultural effort and to the balance of payments. The capital–output ratio for other sectors of the economy differ substantially from those of agriculture. In industry and transport, the ratio may be of the order of at least 3 to 1; in the case of utilities it may be as high as 6 or 7 to 1. In construction and trade, however, the ratio is much lower, perhaps about 1½ to 1. On the whole capital output ratios tend to be higher in the non-agricultural sectors.

Even if we are right about the assumptions we have made with respect to the potential for growth of output in agriculture and other sectors it is not easy to translate these into capital requirements. Overall the capital–output ratio assumed works out at about $2\frac{1}{2}$:1. This figuring, however, relates only to the additional capital investment needed to produce additional output. It is necessary also to provide for replacement of existing capital. Even at the low level of production and capital in Bangladesh, the investment needed to replace depreciated capital may amount to some 3 per cent of output. In these average terms, therefore, Bangladesh at present needs to invest $7\frac{1}{2}$ per cent of its gross national product in order to meet the needs of the expanding population; in addition 3 per cent or so is needed to replace worn-out or depreciated capital. In order to stand still, therefore, Bangladesh needs to invest at least 10 per cent of its current GNP. Only investment in excess of this will increase the amount of capital available per head.

NOTE B TO CHAPTER V: *Costs of Savings and Benefits of Development*

There are a number of reasons for thinking that if things went well it would be desirable to step up the development effort financed out of domestic savings. Most of them are concerned with simple arithmetic. One test of the savings effort that should be made is the time taken to restore the immediate reduction in consumption that is imposed by increased rates of saving. If the capital–output ratio is no more than three, it takes only a few years of saving at the higher level to restore consumption to its previous level and from then on the cost of sustained higher savings for the future would have been paid. Saving and investment of an additional Takas 100 would yield a sustained increase in the level of output of Takas $33\frac{1}{3}$, when it came into operation say after two years; in two further years of investment, making four in all, consumption would be restored. The capital–output ratio assumed for this kind of calculation is important; some types of investment, for example those in agriculture, have lower capital–output ratios, and investment in agricultural improvement can be very well worth while in yielding quick returns and restoring spendable incomes. For the same reason, things like double shift-working or, better, treble shift-working make capital go much further and the pay-off from investment come much more quickly. The concept of the pay-off period is important in gauging how much saving could be made politically acceptable.

Theoretical economics suggests that the size of a development programme should be determined in relation to the extent to which a country is prepared to sacrifice present benefits for future gains.

Three factors affect this: the increase in income that can be expected from saving and investing, the valuation placed on additional increments to income and the extent to which future benefits may be discounted in relation to present ones. All of these concepts present considerable difficulty, and the fact that what is envisaged is a social decision, rather than a set of individual decisions determining the size of the programme, makes for further difficulty. It is arguable, for instance, that while it might be proper for an individual to value future benefits at less than present benefits of the same real amount, it may not be valid to make this distinction for the state, which consists of individuals with finite lives but which in its corporate entity can be assumed to continue indefinitely in the future. Difficulty with concepts is only one problem, quantifying the various factors involved is well nigh impossible and perhaps should not be attempted. Nevertheless the results of studies by R. M. Goodwin[15] are of interest, and throw some light on the size of the development programme that governments might attempt to carry out in the case of countries at an early stage of development.

In working out the theoretical implications of his model, Goodwin takes a fictitious community with certain key economic characteristics which fit Bangladesh quite well. What is less certain is whether his assumptions about the shape of the diminishing utility curve of income are equally applicable. Nevertheless, for what it is worth the model and assumptions suggest that it is plausible to try to attain a level of saving of 8 per cent of GNP quite quickly and to increase it to over 30 per cent in about fifteen years' time and thereafter to reach much higher levels. Very few countries would hope to follow Goodwin's saving path. A 30 per cent rate of saving, while consistent with Japan's economic progress in the post-war period, is not the kind of thing to which Bangladesh can hope to aspire, when it is not even at a stage of evolution corresponding to that of Japan in the middle of last century.

[15] "The Optimal Growth Path for an Underdeveloped Country", *Economic Journal*, December 1961, p. 756.

CHAPTER VI

POPULATION

1. *The Facts*

The facts about Bangladesh's population are not precisely known; censuses are seldom very accurate, and in an underdeveloped country such as Bangladesh they are liable to considerable error, despite all the efforts made to check the data and monitor the work of enumerators.[1] It is usual to find more than one estimate for the population at any particular date, because demographers adjust the basic data in different ways to try to eliminate discrepancies and fill gaps in existing knowledge. Nevertheless, the main characteristics of the size and composition of the population are sufficiently marked for past trends and the likely future evolution of the population to be clearly apparent.

Table VI.1 below shows the evolution of the population in the area of the sub-continent of India that now forms Bangladesh.

TABLE VI.1

POPULATION OF BANGLADESH

Recorded Population		*Illustrative figures of future population*	
	Millions		*Millions*
1881	24	1975	80
1891	27	1980	93
1901	29	1990	121
1911	32	2000	150
1921	33		
1931	36		
1941	42		
1951	42		
1961	51		
1974	77		

[1] The census of 1974 is no exception. First estimates from this census indicated a population of 71·1 million; subsequently it appeared that this might be an underestimate of as much as 8 per cent. In the table a figure of 77 million is used for illustrative purposes but it will almost certainly require revision.

The picture that emerges is of marked but not uninterrupted past growth. The population has roughly trebled since 1881, and roughly doubled since 1931. The growth of population in the Indian subcontinent is essentially a modern phenomenon dating from the nineteenth century. In early time the area was probably underpopulated; the invasions of past millennia seem in part to have been prompted by the desire to move to a land of milk and honey where population was kept in check in relation to natural resources. Checks have also operated in the present century; the influenza epidemic after the First World War at least partly explains why there was hardly any increase between 1911 and 1921; the famine of 1943 similarly explains the interruption to growth between 1941 and 1951; and the growth of population in recent years would have been greater had it not been for the War of Independence.

It is doubtful whether anyone attempting to forecast the present population at the beginning of the present century would have got anywhere near the correct answer; it is perhaps just as doubtful whether present estimates of the population at the end of the century will be near the mark. Those that have been made have assumed that the population in 1974 would be of the order of 75 million and they have concluded that it is extremely unlikely that the population will less than double by the end of the century unless there is widespread famine or uncontrolled epidemics. The spread of estimates made on different assumptions is quite considerable. Those made by the Harvard University Centre for Population Studies appear to vary from about 153 million on the assumption of a drastic reduction in fertility rates to about 229 million on the assumption that no reduction takes place.[2] If the population is to be no higher than 150 million in the year 2000, family planning will have to be pushed with determination, perhaps beyond the limit that experienced observers think possible, given political and other constraints. Perhaps the most disturbing aspect is that it is implicit in the present demographic situation that a rapid rate of increase will be maintained even after the turn of the century.

Crude death rates fell from about 50 per thousand at the beginning of the present century to less than 20 per thousand in 1968.[3] It is this

[2] Quoted in *Some Social Aspects of Development Planning in Bagladesh* Vol. I, *Population Planning*, United Nations Relief Operation, Dacca, December 1972, p. 6.

[3] *Some Social Aspects of Development Planning in Bangladesh*, Vol. I, *Population Planning*; United Nations Relief Operation, Dacca, December 1972, p. 28, gives a rate of 16 only. Other estimates suggest a range of 14–20, e.g. the *Final Report of the Population Growth Estimation Experiment*, Pakistan Institute of Development Economics, 1971.

fall which has led to the present rapid increase in population. In the future there may be a further decline in death rates; the large reduction in the toll of infectious diseases cannot be repeated but there is considerable scope for a further reduction in child mortality and in the death rates of women. As many women as men survive until about age 25; thereafter a much greater percentage of men than women survive, until at the age of 40 the number of men exceeds the number of women by 10 per cent. This is largely the debilitating effect of childbirth—and of abortion. Crude death rates could fall much below those of Western populations, simply because the population is much younger, and it would not be impossible for the crude death rate to fall for a period to below 10 per thousand by the end of the century if age-specific death rates fell to the present levels of developed countries.

Crude birth rates have declined in the present century from about 60 per thousand to less than 50 per thousand. Neither birth nor death rate figures are very accurate but they point to a natural rate of increase of 30 per thousand. The actual rate of natural increase might be greater or less than this and it might increase as well as decrease in the future. It has been found in some countries that economic development increases the birth rate for a time; there is scope for an increase in the birth rate in Bangladesh, which is almost certainly below the biological maximum and might respond to an improvement in nutritional standards. At least it could scarcely be raised by a fall in the age of marriage, for the vast majority of women are already married at puberty or shortly thereafter and few men and women remain single in a community in which arranged marriages are the rule.

Men marry appreciably later than women in Bangladesh; nearly 50 per cent of women in the age group 12–14 are married and about 90 per cent of those aged 15–19. Marriage at 12 is clearly very usual. Only 10 per cent of men are married in the age group 12–14 and only somewhat more than half of those aged 15–19.

Crude death and birth rates are useful statistics because they enable us to gauge by how much the population is likely to increase (or decrease) by a particular point of time. But they are greatly affected by the age composition of the population. The underlying trend of fertility is revealed much more clearly by such indicators as the reproduction rate or the average number of children born to a woman during her lifetime. At the present time in Bangladesh this is about 6–7 for women who live through their reproductive life span. Not all women survive to adulthood and reach their forties, of course, for death rates in the younger age groups in particular are high.

We have made a series of rather simple calculations to derive orders of magnitude for changes in population size and structure that may be in store for Bangladesh. In so doing we are faced with two categories of uncertainty. In the first place demographic statistics of size, age-composition, fertility and mortality of the population for any recent period are largely unknown and at best approximate. Since the 1974 census has still not been processed, we have made our estimates on the basis of the 1961 census supplemented with fragmentary evidence and estimates for subsequent years.

In the second place, future mortality and fertility rates are inherently unknown and predictions are notoriously uncertain. Here we have made alternative calculations reflecting different rates of mortality: one using age-specific death rates at the present time as best we can estimate them; the other using the much lower death rates as now prevailing in the industrialised countries.[4]

With respect to fertility we have made our calculations on the assumption that in each future year the number of live births in Bangladesh will remain at the present absolute level of 4 million annually. Formally this is a very simple assumption, but its realisation would imply a reduction of fertility at unprecedented speed. Yet, the point of our calculations is to show the outer limits of the demographic momentum built into the present population of Bangladesh. The results are shown in Table VI.2.

Expanding populations generate their own characteristic pattern of age distribution; that for Bangladesh today (as estimated) is shown in the first column of Table VI.2. Nearly 45 per cent of the population are under 15 years of age, over 40 per cent are in the reproductive age group, over 10 per cent are between the ages of 45– and 65 and a mere 3–4 per cent are 65 years or more. In a stable and stationary population, as illustrated in columns 3 and 4, only 20–25 per cent[5] of the population (about one-half the share in Bangladesh today) is below 15 years, in the 15–44 age group the proportion is roughly the same (around 40 per cent), while in the 45–64 age cohort the percentage in a stationary population is twice as high, and the percentage of older people is three to five times as high as in the present population of Bangladesh.

The age composition and changes in it clearly make a lot of difference to projections of total population, of labour force and

---

[4] Alternative one in fact uses death rates approximating those estimated for India about 1960; alternative two those for Norway at present.

[5] Depending on mortality rates: in short, the lower the mortality, the lower the percentage.

TABLE VI.2

POPULATION SIZE AND AGE COMPOSITION IN YEARS
1975, 2000 AND 2050

(with alternative mortality rates and constant number [4 million] of live
births annually)

	1975 Estimate	2000 Present rates of mortality	2050 Present rates of mortality	2050 Rates of mortality as in rich countries
	(in millions)			
	1	2	3	4
0–14	35	43	43	60
15–44	33	63	73	117
45–64	9	16	39	72
65	3	5	20	51
Total	80	127	175	300
	(in per cent)			
0–14	44	34	25	20
15–44	42	49	42	39
45–64	11	13	22	24
65	3	4	11	17
Total	100	100	100	100

dependency ratios, of average mortality and fertility. The changes in store for Bangladesh are in all these respects unfavourable: as the large numbers in low age cohorts work their way up over time, unchanged fertility rates in each age group will greatly expand the number of children born; the large number of youngsters coming into the labour force will tend to further increase unemployment and underemployment; eventually the number of old people sharing in the output of the economy will multiply.

From the figures in Table VI.2 we can get an idea of what it would take to contain the number of births to the present level of 4 million annually. It means, for example, that women in the reproductive age group (15–44 years in our table, in fact extending to some younger and also a few older females), who would nearly double in number in twenty-five years, would produce the same number of live births: fertility for the relevant age group would be cut by nearly 50 per cent.[6]

[6] By contrast the crude birth rate would be cut by nearly 40 per cent from 50 per thousand to just over 30 per thousand.

By the turn of the century, however, if throughout the last quarter of this century the number of births could be kept down to 4 million a year, the main part of the job of effecting a sufficient reduction in fertility so as to reach an eventual stationary population would have been done. Perhaps it can be done, but we judge the limitation of births at 4 million would be far too optimistic an assumption. The size of the population in the year 2000 will therefore most certainly be higher than the 127 million implied in the assumption of a constant number of births of 4 million a year.

Another factor making for a larger population is that the high mortality to which the people of Bangladesh are subject, particularly at birth and in early years, but also later in life, and which falls most severely on women, gives scope for a reduction in death rates. Any reduction in mortality rates in coming years will of course also add to numbers. Thus at one extreme: with mortality rates as current in rich countries, a constant level of 4 million births a year gives a population in the under-15 age group as much as 40 per cent or 17 million higher than under present Bangladesh conditions. Child mortality in Bangladesh will of course not decline so rapidly and so far as this example indicates, but at least some improvement in mortality must be expected if prolonged famine on a massive scale can be avoided. This explains why in the development of our scenario in Chapter V population in the year 2000 is put at about 150 million. Such a result will take some doing, particularly since any policy for the containment of new births cannot be made immediately effective.

Finally, reference may be made to the figures in Table VI.2 which show the ultimate size of the population of Bangladesh that will emerge if the number of new births could be kept constant at 4 million a year. By the year 2050, when the last of the present newborn reach their final years, the size of the population would be 175 million provided there is no improvement in mortality rates. Since, however, mortality rates, at least in the longer run, may well decline and approach those now prevailing in rich countries, Bangladesh's population will certainly be over 200 million and could move eventually towards 300 million. All the above conclusions are reached on the assumption that births can be kept constant at 4 million from now on. The prospects are frightening.

2. *The Social Setting*

Social norms and organisation in Bangladesh are not conducive to population control. They might become so if the pressure on land brought the population to starvation point over a period of years, as we discuss later in this chapter in relation to Ireland, but so far food production supplemented by imports, often paid for out of international aid, has prevented prolonged mass starvation. Historically, other societies have not been able to take the same attitude to population control as the people of Bangladesh. Infanticide is a very common characteristic of primitive societies, as A. M. Carr-Saunders described at length.[7] It was not confined to the need to avoid starvation; it was sometimes practised in order to allow an easier life without the burden of supporting unlimited numbers of offspring. Abortion might be regarded as close to infanticide by many and is clearly practised in Bangladesh, but it does not seem to have degenerated into infanticide, except perhaps for the apparent neglect of the health of female children. Infanticide is not in keeping with a modern society, and Bangladesh, although not modern in many ways, has centuries of civilisation behind it. History has given Bangladesh a very marked system of social norms which have changed little over time in response to the accumulation of knowledge.[8]

Education. Almost every aspect of society in village life is against population planning. Probably the most important of these is that of education; one of the few established facts in relation to family limitation appears to be that it is much more likely to be practised by the educated than by the uneducated, as Table VI.3 illustrates for Chile.[9] Of course it is also true that those with higher educational qualifications are likely to be relatively better off and this also may be a factor affecting the relationship.

TABLE VI.3

RELATIONSHIP BETWEEN EDUCATION AND
NUMBER OF CHILDREN

Education level of women	Number of births per couple	Per cent of population
No formal education	4·86	20·2
Some primary school	3·40	46·3
Complete primary school	1·28	13·1
Some Secondary school	1·21	14·4
Complete Secondary school	1·69	6·0

[7] In *The Population Problem*, Oxford University Press, 1922, Chapter X.
[8] Compare, for example, the accounts of village life in Bengal given by Lal Behari Day in *Bengal Peasant Life*, written in the 1870s and reprinted Calcutta, 1970, with that of S. M. Hafeez Zaidi, *The Village Culture in Transition: Study of East Pakistan Rural Society*, East–West Center Press, Honolulu, 1970.
[9] Taken from Ellen Sattar, "Population Problem and the Status of Women III", *Bangladesh Observer*, 9 January 1974.

Education in Bangladesh is at a low ebb, and girls are much less likely to be educated in the villages than the boys. In Monogram, a village surveyed by M. Nurul Huq, of 107 women only 5 had spent 4–6 years at school and 19 had spent 1–3 years.[10] Worse still, the opportunities of being exposed to modern systems of thought, simply by living in the world, are severely restricted by the adoption of purdah, quite apart from the fact that few women move outside their village. Muslim women of low occupational status are not able to observe the seclusion of purdah because they are needed to work in the fields and so are more likely to come into contact with those conducting family development programmes.

Communications. In certain respects the opportunity for villagers to obtain knowledge about the outside world has improved. Development projects have brought them into contact with people from the towns and from foreign countries. There are a few literate persons who subscribe to newspapers and some have transistor radios. Some villages near to roads and the centres of study by researchers, or those concerned with development project work, benefit more than others, but bad communications leave many outside the reach of the information network and while contact with the outside world improves, many villagers, particularly the older ones, have never left their village and are apathetic to happenings outside.

Communication and the dissemination of ideas depend on contact with influential people. Successful farmers who have led the adoption of improved practices will be relied on as a source of information as will others who have made their way in the outside world but still retain contact with their village. Among Muslims "an ordinary person in a village, even today, remains isolated, helpless and ignorant of the outside world; and therefore is obliged, out of necessity, to depend on those who make it their business to keep themselves informed of events and services originating in towns, cities and Government offices".[11] In the case of Hindus, interestingly, this form of dependence seems to be less marked and there is greater reliance on newspapers, reflecting perhaps a higher level of education.

The mass communications media so far seem to have been of relatively little influence. It is here that hope may lie for the future and for a changing structure of beliefs of greater relevance to modern living.

Superstition and Religion. It is often assumed that religion may be an obstacle to the adoption of family planning. Religion cannot

[10] M. Nurul Huq, *Village Development in Bangladesh,* Bangladesh Academy for Rural Development, Comilla, 1973, p. 50.
[11] S. M. Hafeez Zaidi, op. cit., p. 122.

be regarded in isolation from other systems of beliefs. Hafeez Zaidi in his study emphasises the importance of superstition as well as religious teaching, and concludes that 99 per cent of the Muslims and 98 per cent of the Hindus believe that man has no control over his means of livelihood and that God assigns it to him. What is written on his forehead will come to pass. In the face of such beliefs it is clearly very difficult to get people to act as though they had some control over their own destiny, and without this it is not easy to see how they can be persuaded of the virtues of family planning. In many other respects, ritual orders the passage of life. Cultivators do not sow seeds or transplant saplings on Tuesdays or Saturdays. No farmer will cut down his trees on Sunday and Thursday, and other prohibitions exist, including cutting nails or hair at night.[12] It is a pity that such inhibitions cannot be extended to abstention from intercourse outside the safe period!

Fatalism may well be a greater obstacle to the adoption of family planning in the long run than religious beliefs and lack of education the greatest obstacle of all, but religious beliefs also require consideration. Most discussions of the attitude of the Muslim faith towards contraception are at pains to argue that there is nothing in the religious teachings that prevents the adoption of contraception. The arguments that are advanced are many and learned, drawing on authorities of the fourteenth century to show that there is no objection to contraceptive practices.[13] The fact that such arguments have to be advanced is in itself, however, some indication that doubts exist, and this might lead one to suppose that Muslim beliefs are not, on the whole, positively favourable to family planning. Yet the arguments advanced from the writings of the fourteenth century theologians are modern enough. They include the preservation of the life, vigour and beauty of the mother and the desire to avoid the tiresome labour of providing food for large numbers of children.

There is apparently little difference between the religions of Hindus and Muslims so far as family planning is concerned, but the acceptance of family planning (and knowledge about it) is much more marked amongst Hindus than Muslims. In the Comilla-Kotwali *Thana* studied by Stoeckel and Choudhury[14] it was found that roughly 40 per cent of Muslim women, against roughly 80 per cent of Hindu women, claimed knowledge of family planning, and

[12] S. M. Hafeez Zaidi, op. cit., p. 99.

[13] See, for example, Akhter Hameed Khan, *Islamic Opinions on Contraception*, Pakistan Academy for Rural Development, Comilla.

[14] John Stoeckel and Moebul A. Choudhury, *Fertility, Infant mortality and Family Planning in Bangladesh*, Oxford University Press, 1973, Chapter 6.

roughly 40 per cent and 70 per cent respectively approved its use. Against this only 3 per cent of Muslims and 15 per cent of Hindus admitted to ever having practised it. How far these differences are due to actual differences in religious teachings is uncertain. As we have seen, education and exposure to sources of knowledge are very significant factors affecting attitudes to contraception, and Hindu women, on the whole, are better educated and more able to move about freely and to participate in public life.[15] In a survey of four Delhi villages it was found that out of 455 women only 7 per cent gave religion as a reason for not practising family planning.[16] But most of them would be Hindus; for Muslims, religion may be more of an obstacle in practice. It was found that a high proportion of Muslims terminate contraceptive use because of pressures from religious leaders. Among those of higher occupational status this factor seems to have been of less significance, presumably because those affected were able to rely to a greater extent on their own judgement.

  The Desire for Children. One of the difficulties of persuading people that they would be better off with a smaller family is their genuine desire to have large families. The study of the Comilla-Kotwali *Thana* shows that women with no living children desired four. It seems that the presence of children increased the desire for them; those with four children aspired to a total of seven, while those with more than this thought in terms of eight or nine in total.[17] In some respects these conclusions are surprising; the desire for children as shown in the same study is less with older women and it might be thought that as older women would already have a number of children, the relationship would be the other way around. Possibly the reconciliation of these facts is that those who have large families achieve them when young. This would be consistent with the Muslim view that the role of women lies in the rearing of children in addition to caring for the home and being good Muslims. Other well-known reasons for wanting large families are the desire to ensure care in old age by descendants, and the high rate of infant and

[15] Ellen Sattar found in her village survey (*Women in Bangladesh: a Village Study*, The Ford Foundation, Dacca, October 1974) that the education of Hindu women had been better than that of Muslim women. It is interesting that amongst Hindu and Muslim women classified as "unskilled" there is no difference in knowledge about contraception, presumably because the Muslim women in this classification are more exposed to the world.

[16] S. N. Agarwala, "A Family Planning Survey in Four Delhi villages", *Population Studies*, November 1961, p. 110.

[17] John Stoeckel and Moebul Choudhury, op. cit., pp. 78–9.

other mortality that may frustrate this.[18] The risk of losing a son may lead families to desire at least two surviving sons, which is likely to lead to a family of four or more children.

3. *The Experience of Other Countries*

The question of population control in Bangladesh is such a difficult one that it is necessary to consider the experience of other countries to see what can be learned about the strategy that should be followed to bring the population under control. In the following pages we look briefly at experience of India and China in recent years and at the Irish famine and its consequences for population control in the nineteenth century. We start with Ireland—a cautionary tale.

Ireland. There is a strong resemblance between the population problem in Bangladesh and that prevailing in Ireland more than a century ago. "The culture of the potato required little attention except at springtime and harvest, and through the long winter nights the people sat within their cabins, fiddling, talking and telling stories. Firing in the shape of turf-peat cut from the bog and costing little or nothing was plentiful."[19] The Irish by many accounts were a pleasure-loving indolent lot. But, in many other respects, life was hard. There was small incentive and perhaps opportunity for the Irish peasant to better himself at home, for the sway of the landlords meant that very little of the results of increased labour found its way into the pockets of the labourer. According to Connell, "the utter poverty and hope-lessness of life for Irish men and women made them eager to marry young: to delay marriage gave the couple not the least promise of being able to rear their children in less strained circumstances; to marry young was the accepted thing to do; it meant no added priva-tions and might make existing hardships more easily borne; it might, in years to come, be a safeguard against destitution."[20]

With earlier marriage and the ease of providing a nutritious diet based on the potato, population expanded rapidly from about $2\frac{1}{2}$ million at the beginning of the eighteenth century to over 8 million in 1841 (a census year). There was thus little to check the upward movement of population, except famine.

The cause and the form of the famine when it came can scarcely have been anticipated. In its impact, unpredictability and severity, it is difficult to think that there can be close parallels with Bangladesh

[18] See D. Banerji, *Family Planning in India*, Peoples Publishing House, New Delhi, 1971, p. 3.

[19] Cecil Woodham-Smith, *The Great Hunger*, Hamish Hamilton, 1962.

[20] K. H. Connell, *The Population of Ireland*, Oxford University Press, 1950, p. 241.

but the similarities are there. Rice crops fluctuate considerably, though they generally escape the destructive forces of a wholesale failure of the crop as a result of disease. It was disease affecting the potato rather than population outrunning the capacity of the country to grow food that caused the Irish famine and it affected a succesion of harvests; the partial failure of 1845 was followed by the almost complete destruction of that of 1846. Of the 8 million people living in Ireland at the time, $2\frac{1}{2}$ million starved to death. Many others subsequently migrated. The population, even today more than a century later, is little more than half that before the famine. The consequences were exacerbated by the callousness of landlords and by the failure of the British Government to deal with the situation. It is perhaps too much to fear that history could repeat itself in Bangladesh; the record of the international community in dealing with the aftermath of the War of Independence might seem to ensure that measures to avert starvation would be taken if Bangladesh were to experience famine on the scale of that experienced by Ireland in the nineteenth century. The capacity of friendly countries to deal with food shortages is not, however, unlimited as recent events have shown. Starvation in Africa has not been met with the response from the international community that Bangladesh received, and one reason for this is the limited availability of food from other sources of supply. It cannot automatically be assumed that the world will be able to deal with the food problems of the growing population of Bangladesh, and it is in this context that the Irish experience may be relevant to the situation which will emerge if Bangladesh's population continues to increase unchecked.

The consequences of the Irish famine were far-reaching. The immediate reaction was that of mass emigration; most cheaply to Great Britain and more expensively to the New World. This had serious results for the receiving countries in the way of the incidence of disease, including cholera, then endemic in Ireland, in the creation of slum housing and above all in the problems of absorbing an immigrant population that was ill-educated and accustomed to a very inferior standard of life. Such also could be the consequences of famine in Bangladesh if population expansion were to be followed by catastrophic and repeated harvest failure.

The longer-term consequences of famine for the control of population point to one solution of the problem of growth of population that may be applied voluntarily if the shock of starvation is severe enough. Emigration from Ireland to other countries became a continuing feature of Irish life affecting both the pressure on resources and the growth of population itself. Very late marriage became the rule, in complete contrast to the tendency to earlier marriage that had increased the birth rate in the first place. Something of this change in attitude to marriage and the procreation of children has to be brought about in Bangladesh, if it cannot be done in a controlled way it may come about through disaster.

We now turn to the approaches adopted by India and China and consider what lessons they may hold for Bangladesh as a means to avoid famine.

The Orthodox Approach in India. The approach so far adopted to family planning in the subcontinent of India has generally been to enlist field workers to provide information, supplies and medical knowledge. The programmes were started with high hopes. In 1962 it was hoped to reduce the birth rate to 25 births per 1,000 population by 1973; but by 1969 the time limit was changed from 1973 to "as soon as possible" which appeared to envisage a reduction in the crude birth rate from 41 per 1,000 to 23 per 1,000 by 1979. The scale of the task was daunting: it was intended to reach 90 million couples and motivate half of them to adopt family planning. The intention was to establish over 5,000 rural family welfare planning centres and over 4,000 rural sub-centres in keeping with the vast population of India—a formidable task to accomplish, requiring considerable administrative skill. The methods adopted included the distribution of conventional contraceptives and, from 1965 onwards, the intra-uterine device; at the same time mass education and publicity using the radio, visual displays and traditional cultural media were undertaken. Incentives for motivators and doctors, and compensation for loss of time and cost of travel for those accepting family planning were also devices to encourage the acceptance of a population control programme.

The programme appeared to have been put into action with some success and sterilisation figures (6 million) and Intra-Uterine Device (IUD) insertions achieved in 1965–9 might seem impressive were it not for the very size of the task. Examined in greater detail, the results left much to be desired, as Banerji has been at pains to point out.[21] By 1969 the programme seemed to have been losing momentum and even to have entered a phase of decline. Moreover, the achievements had been very unevenly distributed between town and country. Although the urban population of India represents only 17 per cent of the population, about 40 per cent of the sterilisations and IUD insertions had been carried out in urban centres. This presumably reflected both difficulties in establishing the number of clinics planned for the rural areas and the greater difficulty of motivating and convincing people living there.

[21] Op. cit., pp. 31–57.

Dr. Banerji[22] speaks very critically of the formulation of the family planning programme saying that it has greatly overestimated the effectiveness of the "motivators". What, he asks, can you hope to accomplish in preaching family planning to a mass of starving illiterates living in dilapidated huts and insanitary conditions, suffering from diseases and disabilities. Life, he says, is an unending chain of misery, degradation and deprivation for more than 376 million citizens of India for whom a surplus of fresh human stock is the only tangible capital that can be invoked. In such circumstances he endorses Ashok Mitra's observations[23] that the starting-point is primary education and literacy even in the matter of achieving the small family norm.[24]

Another lesson to be learnt from the Indian programme is that it is extremely difficult to use personnel effectively. Banerji hazards the estimate that less than twenty-one sterilisations and less than eight IUD insertions were done for every technical person in the programme. In other respects the programme has been open to criticism. In a study in Uttar Pradesh in 1965–6 it was found that over 60 per cent of the vasectomies could have no demographic effect on the population since they were performed on persons whose wives were either 45 years of age or above, or because they were unmarried, widowed or separated. And as P. B. Gupta has observed,[25] there is also the problem of loops being expelled which must have greatly reduced the effectiveness of IUD insertions. There is not much encouragement to be gained by Bangladesh from considering the Indian experience.

China. China suffered from much the same social attitudes to family planning as Bangladesh. Economic necessity dictated small co-living households in which the influence of the young bride was minimal; marriage took place at an early age; there were traditional reasons for embarking on a family immediately, and a son was needed to ensure the acceptance of a woman by her husband's family; children were desired, and as many failed to survive, there seemed little reason to restrain the birth rate. But, as in other countries the death rate dropped with development in medical science, and population began to increase at a rate which is frequently described as 2 per cent per annum.

[22] Op. cit., p. 26 and the Epilogue.

[23] "The Small Family Norms and Literacy", *Family Planning News*, X, No. 2, p. 6.

[24] Op. cit., p. 33.

[25] In "Population Policy in India", *Bulletin of the Socio-economic Research Institute*, 1969, 3:1.

Official policy towards population planning developed uncertainly and intermittently. Defence against attack was one consideration. So was the Marxist approach which rejected Malthusian doctrine; and the absence of reliable figures of the population and its rate of increase may have meant that the pressure of population on resources was less clearly recognised. In certain respects this may have been beneficial, for it forced the case for family limitation to be presented in positive rather than negative terms. Family planning is advocated not so much because without it there would not be enough to go round, but as a necessary service to the state. Communal pressures are strong; emphasis is placed on the duty of the individual to refrain from early marriage and to concentrate on educational and other training for a full adult life without the distractions of raising a family. Consequent improvement in the health of mother and children is also a strong feature of the ideas that are being advanced.

Postponement of marriage is an important ingredient of the programme of population control. China's Marriage Law of 1950 specified eighteen as the minimum age for women and twenty for men. These were minimum ages; by 1957 the *People's Daily* was suggesting that marriage after twenty-five years was beneficial and did no harm and there was some support for this view from medical circles.[26]

The movement towards later marriage is the keystone to the whole edifice of family planning, but it has to be backed up by the provision of family planning advice, by making supplies of contraceptives available and above all by efforts to motivate people to limit their families. In certain respects, social and economic change is favouring family limitation. One effect of land reform is to reduce the need for children to work large holdings, and the limited opportunities to obtain employment off the land, given the rate of industrial advance that can be undertaken is another factor making for restraint. Some efforts are being made to get the agricultural collectives to make provision for the welfare of old people, and so to reduce the compulsion to have a large family as a means of support in old age.

More widely, new aspirations are having an effect on traditional attitudes. Children are being regarded as expensive to rear, particularly in relation to educational costs. At one time parents were also anxious to save for consumer goods, and the expense of raising a young family must have been considered in relation to this. The extension of mass education and increasing emphasis on the economic

[26] See H. Yuan Tien, "Marital Moratorium and Fertility Control in China", *Population Studies*, No. 3, 1970, pp. 311–23.

independence of women earning their own living are further forces making for family limitation.

The administration of such programmes is no more easy in China than in other places and it is difficult to judge with the paucity of statistical information available, how effective they are. They do have the advantage of being ideologically inspired which means that the efforts of workers in the programme can be reinforced by the educational influence of party workers. Those now approaching marriage or in early married life have been brought up in a wholly communist regime, and new ideas must be gaining increasing ascendancy over those previously all-prevailing. But the fact remains that in China, as elsewhere, it is more difficult to make progress in the rural areas than in the towns.

As in many countries, the family planning programme is regarded as a part of the general health programme. Many deficiencies have had to be overcome, particularly the training of medical and para-medical personnel. Nevertheless it was possible for Han Suyin to report that in every commune that she had visited in 1969, family planning was available in the form of the pill as well as the intra-uterine device.[27]

The Alternatives. In Western countries control of the population has come about as a result of individual decisions, with little, until recently, in the way of state intervention or facilitation to slow down birth rates; indeed, at times the pressures exerted by the state have been directed to trying to raise population as an insurance against war and as a means to escape the economic consequences of a declining population.

It is often assumed that the populations of advanced countries in Europe and other parts of the world have evolved in accordance with a common pattern. The facts do not appear to bear this out. In some countries population growth declined well ahead of the industrial revolution; in others the decline seemed to be a function of falling death rates, and of rising incomes leading to a fall in birth rates. Historically in these countries death rates fell first and birth rates later. Perhaps the same will happen in Bangladesh; but certainly not as night follows day or with controllable results. If there is any relationship between declining death rates, increasing incomes and falling birth rates it is not a simple one. Considerable time-lags are involved: the fall in birth rates follows the fall in death rates very many years later. Moreover, in European countries the difference in birth and death rates was less than in Bangladesh. Restraints were

[27] Han Suyin, "Family Planning in China", *Japan Quarterly*, Vol. 17, No. 4, p. 439.

already in operation. These were evident in social customs. Marriage was not inevitable, or a thing to be undertaken at an early age. Society provided no computerised marriage bureaux; later marriage found favour as an institution; spinsters abounded.

It is tempting to think that in spite of massive cultural differences Bangladesh could follow the declining fertility patterns of other countries automatically. In the views of researchers in the field everything depends on motivation. The real issue is: can the women and men of Bangladesh be motivated? If they can, the passage from high to low birth rates might take place much more quickly than has occurred in other countries; indeed it must be so. In certain European countries it took the crude birth rate over fifty years to decline from levels around 35 per 1,000 to half that amount; even then populations continued to increase because of the fall in the death rate. In Bangladesh's case the problem is much more severe as the existing birth rates are of the order of 50 per 1,000, although the decline in the death rate, when neither famine nor war intervenes, is already well advanced. Without a change in trend, Bangladesh is on the way either to a population of 400 million in sixty or seventy years' time or to starvation.

If motivation is the key, there may be no practical alternative to an effective government population policy: The increase in the standard of living, which is always supposed to be a major factor leading to a decline in birth rates, might proceed somewhat more quickly than it did in European countries either pioneering an industrial revolution or making their way through it at an early stage of its progression, but living standards are already so low that the effects of any likely improvement will in absolute terms be small. Wealthier and, of course, better educated people in Bangladesh, anxious to provide well for a limited number of children, do limit their families but there are not many of them, and the effects of their abstinence will be negligible in relation to the mass of the people. Nor, for obvious humanitarian reasons, can a policy of waiting for an Irish crisis be followed, in the hope that events will lead to control of the situation in the end.

The experience of other countries shows that certain actions and policies are more likely to give results than others, although what is appropriate in some cases will not work in others. The first require-ment for population control may be an improvement in living stan-dards, but this will not avoid the necessity to secure political commit-ment. The intention to remodel society that activates the Chinese is a means of bringing pressure on to people in a way that otherwise would be impossible. Intervention in the affairs of individuals is a thing to be avoided whenever possible, but it simply cannot be avoided so far as population is concerned, if Bangladesh is to survive. At the moment there is no real commitment to the idea of population planning, and while this is part of the general malaise of government it should not be borne with patience, for the consequences of delay in getting family planning off the ground are more serious than the consequences of delays in other government measures needed to ensure the future development of Bangladesh.

There is much in the political philosophy of the Chinese approach to population planning that could readily be taken over. The stress that is laid on the positive aspects of family planning, the development of the individual, the participation of women in the outside working life, and on service to the country as an activating force—all are vital elements. The mere utterance of such policies does not bring them about. A communist philosophy is much removed from the outlook of those in authority in Bangladesh, and there is no machinery so far for inculcating beliefs about the means to secure the appropriate conduct of personal behaviour in relation to the policies of the state. Without the means to propagate these ideas, it will be extremely difficult to put into practice many of the other things that are needed to make a population policy valid, for instance to insist on higher ages at marriage.

The measures taken by Taiwan and Singapore to control their populations show what can be accomplished in suitable circumstances by well-conceived programmes pressed with determination in favourable circumstances. The approaches adopted in the two countries differed: in Singapore those having larger numbers of children are progressively penalised, while in Taiwan the approach is more conventional, and relies on making contraception available to those who wish to take advantage of it. The programme has reinforced a movement previously in evidence towards smaller families; the birth rate has declined by 80 per cent for those covered by the programme compared with a decline of about 50 per cent for non-participants.

In Singapore the birth rate was down to about 22 per 1,000 in 1972 and it was intended to bring it down to 15 per 1,000 by 1975, with the message that two children should be the norm, three acceptable and four definitely anti-social.

The measures taken by Taiwan and Singapore have a more far-reaching appearance than anything that Bangladesh is likely to be able to achieve. In both cases the physical area to be covered is much smaller than that for Bangladesh, communications present no real problem, income is much greater, education more advanced and Western influence more marked. It is most uncertain whether the sanctions employed by Singapore are at all appropriate for a country with the social outlook of Bangladesh; more important, it is doubtful whether effective sanctions could be implemented in the case of people living in remote villages without all the apparatus of a party system to enforce them. Reward for family limitation may be a more useful weapon than the application of sanctions, and this is an aspect of the problem that is examined later. Nevertheless, the experience of both these two countries amply demonstrates that birth rates can be controlled if the right measures are taken.

4. *Approaches to Family Planning*

Education, Information and Motivation. Too little is known about the reasons that lead people to adopt family planning for it to be possible to prescribe a set of measures that will reduce birth rates in Bangladesh sufficiently. There is some evidence, however, that existing arrangements for the provision of family planning facilities fail to reach all who wish to avail themselves of them.[28] Improvement in living standards is not a necessary condition for population control, but it may be judged that it would be likely to exert a favourable influence. Subsequent chapters in the book examine the scope for increasing output and the measures that will be needed to bring this about.

Better standards of education are needed to help in getting family planning accepted. The need for education is general and its effects will be widespread, extending far beyond questions of limiting the birth rate, but within the educational programme special provision needs to be made for explaining why family planning is essential and how it can be accomplished. Family planning programmes use a variety of media for educational purposes. The provision of family planning advice at health centres is one such means; films, theatrical performances and posters are others. The larger the programme of family planning the greater the opportunity to reach people who otherwise would be left in ignorance. In scattered villages the use of the radio and even television, when it can be afforded, are other obvious means of imparting information and attempting to influence opinion. In spite of the fact that not all who have access to radios listen to them, radio might prove to be a powerful tool for the education of those remote from towns or deprived of conventional forms of education, and as such it might make it possible to push ideas of

[28] An impact survey of family planning activities in Bangladesh analysed by Dr. Monowar Hossein in conjunction with others has indicated that there was a genuine unfilled need for contraception facilities which was not being met. With a large number of voluntary agencies now working in the field it may be possible to reach more people.

family limitation on an extensive scale. Most villages possess some radio receivers, but they are not to be found in every house and many villagers are not able to afford them.[29] There is a case for extending the ownership of simple transistor radio receivers in the villages and possibly subsidising this, if necessary, in the interest of imparting information and bringing people in touch with new ideas. The attitudes that it is necessary to inculcate are far removed from those traditionally held as we have seen; they will not be accepted at all easily, for reasons already discussed, unless special measures are taken to make them function.

Age at Marriage. Like Malthus, the Chinese have viewed later marriage as much as a means to allow individuals to realise their potential as a device for reducing the birth rate. In Bangladesh, the limited opportunities for the employment of women outside the home, and the restricted opportunities for them to be educated, leave little alternative and incentive to do other than accept marriage as a career and as a role in life giving status and acceptance to a woman. It is not clear in such an environment what a young woman would do if she did not get married and start to raise a family. Nevertheless, raising the age of marriage is an important aspect of reducing the birth rate and one that must be put into effect in Bangladesh if population is to be brought under control. The following table

TABLE VI.4

BIRTH RATES PER THOUSAND MARRIED WOMEN

Age	1958–9	1963–4	1964–5	1966–7
12–14	193	135	131	144
15–19	283	280	301	248
20–24	333	299	298	279
25–29	300	268	267	242
30–34	253	242	245	199
35–39	219	149	157	126
40–44	198	73	82	62
Total fertility rate	8,529	6,960	7,143	6,212

Source: John Stoeckel and Moqbul A. Choudhury, *Fertility, Infant Mortality and Family Planning in Rural Bangladesh*, Oxford University Press 1973, p. 14.

[29] In the village of Monogram eight radios were owned by the villagers; in the village studied by Ellen Sattar also in the Comilla area, there were more, but in most villages it may be suspected that the radio is not generally available and cannot therefore be used effectively as a means of instruction.

illustrates some aspects of this by showing age-specific birth rates for married women in selected years from 1958–9 to 1966–7 in Comilla-Kotwali *Thana*.[30]

The year-to-year changes shown by the figures may not be significant. There have been many other such surveys and they differ quite considerably in the detail that they show. There does appear to have been some tendency for birth rates to decline, but the Comilla-Kotwali *Thana* has been the subject of much study, and serious attempts have been made there to get family planning accepted, so that it may well be unrepresentative. There may also have been a decline in national birth rates in the 1960s, but this is uncertain and the magnitude is almost certainly less than that apparently experienced in the Comilla-Kotwali *Thana*. Nevertheless, while it is to be expected that age-specific birth rates will vary considerably from *Thana* to *Thana* and over time, the picture presented is probably sufficiently representative for purposes of illustration.

Only about half of the women in the age group 12–14 are married and they remain in the age group only for three years.The births occuring to them amount to only about 0·3 per cent of total births. Almost all women in the age group 15–19 are married and births to them amount to about 20 per cent of the total. Those in the succeeding age group 20–24 contribute about a further 27 per cent of births. The percentage of total births occurring to women in different age groups is shown in the following table.

TABLE VI.5

PER CENT OF BIRTHS TO WOMEN OF DIFFERENT AGES

	1963–5
Under 15	0·3
15–19	19·8
20–24	27·0
25–29	26·7
30–34	15·8
35–39	7·1
40–44	2·5
45–49	0·5
50 and over	0·2

Source: Final Report of the Population Growth Estimation Experiment, edited by M. Naseem Iqbal Farooqui and Ghazi Mumtaz Farooq, Pakistan Institute of Development Economics, 1971. The estimations are those referred to as Chandrasekar-Deming on p. 81.

[30] The Thana is an administrative unit in Bangladesh covering about 100 square miles.

Now it would, of course, be wholly wrong to suppose that raising the age at marriage to twenty-five for women would have the effect of halving the birth rate, or in reducing the number of surviving children by a similar amount. Fewer children survive if they are born to very young and inexperienced mothers who are immature both physically and mentally; early childbirth may well reduce fertility later and reduce the desire for children, leading to some effort at birth control whether by contraceptive practices or abortion; also, in countries where contraception is in use, family size may be largely determined by the number of children couples desire to have. Nevertheless, raising the age at marriage might be expected to have some quite considerable effect, if only because it is clear that contraception is not much practised in Bangladesh.[31] It would also have the effect of delaying births even if it did not affect the ultimate number of surviving children, and this would gain time in which population control methods could be developed more effectively. Raising the age at marriage needs to be carried through both in the interests of population control and as one step to end the centuries-old subjugation of women. In this respect the Chinese have got an effective approach if accounts of their programmes are accurate. Probably a gradualistic approach to it is most likely to meet with success. Documentation of age would be vital. Many women in the villages do not know their age; deception could be easy.

It is one thing to advocate an increase in the age at marriage as a method of reducing birth rates, but another to get it implemented. Passing a law would not be enough; custom is too deeply ingrained for early marriage to be easily reversed by an addition to the statute book.

Abortion and Vasectomy. There is a case for legalising abortion and facilitating it. Conditions in Bangladesh are vastly different from those in Western countries but there is no doubt that in those countries the pill and, where it has occurred, the legalisation of abortion have been powerful means of population control. It is probably not too optimistic to suppose that both have their place in Bangladesh. Japan is often cited as a country halving its birth rate in a decade by giving abortion facilities to all that wanted it, but legalisation of abortion was not really adopted by Japan as a conscious population control policy. There can be no doubt that there is a demand for abortion in Bangladesh and that it is practised

[31] S. N. Agarwala is reported by Syed Iqbal Alam in "Age at Marriage in Pakistan", *The Pakistan Development Review*, Autumn 1968, p. 489, as estimating that in India an increase in average age at marriage from the existing 15·6 years to 19·2 years would result in an annual crude birth rate 30 years later of 33·9 births per thousand instead of 47·8.

in spite of all the prohibitions that may exist and reluctance to admit to it. In an enquiry in Puerto Rico in 1965 it was found that 28 per cent of mothers aged 20–25 had had at least one abortion. Can it be so different in Bangladesh?[32]

Abortion is, of course, in one sense an action of last resort representing failure to get conventional methods of protection into use by those who need them, but it must be remembered that the use of contraceptive devices is not easy in conditions in which little privacy can be found, as in living conditions in villages. The need for the conventional approaches to family planning and population control is no less necessary if abortion is permitted or birth rates reduced by other social measures. Vasectomy is given a prominent place in the programme outlined in the First Five Year Plan with a threat to resort to punishment by withholding benefits in respects of younger children in large families, and to compulsion.[33] However, as we have seen, experience in India is such as to suggest that not much is to be expected from vasectomy where all too frequently those accepting the treatment are nearing the end of their reproductive life.

Fiscal Incentives. There is no divine ordinance why girls should marry at twelve or women at twenty. In West Pakistan in 1964 the average age at marriage was nineteen, compared with fifteen in East Pakistan.[34] In many other countries today, and in earlier times, marriage under twenty was exceptional or, if allowed, dependent on the ability of those contracting it to earn a suitable living.

Taxation might be used as a means to bring about the postponement of marriage, and it is not difficult to sketch the outlines of schemes that might be considered. One scheme might be to tax those women who marry young. The tax might be prohibitively severe for those contemplating marriage under fifteen or even under twenty, and it might gradually decline in its severity from some age, which could be fifteen or twenty until at, say, twenty-five it might fall to zero. After that age, marriage would be free. There is no doubt that such a tax would be immensely unpopular and that it would be resisted and evaded. It is difficult to see the present government introducing it.

It would be possible to combine a tax on marriage with a system of rebates related to the number of children resulting from it. For

[32] See Harvick B. Presser," Rate of Sterilisation in Puerto Rican Fertility", *Population Studies*, November 1969, p. 355, table 12. Note also the statement by A. E. Shafiullah in the *Bangladesh Observer* for 6 May 1974 that a large hospital in Dacca receives 120 cases of incomplete abortion per month.

[33] *The First Five Year Plan*, Planning Commission, Government of the Peoples Republic of Bangladesh, November 1973, p. 539.

[34] Syed Iqbal Alam, op. cit., p. 494.

those with no children the whole of the tax might be refunded, either as a lump sum at some appropriate age, or in the form of a pension. With more children less of the tax would be refunded so that with say four children nothing would be given back.

Other schemes of similar general character have been proposed. Ridker and Muscat have put forward a proposal which links the payment of a pension to a couple with the number of surviving children and they have shown how it might work in a country such as Malaysia.[35] The pension would vary inversely with the number of surviving children, becoming zero for families of four or more children. Many variations of the scheme are possible and various scales of incentives could be adopted. In terms of social accounting there would be no difficulty in demonstrating that only a modest reduction in the birth rate would be necessary for the operation of such a scheme to show a substantial surplus in the kind of economic conditions that prevail in Malaysia.

Such ideas are attractive but very little can be hazarded as to how they would work in practice. Malaysia is at a very different stage of evolution from Bangladesh. It had a *per capita* income of $430 in 1972 against $70 for Bangladesh, a population today of 11 million against 80 million, and a system of issuing birth certificates for children which is widely observed because such certificates are vital documents for establishing citizenship, school eligibility and other matters. In Bangladesh there is no such system, although presumably one could be established given time.

From the financial point of view such schemes have the advantage that they do not automatically involve the state in making payments of a substantial amount unless they produce results. It is only families with less than four children that are entitled to a pension, and initially many families would continue to have families of four or more children. The payment of pensions would in any case be delayed for a number of years when incomes would have increased. The upper limit to the cost would be set by the need to provide pensions for all couples after the age of, say, sixty (retirement takes place early in Bangladesh and it may be more realistic to take sixty as a retiring age than sixty-five). In an expanding population with high mortality, the percentage of older people is comparatively low. In Bangladesh only 7 per cent of the population is aged sixty or over, although in relation to the employed population aged 15–59 the proportion is about 15 per cent.

[35] Ronald G. Ridker and Robert J. Muscat, "Incentives for Family Welfare and Fertility Reduction", *Studies in Family Planning*, January 1973, The Population Council, New York.

The cost of pensions has to be related to the burden it imposes. If pensions were to be paid at the average rate of earnings of the working population the cost involved would be of the order of 15 per cent of the GNP. In practice, pensions are much less than average income received when working, but even if they were to be only one-third of that level, the cost would amount to about 5 per cent of GNP. It is difficult to see how even this amount could be raised for the purpose. It may be true that a large family is often desired to provide for old age, and that if provision were made for this, through a pension scheme, one reason for having children would be removed; it may also be true that the old are by and large maintained by family subvention and that the formal provision of a pension would not greatly increase the demand for necessities. But it would add to incomes, the fiscal burden remains and it is difficult to see how this could be overcome. So either non-contributory pensions succeed in reducing population growth but are probably too costly to finance without contributions, or they fail and so prove to cost little. The ideal solution is to link pensions and contributions, as a tax on marriage might be designed to do. Nevertheless, on fiscal grounds (unless all else fails) it seems doubtful whether a reduction in population growth can be brought about by financial measures.

On other grounds it is also uncertain whether schemes linking family planning to pecuniary rewards are likely to succeed. The links between behaviour and economic incentives are often weak. In conditions of declining population experienced or feared by some countries in the 1930s, the conclusion was that efforts to increase the birth rate by offering rewards were not likely to be very effective. In the other direction the same conclusion might well apply: a reduction in the birth rate cannot be bought.

Administration and Finance. Past experience of conventional programmes of family planning in the Indian subcontinent is not encouraging but one reason is that the programmes were badly implemented. Reducing the birth rate deserves to have the attention of first-class administrators who can be persuaded to work actively in a field programme. For this to happen it would be necessary to depart from the general policy of restricting the salaries of state employees to unrealistically low levels and to offer more to those who are recruited into the family planning progamme. This would almost certainly be abused unless the most rigorous selection procedures were carried through to ensure that the staff recruited were of the highest calibre and properly motivated to achieving a reduction in the birth rate. If programmes are to succeed, they must be properly monitored and falsehoods in reporting exposed. Births and deaths need to be recorded. It should not be too difficult to bring this about.

Births, at least of sons, are an occasion for celebration, and they attract attention, so that there is little difficulty in taking note of them. Perhaps this might be one of the duties of religious teachers or of the village schoolmaster if one exists.

There is a limit to the rate at which any programme can be got off the ground and facilities established and trained workers provided. This perhaps explains why present expenditure on the population control activities seems so small in relation to the critical nature of the effort in this field. The population planning programme envisaged in the First Five Year Plan required an expenditure of only Taka 70 crores, about $1\frac{1}{2}$ per cent of the total expenditure envisaged over the five years.[36] Finance is less of a limitation in programmes of this kind than might be thought; there are many international donors who would quite willingly provide large amounts for the purpose of population control.

Some idea of the financial effort needed may be gained by reflection on the number of married women that it may be desired to reach. There are about 15 or more million married women in the reproductive ages. The most urgent need is to reach those within the most fertile age groups, say the 10 million youngest of them. The number of workers in the field needed for this depends on the ratio of potential clients to workers. Ideally this should not be more than 500 to 1, implying a full time workforce of about 20,000. The costs of such a force might amount to about Taka 50,000 per year per worker, which suggests that a programme of about Taka 100 crores per year should enable a reasonable coverage to be made. It might be helpful if donor-countries were to indicate their willingness collectively to support a programme on this scale, provided a suitable one were devised. It is a large programme, but it is no more than the situation demands.

As always, a programme of this kind should try to deal with areas of work where it is reasonable to expect that results can be obtained relatively easily. Geographically this may mean starting with the towns and going on to areas of the countryside that are believed to be receptive. In terms of the age of the eligible couples, there is not much point in attempting to educate those who will speedily be beyond the reproductive age groups, although they may be amongst the most receptive because of the burden of large families. Equally it may not be easy to make much impact if couples are childless, or to do much more than to attempt to persuade them to space their families if they clearly want a larger family.

[36] In the Annual Development Programme for 1975–6, $2\frac{1}{2}$ per cent of expenditure is scheduled for population planning.

5. Conclusions

The population problem of Bangladesh is nowhere near solution. In present circumstances the most likely check to population growth is famine possibly followed by some reaction along the lines of the Irish model, although this is less likely in Bangladesh, enured as it is to hardship and catastrophe, than in nineteenth-century Ireland suddenly subjected to a famine of cataclysmic proportions. There is little reason to think that a steady and sustained increase in incomes will act fast enough to stem the continued increase in people. Nor is there any reason to suppose that the approaches so far attempted in the Indian subcontinent are likely to succeed unless they can be implemented vastly more effectively.

No one set of measures is likely of itself to bring population under control. Population planning is only one aspect of planning for the future, and it must be regarded as part of a series of concerted endeavours of a reinforcing nature designed to change the future of Bangladesh. The approach advocated in the First Five Year Plan is in most respects conventional. It is hard to judge from it whether the measures delineated on paper are really capable of being translated into action in the remote areas occupied by many of the villages. The policy advocated is that of dissemination of information, and furnishing supplies, concentrating on the most fertile section of the population through clinics where "eligible couples" can be subject to persuasion.

There is no shortage of ideas in the chapter of the Plan devoted to family planning, but little that gives confidence that such ideas can be put into effect. The suggestions held in reserve, those of later marriage and legal access to abortion, may well not even reach the statute book during the period of the Plan. The position will remain hopeless unless drastic measures are taken and unwonted determination is exercised to put them into effect.

The social changes that are needed will not be easily brought about. Bangladesh is no China given to social engineering on a grand scale. But somehow education, employment and improvement in the status of women has to be brought about if Bangladesh is to emerge from the Middle Ages in the matter of population. There will not be much to show by the year 2000 for all the efforts that are needed. The population will be nearly twice its present level and still growing. It might just be possible to approach a net reproduction rate of 1 at that time, but only if great pressure is exerted to promote population control now.

CHAPTER VII

AGRICULTURE

1. *The Land*

For centuries the land which is Bangladesh was an area of relatively ample food self-sufficiency, even of surplus in good years. In recent decades, however, it has become a region of growing food deficits. While grain output has continued on an upward trend, it has been outpaced for a quarter of a century by the growth of population; imports of increasing magnitude, both in absolute quantity and in relation to overall consumption, have been required. The fact that food production is losing out in the race against human reproduction is the dominant problem of Bangladesh agriculture, and it is also the single most important factor explaining the poverty of Bangladesh and its persistently depressed economic and financial situation, internally and externally.

Agriculture is easily the dominant mainstay of economic life in Bangladesh. As much as 90 per cent of the total population live in the rural areas; over 80 per cent of all employment is in agriculture; about 60 per cent of national product derives from agriculture; and 90 per cent of exports are either agricultural products or manufactures of them.

Currently about 22 million acres are cultivated, of which half is land suitable for double—in some cases triple—cropping; the other half consists of low-lying areas which are deeply flooded by the water of the rivers or inundated by salt water for much of the year. In the dry season effective cultivation requires irrigation for most of the crop area. The main thrust of agricultural expansion can come only from increased productivity through the application of modern technology: new and better seeds, better and fuller use of fertilisers, pesticides and water control; as well as more effective institutions for organisation of production, distribution and marketing.

The population density is already very high, averaging 570 persons per square km., and it is deteriorating rapidly. In the early years of this century there were on average four persons to 3 acres of cultivated land. Forty years later at the time of the Bengal famine, four persons shared 2 acres; today there are four persons to 1 acre of cultivated land; by the end of the century there will be only ½ acre for four persons. In face of the accelerating change in population density, particularly as it has been seen in the second half of this century, rural economic and social life in Bangladesh can no longer maintain its timeless traditional character. Change there must be; the question is whether life in Bangladesh, which is now so precarious can be secured and ameliorated in circumstances of rapidly increasing population pressure on the land.

The inevitable increase during the second half of this century in the ratio of population to land gives a measure of the increase in output per acre required to provide sustenance for the population. In addition, account must be taken of the fact that even when harvests are good and supplemented by imports of foodgrains the people of Bangladesh are seriously undernourished.

Land is largely cultivated in small plots; it is estimated that there are 7 million farms. In the circumstances of Bangladesh, even a very small-sized farm provides an important basis for the survival of a household; one out of every four farms in Bangladesh is in fact of only 1 acre or less. Such farms, nearly all of which are owner-operated, are of course insufficient as an exclusive source of employment and of income for the whole household of typically six or more members, but they do provide an element of security and of standing in the community.

Two out of four farms are between 1 and 4 acres. In contrast to the smallest farms, only 60 per cent of these medium-sized farms are owner-operated. Depending on the quality of the land and on its exposure to flooding, drought and salinity, owner-operated farms may provide a marketable surplus in addition to subsistence. Tenant-farmers surrender part of the produce for rent, sometimes as much as half the crop. While this will increase the volume of agricultural produce that enters the market, it also means that members of tenant farming families must try to supplement their income as agricultural labourers and as participants in non-agricultural rural activities.

Only one out of four farms in Bangladesh is of 4 acres or more. These are the farms from which most of the marketable surpluses are derived, though for most of them only when harvests are good. These also are the farms where technological improvements through better seeds, plant control, fertilizers, capital investments, etc., are most likely to be adopted. Rather more than half of them are owner-operated, providing an existence which, in relation to life in Bangladesh, must be considered secure and well-to-do. Such owner-farmers and their families constitute the core of rural society.

2. *Foodgrains and Population*

Bangladesh is a rice economy: half of all value added in agriculture is represented by paddy production; the next important item being jute. There is some domestic production of wheat, pulses, edible oils and other crops which provide important additions and supplements to the diet, as does fishing—mainly pond and other inland fishing.

Paddy is grown on 4 out of every 5 acres of the total area cropped in Bangladesh. The relative share of paddy fields in total acreage will decrease as other products, including wheat, gain importance. For the foreseeable future, however, rice production will provide the main source of income and livelihood, the main source of calories in the diet and the main indicator of economic and even political viability of the country.

In the 1960s imports of grains from West Pakistan and foreign countries increased markedly and reached a level of about 1·3 million tons in 1969–70. In spite of domestic output of rice being outpaced by population pressures, growing imports of foodgrains in the 1960s prevented *per capita* consumption from falling below the average level of about 1 lb. a day maintained since the Bengal famine.

During the liberation struggle and the early years of independence, Bangladesh suffered a serious reduction in rice output. It was a period of very large foodgrain imports, nearly all wheat grains, financed initially as humanitarian assistance, but increasingly by Bangladesh's own resources. In 1971, when millions fled to India and lived there, imports of grains to Bangladesh amounted to an estimated 1·3 million tons. In 1972 and 1973 grain imports amounted to nearly 2·5 million tons each year and in 1974 to about 2 million tons. In recent years domestic output of foodgrains has been supplemented by imports to an extent which corresponds to the consumption by one person in every five or six.

In the early 1970s Bangladesh was hit by cyclone, war, drought and floods. In spite of efforts to introduce technological improvements, estimated rice output in the five-year period 1970–5 was no greater than in the previous five years 1965–70, leaving nothing to meet the needs of the rapidly growing population. Even with record imports of food in the early 1970s, the total volume of grains available from domestic production and imports was insufficient to maintain the low average level of *per capita* consumption of the 1950s and 1960s; the already meagre diet of up to 1 lb. of foodgrain a day on the average for the whole population was further reduced. Moreover, during recent years there has undoubtedly been a large, unregistered outflow of foodgrains across the border to India. The quantities involved are very difficult to estimate with confidence, but most observers believe that at least ½ million, possibly more than 1 million, tons a year have been smuggled across the border. Whatever the amount, domestic consumption levels in recent years have been even lower than indicated by data of imports and domestic output.

Foodgrain production in Bangladesh in the three years since Independence has been about 10 million tons per year or even less (deducting 10 per cent for seed, wastage, etc.). For Bangladesh to be able to feed its population by the mid-1980s, and then only at the present average level of daily intake, domestic grain production would have to nearly double in ten years as compared to the harvests of the early 1970s. The achievement and maintenance of the goal of foodgrain self-sufficiency will require a transformation of agricultural production practices, very large public investments, particularly in water control, and new social and economic institutions. None of these requirements are easily met; far-reaching social and political changes are needed in Bangladesh to provide the framework for the realisation of any one of them. The odds certainly are against success; yet with persistence and determination and with some luck and fair winds the race between food output and population may be won, even in Bangladesh.

3. *The Advent of a New Technology*

Output per acre of rice in Bangladesh is low in relation to potential. There is scope for very significant improvements through modernisation of agricultural processes and by the much more intensive use of supplementary inputs in current production, and with the help of investments to deal with the basic need of water control.

Agricultural practices in Bangladesh have undergone some adaptation to new technologies. The use of fertilisers has always been very low. This is explained by the fact that traditional rice varieties, which in other respects are well suited to the soil and growth conditions of Bangladesh, are tall but weak-stemmed plants. If nitrogenous fertiliser is added, the heads of the plants get heavier and the stems taller and weaker, and the plant therefore tends to fall. It is only in recent years, after the breakthrough in plant-breeding technologies at the International Rice Research Institute in the Philippines (IRRI) and the initiation of adaptive research in Bangladesh, that cultivation based on new varieties and new practices has become a realistic possibility.

The first attempt was made in the mid-1960s with the introduction of a new seed, called IR 8, this proved moderately successful for the winter (*boro*) crop. For the two other main crops, *aus* and *aman*, IR 8 turned out to be unsuitable, particularly because of the great variation in yields and thus the high element of risk involved for individual farmers. *Boro* season yields were generally satisfactory; three times the output from traditional varieties was obtained in many instances and farmers soon appreciated the opportunities offered by the new seeds.

Farmers rapidly realised that new seeds require adaptation and change in cultivation methods. In order to derive the full benefit of the new varieties of rice, more water and better water control was required, better plant protection against blight and cold damage, and the growing season had to be extended. While further adaptations of IR 8 to shorten the growing season and make the plant less susceptible to damage could be hoped for from further research, the basic need for effective irrigation is likely to remain. Since water control in the circumstances of Bangladesh is physically and institutionally difficult to provide and expensive to construct, the new seed technology opened up in the mid 1960s for the *boro* crop could not go very far in effecting a real change in the Bangladesh rice economy.

The introduction in 1970 of IR 20, however, was a major breakthrough for paddy technology in Bangladesh. This seed variety is very much better suited for the main *aman* crop than are traditional varieties. With average monsoon conditions, yields are high, and the plants are moderately resistant to pests. Since 1970 several other new rice seed varieties have also been developed by IRRI and introduced in Bangladesh, covering all three main crops and different conditions within each crop.

As these technological innovations have become available the Bangladesh farmer appears to have responded. According to official estimates, the area planted with the new high-yielding varieties in 1974 covered some 1·7 million acres. While this may well be a considerable exaggeration, it is significant that such acceptance of the new seeds as has in fact taken place has occurred in spite of limited experience with the new seeds in the conditions of Bangladesh, in spite of very limited extension services and notwithstanding the fact that farmers have had to adopt new cultivation practices. Generally, for the full realisation of their potential, the new seeds require better land preparation, better weed and pest control, more attention to transplantation (right time, right spacing), more use of fertiliser and better drainage and irrigation facilities and water control. The new seeds give opportunities for other activities arising from the new cultivation practices since they require both more labour per acre of land and more supplementary inputs, many of which the farmer will have to purchase.

The prospect of applying new technologies to all three main paddy crops (as well as for wheat) in Bangladesh gives a fresh start for the country in the population–food race.

4. Development Strategies for Food Production

The coming of a new agricultural technology has a profound significance for the agricultural development strategy that may be adopted. For centuries, foodgrain supplies for the survival of the population in the delta have depended on the fertility of the soil as determined by the annual floods of the rivers. As population has increased with increasing rapidity, more and more difficult land has been settled and cultivated, the deeply flooded areas upcountry and the exposed low-lying, ever shifting terrain in the river mouths. This population pressure on the land, combined with an apparently fixed traditional rice cultivation technology, dictated a two-pronged strategy: in the first place, large-scale efforts and investments to install irrigation and drainage structures and even to control the vast flow of the rivers themselves; in the second place, the allocation of foreign exchange for large and growing quantities of foodgrain imports financed through industrialisation, import saving and export-earning developments, and by foreign assistance.

This, in fact, was the declared strategy in the 1950s and 1960s, but it was a strategy implemented only in part and without persistence. In actual fact, irrigation and drainage investments were totally inadequate, while major water control schemes, with one or two unfortunate exceptions, never left the drawing boards. Industrialisation, except for some jute manufacturing, never amounted to very much in East Pakistan, import-saving efforts did not extend to substitution of home production for imports from West Pakistan, and export promotion was largely ineffectual. As a result East Pakistan's overall balance of payments which was strongly positive in the 1950s, registered increasing deficits in the 1960s. While the above two-pronged strategy dictated by increasing population pressures and stagnant food production technology was rational in conception, it was largely ignored in implementation.

By the early 1970s, at the birth of Bangladesh, the development strategy called for by the technological innovations and adaptations of rice cultivation was different. In two important respects the situation was very much worse than twenty-five years earlier: first, the population pressure and the momentum of its growth was much greater, and secondly, the balance of payments situation which had been very strong in earlier years had turned into one of desperate shortage. In two major respects, however, the situation was clearly better: first, the country was on its own, allowing its policies and future to be decided fully by its own people, and secondly, traditional rice cultivation could be superseded by a whole range of new and dynamic technologies.

In terms of development strategy, the significance of the new rice technologies is that they allow not only higher yields but also much greater choice and flexibility. While the development of basic technology is largely determined by international efforts, the application and specific development of the various seeds are matters for national efforts. Moreover, the creation of the circumstances in which given seeds are most effective depends on national decisions: on investment programmes for physical structures and for training and extension, on import and production arrangements to provide the inputs needed to make the new seed technology effective, and on the establishment of institutions and facilities for marketing the output. The new rice technologies, therefore, open up options and opportunities; they are not in themselves new or additional supplies of food.

For Bangladesh the introduction of an element of flexibility is critical. The old strategy would not have had any chance of success in the country's failing economic situation in the early 1970s. A strategy which depended for its success mainly on the taming of large rivers would be incapable of fulfilment, given the immense technical, organisational and financial problems involved. Eventually, say in a century or so, and gradually from small beginnings in the near future, control of the waters of the Ganges and the Brahmaputra must be achieved, but for the present and the next few generations, physical survival must be assured principally by other changes not dependent on control of the major rivers. The new rice cultivation technology may well provide the basis for this.

The increase in rice output which is possible with the new seeds and technology is very large for each crop. For good results supplementary inputs of fertilisers, pest controls, irrigation, drainage, etc., are essential, most of the seeds yielding output in rough proportion to the extent of application in the initial stages. Major irrigation and drainage schemes, however, and indeed control of the major rivers and installation of effective coastal embankments, require very large investments and have long gestation periods for their completion and before they contribute significantly to current crop production. The fact that current output can be increased very considerably by concentrating on new seeds, other inputs and relatively small-scale investment programmes, rather than on large-scale, indivisible investments which are very costly in terms of both time and finance, provides the basis for an "inputs" strategy for the medium-term future. This inputs strategy leaves major water control investments, if not their planning, to the future. The strategic decisions in terms of concentration and timing of effort become choices between crops and between the several elements of an input package. The great advantage of the new technology for Bangladesh is that it not only allows deferment of the immense major water control schemes but also provides variety and options in the introduction of a new technology.

5. Potentials for Foodgrain Production

In its First Five Year Plan covering the years to 1977-8, the government outlined an agricultural development programme which sought to draw the maximum benefit from the quick yielding potentials inherent in the new technologies as they could be applied in the actual economic, social and political circumstances prevailing in Bangladesh. The Plan in fact foresaw the achievement of foodgrain self-sufficiency by 1977-8, a prospect which in the light of subsequent developments (the Plan was prepared in early 1973) is certainly unattainable.[1]

The Plan made its target dependent on an effective input strategy. Compared to an "average" pre-Plan year (in the First Five Year Plan this is referred to as "benchmark" quantities) a small increase in the multicropping of agricultural land was foreseen, the major emphasis being on an increase in yields by over 5 per cent annually. This was to be obtained by shifting to new seeds for all three major crops and by greatly expanding the area for the *boro* crop for which additional yields with new seeds are higher than for the two other crops. The combined effect of the successful implementation of the Plan programmes was expected to result in a total rice output in 1977-8 of over 15 million tons which (together with projected wheat output and allowing for "normal" deductions for seeds, feed, waste) would roughly correspond to the expected demand, thus eliminating the need for net imports of foodgrains.

The First Five Year Plan included quite heavy allocations for major water control projects, but they cannot be expected to make much of a contribution to output within this decade. They appear to have been included in the First Five Year Plan in response to pressures from the community of flood and irrigation engineers and their institutions for a longer-term strategy, and also as a reflection

---

[1] The World Bank in a report prepared a year later suggests a more modest target, but still foresees foodgrain self-sufficiency attainable within this decade.

of the need for allocation of resources for flood protection of life and property, not just to enhance agricultural output. Whatever the wisdom or political necessity of such allocations, the success of the drive for early self-sufficiency depends on the fullest possible implementation of the input strategy, not major water investment. The latter is no substitute for the former in terms of food output in the intermediate future, and therefore cannot be allowed to pre-empt financial and administrative resources at the expense of the input programme, if the aim of food self-sufficiency is to be reached at the earliest possible time. Given that proviso, however, an early start on major water projects may be critical for maintenance of food self-sufficiency in later decades.

The analysis underlying the First Five Year Plan builds on a long series of reports and studies in the 1960s undertaken by domestic and foreign experts. A major advance of the analysis (and a summing up) of the agriculture and water development potentials and policies of Bangladesh was undertaken by World Bank staff and consultants in 1971.[2] The Bangladesh Plan, while of course it differs in some important respects from the strategies in the World Bank report, in fact also builds on the insights and analysis in that Report.

The conclusion of the World Bank report, looking to a longer-term future than does the Plan, was that the productive potential of the new technologies is indeed large. While current rice production runs at a level of 10 to 11 million tons annually, known technologies, coupled with the gradual development of irrigation and drainage facilities and of course adequate institutional support, could quadruple output by the end of the century. But the difference between trebling and quadrupling output would be very expensive, involving moving into costly projects of water control with long gestation periods. Rice production strategies for Bangladesh may therefore be considered as being composed of three distinct—though partly overlapping—stages: first, concentration on improved agricultural inputs (seeds, fertilisers, pesticides and extension services); then a combination of improved inputs and irrigation from tube-wells and low-lift pumps (but no flood control and flood drainage); and eventually—if ever—improved inputs plus complete water control (full irrigation and drainage). Table VII.1 summarises the potential for rice production as it emerges from analysis based on such a three stage strategy.

[2] The massive report from this exercise has not been published, but is used extensively in Bangladesh and by national and international foreign aid agencies. Access to the report has also been given to some students of the Bangladesh economy.

TABLE VII.1

POTENTIAL RICE PRODUCTION

(million tons)

Year	Inputs Only	Inputs plus Irrigation	Inputs plus Full irrigation and Drainage
1983	16	26	35
1993	19	32	42
2003	22	38	51

The economic rates of return on the production and distribution of the new seeds are high, and the same applies to the provision of fertilisers and other elements of the input package; in suitable combinations, rates of return above 50 per cent are not untypical. At the other end of the scale, longer-term projects have much lower returns; investments for irrigation and drainage projects have rates of return varying typically from 5 to 15 per cent.

The flexibility and range of new options provided by the new technologies present planners with difficult and important choices. These require consideration of agricultural technologies which are both technically complicated and largely untested in the special circumstances of Bangladesh. Moreover, the fact that agricultural technologies themselves must be expected to be further developed in coming years, perhaps in new and unexpected directions, makes the task of decision-makers even more difficult and hazardous. The need clearly is for strategies and policies that can be reviewed and adjusted as experience is gained and circumstances alter; heavy investments in large-scale indivisible water control projects are questionable.

The new seeds and technologies of foodgrain production thus appear to provide the basis for the people of Bangladesh to regain overall balance between population and domestic grain production. Estimates of the time required to do this differ; the Plan sets out a policy to achieve this by 1977–8; others judge that it would take much longer. Having analysed the facts and the arguments, we share the view that the production potential over the intermediate future is sufficiently large, and the programmes for the realisation of this potential are on the whole sufficiently realistic, for total grain production in Bangladesh to reach a level of total consumption by perhaps the mid 1980s. Moreover, and here we differ from many knowledgeable analysts, we also judge that in the longer term, grain production could continue to grow more rapidly than population. If by 1985 production could be brought into balance with consumption, sufficient momentum would have been gained for further advance in Bangladesh. It might easily be possible to increase output at the rate of 3–4 per cent annually until the end of the century: there will be further room for intensified multi-cropping, for wider application of inputs, for irrigation and drainage, for some major water control schemes and for further development of technologies. Such studies as we have seen all give support to this conclusion, even though they do not all draw that conclusion.

Clearly any judgement of this nature and for such a period must be highly conjectural and we do not hold our view with absolute certainty. Even if the trend is as we suppose, it seems very likely that there will still be individual years, perhaps even series of years, in which food will be short due to unfavourable crop conditions. But on balance we expect that Bangladesh will cease to be a net importer of foodgrains by 1985. Seen against the background of the last few years, when Bangladesh has been desperately short of food and in a state of economic and financial collapse, and highly dependent on international readiness to provide support, the achievement and maintenance of food self-sufficiency would be a dramatic change.

6. *Potentials for Other Crops*

In this chapter we have concentrated most of our attention on the production of rice because without rice everything will fail. Rice, however, accounts for little more than half of agricultural output, and other crops and products must be produced in larger quantity in the interest of providing a balanced and adequate diet, improving export potential, creating employment and providing inputs for industry.

Tea. Until Independence, the tea estates enjoyed a privileged position in Bangladesh. Output was sold at high prices, particularly in the captive market of West Pakistan. Profits were good and the cultivation of tea prospered financially. The loss of the West Pakistan market exposed the industry to world competition, and brought out many shortcomings. Yields are low, about two-thirds to three-quarters of those of the other major producing centres of India, Ceylon and East Africa, mainly because of the uneven rainfall. The quality of the tea is not very good and so it does not command the best prices. The tea gardens suffered considerably from the War of Independence, and the disorganised state of the Bangladesh economy subsequently affected production adversely because it was often difficult to get the supplies needed to run the estates and move the tea to market. It is scarcely surprising in the circumstances that the production of tea proved for a time to be unprofitable and that it was necessary to subsidise the industry. Devaluation should go a long way to improving the financial position.

The increase in world prices for tea in 1974 was also a favourable factor. The tendency is for world supplies of tea to be relatively plentiful in relation to demand, and it is probably best to assume that a buyers' market will be characteristic of market conditions during much of the rest of the century. But whether or not this is the case, Bangladesh simply cannot afford to get pushed out of the market for tea; too many workers are dependent on the cultivation of tea, and export earnings are too important for the industry to be allowed to run down. Fortunately there seems no reason why it should. There are opportunities to increase output and yield by infilling; in many of the estates, tea bushes have not been replaced when they died, and while it takes some time for new stock to reach a full yield, some worthwhile production is possible in the fourth year. It is generally assumed that the quality of tea grown in Bangladesh cannot be improved because the tea areas are low-lying; while this may be a factor, picking methods also have an important effect on quality. If the leaves are picked at more frequent intervals when they are smaller, quality can be greatly improved, and for this reason new regimes need to be introduced in many of the gardens.

In some areas, diversification of crops may well prove to be profitable. Experimental plantings of coffee trees are doing well in the Sylhet area, and while it is not proving possible to produce coffee of the highest quality it will be possible to provide for the needs of the domestic market. Other possibilities include the cultivation of rubber. The existence of the tea gardens, with the organisational capacity to work on a large scale, should make it possible to introduce new types of cultivation relatively easily, and if these proved to be more profitable than the cultivation of tea, it would be possible gradually to divert the use of land to alternate crops. If the tea gardens are to play this pioneering role, efforts will have to be made to maintain and develop managerial efficiency. Many gardens were run by expatriates, often Scots, but there will soon be no expatriate managers working in Bangladesh. There is, of course, no reason to think that this should affect the management of the estates adversely in the long run, but there appears to be a problem of transition in which it may be necessary to make special provision for the training of managers.

Jute and Other Products. The production of jute at competitive prices is vital if export earnings are to be maintained. Some important aspects of this have already been examined in Chapter IV in relation to the exchange rate. Jute production has got to be revived and maintained in the face of food shortage and high rice prices, and jute cultivation must be made attractive to the farmer in spite of this. If rice output expands at the rate indicated, the present extreme pressure to grow foodgrains will gradually diminish and there will be more room for the cultivation of jute. Besides attention to relative prices to the producers, other well-known measures needed to improve the competitive position of jute are needed. Better types of jute have to be developed, improved systems of cultivation have to be made known to farmers and complementary inputs made available. Research into jute cultivation is unfortunately far behind that devoted to the cultivation of rice, and negligible in relation to what has been spent on synthetics; but for this, jute would not be in danger of being driven out of world markets. A great deal of time has been lost and it is very doubtful if this can be made good. Nevertheless a determined effort must be made to try to preserve jute production by pressing ahead with research and applying its findings in the fields.

Like jute, other crops have been affected by the need to devote land to the cultivation of rice and would be helped if less land were needed for this purpose. Even in present circumstances it ought to be possible to produce more fruit and vegetables; the importance of these as ingredients of the diet does not seem to be fully appreciated, and land that could be used for this purpose is sometimes left as waste. As well as shortage of land, bad communications, lack of marketing facilities and the limited knowledge and experience of farmers restrict production. More cotton, tobacco, potatoes, oilseeds and pulses would be consumed if resources could be devoted to producing them. It would also be possible to produce more coffee and quite probably rubber and palm oil. The prospects for all these products would be improved by suitable programmes devised to develop better varieties, change cultivation practices and demonstrate their possibilities.

The opportunity to increase the output of fish is good. So far most fish has been taken from inland waters, and the possibilities of the Bay of Bengal have been largely neglected. However, a start has been made with exploiting these resources, and there is considerable potential for increasing the domestic consumption of fish and for expanding exports. Inland fisheries are by no means used as efficiently as they could be; overfishing is a problem and the use of pesticides endangers the fisheries in some instances. Also, as is discussed in the next chapter, the neglect of village tanks has affected fish production adversely.

More animals will be needed to provide the increased amount of soil preparation needed with the new technologies, and this will help to increase output of milk and other products, including some processed by industry. The basic problem of increasing the output of animal products is, of course, that of feed; as in nearly every other case, poor rice yields react adversely on other production possibilities.

At present cattle, as well as men, suffer from malnutrition and this is one reason why livestock output has declined in the last ten years. Something can be done to improve the output of livestock other than cattle by improving strains, for example in poultry. Realistically, however, efforts to increase the output of livestock products are unlikely to be of any great significance for some considerable time. Improvements in rice production come first and must be given administrative priority; more complicated programmes of greater difficulty will, for the most part, have to be held in abeyance.

7. *Policies for Application of New Technologies*

The increase that could be got by a proper application of the new, known technologies is great. Problems arise not from dearth of suitable techniques but because of difficulty in creating the right conditions in which they can be speedily adopted. Basically it is a problem of political and economic organisation. Farming methods should not stand in the way of a large increase in output. It is believed that techniques are quite widely known, but if they are not, it is not an impossible or lengthy business to teach farmers rice technology. A suitable person may need only a few weeks' training to become an effective farm level instructor; it should not be too difficult to make the new technology familiar to large numbers of farmers.

The key ingredients of seed, fertiliser, pesticides and water control need to be combined in optimal proportion, if they are to achieve maximum impact, but substantial progress can be made even under much less than optimal conditions. In the short run, it is likely to be easier to make seeds available than fertilisers and to provide some water for small-scale irrigation than to develop large-scale flood protection arrangements. The provision of some inputs requires direct intervention by the state because the scale and complexity of the operation is beyond the resources of private enterprise, but many improvements are quite capable of being carried out without state assistance or intervention.

Success depends on the actions of millions of farmers, but also on basic and, particularly, applied agronomic research and development, on the provision of the inputs required in adequate quantity and at the right time, on institutions and trained manpower for agricultural extension, on appropriate storage and marketing facilities being developed, on credit facilities being made available and effectively operated, and on a host of associated matters. In all this the role of government is crucial.

Many of the measures to increase agricultural output will have to be implemented over several years, and much of what is now foreseen as technically possible and desirable cannot even be started straight away. There are, however, some measures that might be introduced in the next few years with considerable effect if current policies were modified. In the discussion below only some aspects of this are examined and certain desirable measures highlighted.

Fertiliser. When the significance of the use of fertiliser, pesticides and water with new seeds was first appreciated, it was felt that they would not be used readily if they were sold at world prices. The practice was adopted either of providing them free, as was done with pesticides, or of selling them at much below cost, as was the case for fertiliser. Ten years ago this was probably the right approach. Some farmers had disastrous experiences from using the wrong quantity of fertilisers, or using them in the wrong form, when they were first introduced. There was little practical experience of the effects of fertilisers under controlled conditions, and farmers were naturally disinclined to take a step in the dark. Since then, there has been a radical change in the understanding by farmers of the possibilities of new methods of cultivation. By 1972 there was convincing evidence of the acceptance of the use of fertilisers and the readiness to pay an economic price for it which was clearly illustrated by the fact that farmers bought on the blackmarket. It was also evident that the availability of fertiliser in Bangladesh at subsidised prices was giving an additional incentive to smuggle part of the fertiliser to India. The price of urea towards the end of 1973 was about Rs 60–70 per maund in West Bengal while it was being issued at Taka 30 per maund in Bangladesh. The Rupee and the Taka were then nominally at par. In fact, the blackmarket exchange rate was more like 2 Takas to 1 Rupee, and this made smuggling even more attractive. Against such a large disparity in the exchange rate, there could be little hope of removing the incentive to smuggle fertiliser by a price increase on the Bangladesh side of the border; but it was also evident that fertiliser was underpriced in relation to its value in agriculture. Smuggling apart, fixing a price for fertiliser below its economic price, far from favouring the poor farmer (as it might be thought was intended), had the effect of improving the position of richer farmers who were likely to be more adept at getting it.

Yet the fact that fertiliser could be sent to India is itself an illustration of failures of the agricultural programmes. Combined with suitable inputs, fertiliser increases yields very greatly. When it was in scarce supply in 1973 and 1974, the world price exceeded $200 per ton (roughly Taka 70 per maund at the official exchange rate), but even then it paid for itself several times over. If all had been well with Bangladesh agriculture, there would have been very little incentive to sell fertiliser to India by the back door or for any farmer to be prepared to sell the limited supplies he could get to a neighbour. In terms of agricultural economics, fertiliser for most farmers would have been too valuable to go without.[3]

The government has come increasingly to recognise that the time is ripe to reduce and, it may be hoped, permanently to abolish subsidies on fertilisers and to start to charge for pesticides. The price of urea was increased by two-thirds in 1974 and began to approximate world production costs at the official rate of exchange; the price of other fertilisers was doubled. This change of policy has the effect of helping the government's financial position but from the point of view of increasing food production its major significance is that it should help to improve the distribution of fertiliser and hence the output of rice and other agricultural outputs. The extent to which it will do this will depend on the methods of distributing fertiliser that are adopted. At present fertiliser is distributed by the Agricultural Development Corporation, but this has not always worked smoothly. Such was the disruption of transport and its organisation in the spring of 1973 that there was something like 30,000 tons of urea held in store in the Ghorasal fertiliser plant. It might have seemed possible at the time to have transported the fertiliser to market using country boats; the obstacles in the way of this were, first, the decision that the fertiliser should be distributed by the Corporation and, secondly, the fear that if the fertiliser were moved privately it would be "lost" in transit; as it was underpriced, this might well have happened. If, however, the fertiliser were sold at its scarcity price it might be possible to distribute through private trade—quite possibly a much more efficient way of dealing with it, at least in the short term.

Irrigation and Water Control. The changes in pricing policy for fertiliser should help in the more efficient use of this scarce commodity. So far the same policy has not been applied to the distribution of water for irrigation.

The simplest forms of irrigation are well within the capabilities and resources of individual farmers and have been practised since prehistoric times. There exist many primitive devices for lifting water out of lakes or rivers, but surface water is distributed irregularly and is available in only limited areas during the *boro* season. In many areas the potentiality of surface irrigation can be extended by using

[3] Investigation of the variation of yields of rice with the application of fertilisers in suitable combinations shows that by increasing the application of fertiliser from 1 to 5 maunds an acre the yield of paddy can be increased from 20 to at least 40 maunds. When paddy fetches Taka 50 per maund, any price for fertiliser less than Taka 250 per maund will pay off.

low-lift pumps and suitable irrigation channels. The next step in the development of water resources consists of sinking tube-wells. These may be shallow or deep, depending on the depth at which adequate supplies of water are available, and the deeper they have to be the more they will cost. Cost will also depend on the methods which are used to sink them and the type of contractor who is used to do the job. A further stage in the complexity of providing water supplies consists of large-scale irrigation works in which water storage is linked to much more extensive distribution systems. Finally, there are still more grandiose schemes covering the total hydrology of rivers or major areas, often in India, and crossing the boundaries of countries.

The benefit that accrues from irrigation is large since it can make it possible to grow an additional crop during the dry season and sometimes two additional crops over the year. It is calculated in the First Five Year Plan (p. 150) that the annual net benefit per acre from irrigation works out at Taka 1,000 to Taka 1,200 per acre against costs of furnishing the irrigation facility, ranging from roughly Taka 150 to Taka 300 per acre. There is clearly a case for charging prices that will ensure at least a recovery of costs, and it is arguable that this should go further to tap a greater proportion of the increased production that results. The approach advocated in the Plan was gradually to increase the scale of charges made for water, starting with Taka 50 in the first year of the Plan and terminating with Taka 150 in the final year. Since in the last year of the Plan it was hoped to have about 4 million acres under irrigation, charges on this scale would produce very considerable revenue, in fact about Taka 60 crores in the final year. It may be thought, however, that this is not enough. Even in the last year of the Plan, the supply of water would still be greatly subsidised. In terms of the productivity increase resulting from irrigation, it would not be unreasonable to increase the charge per acre to, say, Taka 300. This would still leave a large additional return accruing to the farmer, more than sufficient to allow him to reduce indebtedness to some degree and still to increase his standard of living considerably.

The increase in charges for the use of water is important from the point of view of production, because when water is free there is no incentive or compulsion to use it economically. Many of the tube-wells are nowhere near to irrigating the area of land that they could do. Often only a few farmers benefit from them when many others could also be supplied. To charge for water in relation to the cost of supplying it would give an incentive to bring more farmers into the circle of irrigation water in order to meet costs. It is clearly necessary to relate charges to the capacity of the tube-well (having regard to its command area) in order to ensure efficient and economical use of the water. To charge would also help to ensure that pumps and engines were maintained by building up pressures to obtain value for the money paid. Another effect of stopping the policy of giving water away might be to encourage the greater use of cheaper and smaller facilities for the provision of water, such as simple hand pumps capable of irrigating 1 or 2 acres.

Rural Credit. The adoption of new technologies of cultivation requiring increased amounts of purchased inputs, coupled with decisions to increase the price of some of these inputs as suggested above, have meant that the farmers need more money to purchase them. This might seem to require an increase in the availabilities of institutional rural credit. We are not convinced that this is really necessary on any large scale. It is true that institutional rural credit so far provided has been very small in relation to the various measures of need that have been advanced from time to time. But the magnitude of the need is very uncertain. Guesses are made about it and are often arrived at by taking estimates of agricultural output and applying some rather arbitrary credit requirement factor to this figure. The extent of the real need for credit may reasonably be doubted. The first requirement is for credit to purchase fertilisers and perhaps seed. The use of fertiliser is unlikely to exceed 1 million tons a year for some time, if only because of supply difficulties. At a long-term price of, say, Taka 1,000 per ton, the cost of this would amount to Taka 100 crores. This is a considerable sum, but it is not to be supposed that the whole of it would have to be met out of credit. The amounts of fertiliser already in use, rather less than $\frac{1}{2}$ million tons, are purchased out of the farmers' existing financial resources.

In large measure fertiliser is a self-liquidating input; a loan is seldom needed for more than 6–8 months, and the increase in output that results from its use is generally more than enough to enable sufficient to be saved to pay for the fertiliser several times over. There may also be requirements for credit to pay for the input of water if, as is suggested, this were charged for on a scale more closely approximating to the cost of providing it, but here again it should always be possible to recoup the cost of the water out of a single crop with a lot to spare. Credit requirements might increase very considerably if the farmer were asked to finance some of the less quick-yielding forms of investment in the provision of water; at present this is being financed, rightly or wrongly, by the state, and the capital cost does not fall immediately on users. Many of the minor improvements needed on farms can also be carried out without much more than the use of the farmer's own labour.

In fact it is more than likely that any attempt to increase rural credit for general productive needs would fail in its purpose because the money would be diverted to other uses. In his study of the Comilla programme,[4] Ali Akhtar Khan demonstrates that, while applications for loans show the purposes for which the money is required as being wholly productive, borrowers in fact admit to having borrowed, at least in part, for other purposes. Presumably the figures collected understate the extent to which this occurs. They show, for what they are worth, that 14 per cent of the loans were used for non-productive purposes and roughly half for the release of mortgaged land. While among societies making high amounts of loans, the amount planned and utilised for mortgage redemption was also about 50 per cent, the proportion used for purposes not revealed in the borrowing plan was over 20 per cent. The figures seem to suggest that the larger the loan, and by implication the richer the farmers involved, the greater the percentage of borrowings directed to non-productive purposes. The diversion of loans from the nominal purpose for which they were made is scarcely surprising in view of the general pattern of borrowing needs. As Ali Akhtar Khan has shown in another publication,[5] in Gazipur village over 70 per cent of current debt had been contracted to cover family expenses. Moreover, the record of repayment of loans made to rural borrowers has been almost universally bad, and much of what is lent may better be regarded as a subsidy to consumption than as a means to increase production.

The conclusion we have reached about the need in the next few years for increasing institutional rural credit is largely negative. For the most part borrowing is for non-productive purposes, the rate of recovery tends to be low and the money to be wasted. Currently perhaps half of rural credit is provided by friends and relatives, and as much as one-third by landlords and money-lenders. Moreover, the ability of local personal lenders to increase the amount of credit they extend will increase quite rapidly as the new technologies of rice cultivation get under way. The proposal in the First Five Year Plan to disburse about Taka 200 crores on balance after allowing for recoveries seems to be misplaced, and is the more difficult to justify in the light of present financial stringencies. If, however, there is any real evidence—which we have not found—of sales of fertilisers to farmers being held up for lack of credit, then

[4] *Rural Credit Programme of Agricultural Co-operative Federation*, Bangladesh Academy for Rural Development, Comilla, Bangladesh, 1971.

[5] *Rural Credit in Gazipur Village*, Pakistan Academy for Rural Development, Comilla, Bangladesh, 1968.

existing institutional rural credit facilities or expansion thereof could be used to meet the need. It may be possible to justify greater availability of institutional rural credit on other grounds and in relation to the general and long-term rural development that needs to be undertaken; it is much more difficult to regard it as one of the more important means to get an immediate increase in agricultural output.

Administration. There is a hollow sound to every exhortation to improve efficiency in the administrative sphere, but this does not prevent us from observing that Bangladesh is failing to do what is within its competence to ensure and speed up the adoption of new methods of rice cultivation. At the moment the efforts of Bangladesh's administrators are too widely spread. Concentration of administrative talent is needed to overcome the obstacles to progress in agricultural production. Detailed targeted programmes that can be monitored month by month need to be enforced. Such targets should include the amount of fertiliser to be distributed, the amount of seed to be made available, the number of tube-wells to be drilled, and so on. They should include a few targets of a type that would help to mobilise village resources, such as the restoration of tanks, construction of godowns or the development of co-operative activities. This could become the beginning of a nation-building activity.

Monitoring programmes call for a new approach involving independent appraisal. It is common experience that reports by agencies on their activities often cannot be relied upon and may exaggerate performance. For example, serious doubts are felt about whether as much land is planted with IRRI (high-yielding) varieties of rice as is reported. Such things must be verified. It is hardly wise to base decisions on inaccurate information of a critical nature when the facts could be ascertained.

8. *Implications of New Technologies*

Even if it were possible to attain the foodgrain balance discussed above, Bangladesh would nevertheless have to grapple with tremendous problems inherent in the very success of the foodgrain production programme: greater output gives rise to greater consumption by the farmers themselves and their own household, and may reduce the relative quantity marketed; policies are needed to ensure sales of rice to other sectors of the economy; there is a growing need to establish stocks and to ensure more effective, rapid and economic physical movement of products; and problems will arise and intensify in respect of the uneven impact of technological improvements.

The new technology, particularly of rice, on which hinges any hope for amelioration of living conditions in Bangladesh, brings in its wake large and adverse distributive effects which are difficult to counter without "killing the goose that lays the golden eggs". For reasons of physical characteristics of the land and agronomic conditions, the introduction of a new productive technology in the most rapid and effective manner means concentration over the next five or ten years on areas in the north-west and south-west regions of the country, much less in the central and eastern regions; and within each region there will be large further differences between rapid and slow-moving agricultural advance. By adopting suitable policies and by planning the differential application of new technologies and intensified input programmes, the impact can be modified, but unfortunately the scope is not large; the rewards of successful agricultural development will be reaped in some localities and by some farmers: for other areas and farmers life will go on as before.

The new technologies which permit the advance in production are in most, but not all, of their elements neutral to scale, i.e. they can be adopted with roughly equal proportional advantage for small and large farms. Irrigation and drainage development, however, typically requires organisation extending beyond the level of the individual small farm, often involving development of institutions for marketing of inputs and outputs. The new technology requires— in fact is characterized by—the use of purchased (or external) inputs. Farm economics clearly demonstrate that the switch-over to the new technology is highly profitable, but it also requires a much deeper involvement by the farmer in finance, and in the markets for the inputs he needs and for his output. The rural market (perhaps particularly at farm and village level) is notoriously imperfect, leaving a great deal to depend on tradition, social class, initial position, contacts, financial resources, ability to act and to wait, and on chance and circumstance. The small farmer has a hard time under present traditional conditions; he seems bound to lose out under the new market-oriented and market-dominated production system, unless very strong and effective measures are taken to strengthen his position.

While agricultural and rural development will benefit a large number of people and to this extent may be more widespread in its effects than industrial development, it will give rise to an increase in inequality of income within the rural area itself. The effects in terms of helping the landless labourers will be rather small; nevertheless, if progress could be intensified there would be some enlargement of work opportunities outside agriculture and the opportunity for greater specialisation among different occupations. Increased income and wealth of cultivators will create demand for non-agricultural products. With greater supplies development will also open up opportunities for improved diet. Unless, however, there is parallel development in other sectors in town and country, success of agriculture will increase income inequality and unemployment will rise, it seems, very rapidly. Rice production would be a highly profitable market-oriented activity for relatively few; it would tend to become an export industry (through smuggling and economic and political pressures to allow sales abroad) rather like jute. The rice producer would want to sell to whoever could pay the most, which is not likely to be his unemployed and poverty-stricken compatriots.

CHAPTER VIII

EMPLOYMENT, RURAL DEVELOPMENT AND EDUCATION

1. *Employment*

With regard to Asian countries, Gunnar Myrdal has cautioned against examining questions of labour utilisation from Western points of view which, he maintains, are inappropriate for many of them. He suggests that to set as an objective the creation of as many jobs as it can be presumed there are people to fill them is both a vague and often an unhelpful concept. In Western, largely industrialised societies, it may be appropriate to count heads to be gainfully employed unless incapacitated or, in some cases, of idle disposition; but in agrarian societies with vastly different social customs and objectives, relying mainly for employment on cultivation with its attendant seasonal patterns of work, it is extremely difficult to identify persons who can properly be regarded as unemployed or much less than fully occupied in gainful activity. Myrdal concludes that the view that employment for a certain number of hours per week is the norm may not be appropriate in village societies.

Nevertheless, there can be no doubt that there is unemployment and under-employment in Bangladesh. Many of the population would work, or work harder, or for more hours if they could see an opportunity of doing so. Concern about unemployment arises not from any ethical considerations about the virtues of work or of a forty-hour week, but because the opportunity to work is a means to ensure independent livelihood to those who might otherwise be destitute or totally deprived of the opportunity to make their own way of life. There is no system of unemployment benefits for those living in Bangladesh; there is no organised system of support for those who are unable to earn their living. The unemployed are either looked after by their friends and relatives, survive by begging, or die.

Even at the risk of being accused of looking at problems of employment in Bangladesh through Western eyes, it seems to us right to lay stress on employment creation and to agree with Robert McNamara, President of the World Bank, speaking about the failure of development policies to reach the poor, that

given the intimate link between poverty and massive unemployment, unemployment and underemployment must be tackled head on. With twenty per cent or more of entire populations already jobless or virtually idle—and with the population explosion producing a growing stream of new entrants into the labour pool each year—unless policies and programmes are devised to absorb surplus labour into productive jobs, little can be done to improve the lot of the desperately poor. Job creation must therefore become a direct objective in itself. It will be necessary to organise rural and urban public works—the building of market roads; construction of low cost simple housing; reafforestation programmes; expansion of irrigation and drainage facilities; highway maintenance, and similar low-skill, labour intensive, and economically useful projects.[1]

In the circumstances of Bangladesh, job creation is even more vital than in the developing world at large. As we have suggested in Chapter V, by the year 2000 there could be as many as 20 million persons completely or partly unemployed, unless special efforts are made to create jobs and mobilise labour resources into productive activity. Without such measures, it will be very difficult to keep the social fabric intact; law and order will finally collapse and quite likely revolution will intervene. Rural development is a political necessity.

It is by no means certain that a solution to the employment problem can be found within the context of a market economy. Economists have put forward some ideas as to how it might be done, but the suggestions so far advanced fail to carry conviction. It is generally assumed that the price mechanism is at fault and that modifications to it can bring about the desired result. Labour, it is often argued, is over-priced because it is supported in unemployment by the extended family system and will not work for less than can be gained through this system plus some allowance for the disturbance of going to work and for the disutility of the work itself. The answer, it is maintained, lies in subsidising labour, so leading entrepreneurs to adopt more labour-intensive production methods. Since combining more labour with capital would increase the productivity of capital, a tax on profits could be imposed to cover some of the cost of the subsidy. A correct view, perhaps, but such solutions are not really practicable. In spite of offsetting taxes on capital, any massive improvement in employment would be too costly to finance; and it would be virtually impossible to prevent fraud on a substantial scale as employers claimed the subsidy on behalf of relatives and friends. It is hard to see any answer to the problems of Bangladesh in such theorising.[2]

[1] In his 1972 Address to the Board of Governors of the World Bank.

[2] For a rigorous treatment of the theory behind these views see A. Qayum, *Theory and Policy of Accounting Prices*, North-Holland Publishing Company, 1960.

Sometimes it is suggested that the same results could be achieved more directly if planners were not so blind to alternative methods of production that are less demanding on the availability of capital. We discuss some aspects of this in Chapter IX and suggest that it is not easy to improve the use of capital by a policy of developing small-scale rather than large-scale industries. The facts do not seem to give any strong support for supposing that alterations in production techniques can contribute to the reduction of unemployment in a significant way.[3] The ILO report, *Matching Employment Opportunities and Expectations; a Programme of Action for Ceylon*, for example, is not encouraging about the use of handlooms for this purpose. It concludes: "In principle, since the ratios of both capital to labour and capital to value added are lower for handlooms than for decentralised power looms and automatic power-looms, both output and employment could be maximised by choosing this technique. However a number of factors reduce the practicality of such a policy, namely the inferior quality, durability and higher cost of production of handloom cloth and the consumer's preference for cheaper mill-made cloth." The report goes on to point to the fact that it probably overestimated the output of the handloom weavers and that it assumed single shift working for power looms when three shifts could be worked. In fact, correction of the estimates in this way suggests that handlooms were inferior by most if not all standards of comparison.

We mention this example at length because Bangladesh is adopting a policy of encouraging its handloom sector. Conditions may be different in Bangladesh from those in Sri Lanka, for the scarcity of foreign exchange is so great as to suggest that machinery imported at an equilibrium exchange rate would be more expensive in Bangladesh relative to labour costs, but even so it may be necessary to justify the employment of handloom weavers as much on political and social grounds as economic ones. There are other industries in which employment might be increased by the use of technical methods of production that make heavy demands on labour, but we judge that the opportunities are rather slight, and that where such methods are feasible, opportunities are probably fully exploited. Road construction is another case for which labour-intensive techniques are often advocated. The opportunities to substitute labour for capital in this area seem also to be limited. This may be because suitable techniques have not been developed, but it appears that

---

[3] For a summary of the present state of knowledge on the employment implications of industrialisation in developing countries see D. Morawitz's article of that title, *Economic Journal*, September 1974, p. 491.

construction tends to be either highly labour-intensive or highly capital-intensive. Intermediate techniques do not appear to be available, and attempts to mix labour- and capital-intensive activities have so far appeared very inefficient. Very often traditional highly labour-intensive methods are not economically competitive, even in countries such as India or Bangladesh, because of low labour productivity.

More recently, economists seem to have been coming to the view that there is a trade-off between jobs and output in the sense that if output is sacrificed, more jobs can be created by using less efficient but more labour-using processes. In spite of the loss of output, they appear to argue that the operation might be beneficial if it resulted in redistribution of income, within a smaller total income, to the poor and underprivileged who would value it more highly.[4] Redistribution of income is an important objective of economic policy; it is clearly undesirable to act on policies which have the effect of spreading their benefits very narrowly. But equally it seems very undesirable to forgo output in order to achieve a more widespread effect unless this is the only way to achieve the required distribution of income, and provided of course this lower level of output, properly distributed, contributes more to total welfare than other alternatives. More often than not, we submit, it might be possible to eat the cake and have it, too.

2. *Rural Works*

In East Pakistan before Independence, an attempt was made to create employment opportunities in the countryside by instituting rural works. The programme launched in the early 1960s used surplus commodities imported under the United States P.L. 480 programme as a source of finance. Besides creating employment, it developed local initiative and encouraged the construction of rural roads, bridges, drainage schemes and buildings. Its impact, as with so many other things, was limited by the amount of finance available, and after the programme had been in operation for some years, we suspect the planners were finding difficulty in devising projects that provided a high ratio of employment to the amount of expenditure involved. For the re-excavation of rural tanks 95 per cent of the cost involved consisted of the hire of labour; for the construction of *kutcha* roads and their repair the labour content was 90 per cent; while for the excavation of small canals and their construction and repair it was 85 per cent. But for *pucca* roads, buildings and bridges

[4] For example, Frances Stewart and Paul Streeten, "Conflicts between Output and Employment", *Oxford Economic Papers*, July 1971.

the labour content was only about 15–20 per cent. By 1970 the planners were reviewing the opportunity to continue the construction of *kutcha* feeder roads and ruefully calculating that there were 2½ miles of such roads for every square mile of territory in East Pakistan and that the scope for further construction of this type of road was limited.[5]

It was estimated that about 400,000 man-years of work were provided in 1969–70 by the works programme in East Pakistan. Almost three-quarters of this employment was given by the Thana Irrigation Programme then in operation. The essential justification for this programme was to increase agricultural yields, and employment creation was a subsidiary issue. The works programme proper was expected to provide only 100,000 man-years of work in 1969–70.

It was hoped that employment given by the two programmes could be doubled during the duration of the Fourth Five Year Plan for Pakistan, i.e. by 1974–5, but what could be done depended on available finance which could just as well have been used for the finance of other development programmes. Such programmes might not have created the same amount of employment in the same places, but otherwise there was nothing that particularly singled out the rural development programme as a means to overcome the problem of unemployment and underemployment in any fundamental way. Experience with the works programmes confirms the view that it is difficult to obtain sufficient employment from them in the face of financial constraints, and it is not always easy to devise suitable schemes of work.

A recent suggestion by Dr. S. V. Allison of the World Bank outlines a new possibility for productive works programmes. The cost of major flood protection schemes is so great that they cannot be afforded at present. This has led to reflections as to whether there are alternative possibilities which might be both less costly and also labour-intensive. Dr. Allison has proposed that the topography of substantial areas of Bangladesh should be restructured into a series of effectively flat terraces. The highest of them would hardly ever flood. Successively lower ones would flood with increasing but statistically predictable regularity, to varying degrees. The lowest level would probably be below winter river levels, so it could be irrigated by gravity flow through sluices during the dry season; there would be no attempt to keep water out of such levels during the flood season. Besides providing flood-free land for residential purposes at the highest level, restructuring the topography would greatly improve

[5] See *The Fourth Five Year Plan, 1970–75*, Planning Commission, Government of Pakistan, July 1970, p. 342.

water control and enable agricultural output to be increased by planting additional crops and, in the lower reaches, by cultivating fish. Dr. Allison suggests that there would be about 7 million acres of land over which restructuring the topography would be fully justified, and that about 50 million man-years would be needed for the task. This would give employment for 1 million people for 50 years or 2 million if the job were to be completed by the end of the century. This seems a large amount of employment, but it must be related to a labour force of about 27 million people at the present time and to one of 56 million or more at the end of the century. Even a scheme of this magnitude would not cure unemployment. It also would need substantial funds to pay for it, even if some labour could be mobilised without payment.

3. *Approaches advocated in the First Five Year Plan*

It was one of the virtues of the First Five Year Plan for Bangladesh that while advocating rural development for its own sake it recognised the limitations of traditional attacks on the employment question. Proposals were made for the establishment of cadres and the direct mobilisation of labour that otherwise would be totally unemployed or insufficiently employed. The actions proposed in the Plan hinge on the fact that most of the underemployed and most of the unemployed are assumed to be able to subsist through the charity of relatives and friends and to be ready to provide labour free, although other costs such as the provision of additional food would have to be met before many of the unemployed were capable of putting in a full day's work, and they would certainly require some additional "sweeteners" before they would be ready to participate in a works programme. It might also be unrealistic to suppose that their friends and relatives would continue to support them once they were in employment offered by the state, even if this were in fact without pay. Apart from this, money would be needed for tools and perhaps more complicated capital equipment. Transportation to the scene of the work and living accommodation of some kind would often be necessary in addition. Some costs of employment are quite unavoidable, but it was proposed in the Plan to keep them to a minimum by a programme of labour mobilisation.

The Plan suggests that all males of working age should be required to donate a given amount of labour in a year with the option to commute on payment of a given sum of money. A special programme was proposed for students, who would be expected to use their vacations for voluntary work in their own neighbourhood or village, utilising their special skills whenever these could be used with advantage. Such a programme would make it possible to use labour which otherwise would be idle, but it would not directly affect the persistence of unemployment. To do so it would have to be greatly extended. One or two years of national service, applied to all sections of the community, would have a bigger impact on unemployment if it could be assumed that all the employment provided by the programme was additional to that which would have been provided in its absence. On this assumption the effect could be appreciable.

Schemes for the mobilisation of labour into compulsory workforces are difficult to organise. The experience in Sri Lanka was not very encouraging. Under-twenty-fives were offered 3 Rupees per day in 1967 for work in development schemes. By the time the scheme was suspended in May 1970, 40,000 youths were registered, with a maximum of 27,000 reporting for work on any particular day. Infrastructure costs were heavy, administrators and teachers difficult to find, and morale hard to maintain. It would be surprising if Bangladesh fared any better.

An alternative way—perhaps an additional way—of occupying those who might otherwise have nothing to do might be to try to keep children at school for a longer period. This could be a less costly proceeding provided that parents were forced to maintain their children. But it is scarcely realistic to suppose that, with an educational system so obviously deficient as that of Bangladesh, it would be possible to make such an alternative work in a satisfactory way, or even work at all.

The above analysis suggests that not much can be done in the short run to increase opportunities to work. Measures that would greatly alter the rights and obligations of individuals would ameliorate but not solve the problem. While a number of less radical efforts to improve employment opportunities will have the effect of creating jobs, as will the development effort itself, it may well prove quite impossible to prevent a rise in unemployment and underemployment from taking place as more and more people depend on the limited amount of land available.

4. Rural Works Opportunities

The above rather depressing analysis notwithstanding, there is a great deal of useful work that could be done if peoples' energies could be harnessed and financial problems overcome. Ellen Sattar relates her experience in carrying out a village survey:

One Hindu woman begged our help because her house was literally falling down and there was no male member of the family to repair it. As always we were followed by a crowd of children and young men. Turning to them

I remarked that these healthy young men could surely repair the house for her. They actually all took two steps backwards and looks of blank amazement appeared on their faces. Excuses poured in and the upshot was that after giving the widow some money in order to enable her to hire labourers, the crowd thinned rapidly and followed us no more.[6]

It would be wrong to conclude that laziness is a universal characteristic in Bangladesh any more than in any other country. Most of the village women work very hard and are fully occupied with the chores of looking after the household. In Ellen Sattar's survey very few of them appeared to have any leisure time to speak of. The rickshaw pullers, the coolies pushing their carts, the labourers engaged in digging trenches for drains, all work hard to the eye of the casual observer. The top civil servants, the businessmen and the professional workers likewise are fully employed and generally hard at work. But that there are great difficulties in arousing village initiative and organising productive activity in the villages which would improve the standard of life is undoubted. Professor Dumont, another observer of village life in Bangladesh, has much to say on the subject. In his view a major obstacle to the better exploitation of village resources is failure to make the best use of available land. Tenant farmers have little incentive to improve systems of cultivation when much of the product goes to landlords, small farmers in the hands of moneylenders see much of any increased output being used to repay their debts so that extra effort may not be worth while, communal ownership of tanks stifles individual initiative, while the large landowners, comfortably off, play no part in the cultivation of their fields which are farmed inefficiently. Hill farming is almost unknown in Bangladesh and the use of such areas only for the production of timber is inefficient. Dumont maintains that the cultivation of orchards, tea and mulberry would use the land much more efficiently and still make it possible to produce bamboo for the manufacture of paper, provided that it were cut at the right height.[7] Much of the land in the village itself is badly utilised, and if more emphasis were laid on the cultivation of vegetables and fruits, it would be possible to augment dietary standards in a worthwhile way.

A major improvement in the productivity of land could come through a better utilisation of water resources, using village rather than government initiative to get things going. Better use of tanks

[6] *Women in Bangladesh: a Village Study*, The Ford Foundation, Dacca, October 1974, p. 32.

[7] Réné Dumont, *Problems and Prospects for Rural Development in Bangladesh, Second Tentative Report*, The Ford Foundation, Dacca, 30 November 1973, p. 39.

is one way in which, Dumont maintains, village action could transform the situation, although this is contested in the First Five Year Plan. The starting-point of the discussion is that there are 633,000 acres of tanks in Bangladesh, of which 75 per cent are derelict. On this point there is no dispute. What is in question is the contribution that such tanks could make to irrigation, while at the same time being used for the raising of fish. The issue turns largely on the depth to which the tanks can be excavated. The Planning Commission assumes that a depth of 8 feet of water should be considered and that during the dry season about one-quarter of this would be lost through evaporation and seepages. The minimum level that must be maintained for fish cultivation is said to be 3–4 feet. On this arithmetic, only some 2 feet of water could be used for irrigation.

It is clear that the depth to which the tanks can be excavated is crucial to the argument. Dumont assumes that it would be possible to accumulate 10–12 feet of water by the end of the rainy season. In many cases the same effect could be created by raising the sides of tanks by a higher earth embankment, as would probably be done anyway if the spoil from excavating the tank to a greater depth were deposited on the bank. In this way it should be possible to utilise 4–6 feet of water for irrigation. The effect of this change in assumptions is to double or even treble the irrigation payload of bringing derelict tanks back into production. The Planning Commission appears to assume that water derived from tanks should or would be used for the cultivation of rice and so would not go very far. Dumont assumes that if it were used for this purpose it would nevertheless be possible to keep requirements down to about 2 feet multiplied by the cultivated area, if maximum economy were made of water by levelling and constructing bunds. On this basis 633,000 acres of tanks might be able to irrigate double their area of land. This is not all. Other crops are much lighter on water than rice. The cultivation of Pak Mex wheat (a new high-yielding variety originally developed in Mexico) instead of rice might enable five times the area of land devoted to tanks to be sown in the dry season. Dumont maintains that if leafy vegetables were grown during the dry season, two or three crops might be raised. It is difficult to decide in the face of dispute about the underlying figures how effectively reclaimed tanks could be used. On one point at least there is agreement. The output of fish might be greatly increased. A well-kept tank can produce $\frac{1}{2}$ ton of fish a year; with improved techniques, and to a much greater extent with artificial feeding, yields could be greatly increased.

The construction of *pucca* canals as opposed to *kutcha* ones[8]

[8] The term *pucca* is used to denote something substantial and permanent and the term *kutcha*, in contrast, something impermanent or makeshift.

would improve the distribution of water, whether derived from tanks or from other resources. Such canals could be combined with the construction of footpaths or bicycle paths, thus improving communications.

The importance of Dumont's suggestions is that they reveai several areas for communal village action. Rural development could become something to be organised by the villagers themselves. More might have been done along these lines had it not been for the fact that most major development programmes such as irrigation programmes have been mainly the responsibility of the central government, leaving very little to local organisation. It is scarcely surprising that the result has been that pumps have been badly maintained and utilised and that they have done little to improve the lot of the really poor.

It is not just in the better utilisation of land and water that there is scope for improvement in village life. There is a great need to improve the performance of education and make it more relevant to the needs of village life. There is a vast need to improve agricultural techniques and agricultural implements. There is, as must be emphasised repeatedly, a need to improve the status of women and to benefit from the contribution that they could make to improving production and living standards.

5. *Rural Development Organisation*

To recognise these needs is to realise the difficulty of finding a solution to the problem of motivating those who have to be involved and of developing the organisation that is needed to promote rural development. In organisational respects Dumont draws very unfavourable comparisons with the Chinese. He comments that in a South China village scene "everybody in the the village, men and women, ex-rich and poor, staff and peasants, would be working with his own hands. Excavation of tanks, minor irrigation and drainage would be realised in a few years, without any state participation, which will be limited to big works. In a Bangali village, one-third of population works two-thirds of the time. In a Chinese village two-thirds of total population works 3/3 of the time: three times more."[9]

The problem is how to arrive at activity on this scale. The approach developed by the Academy for Rural Development at Comilla is the basis of present policies. In this approach co-operative activity is

[9] R. Dumont, *A Self-reliant Rural Development Policy for the Poor Peasantry of Sonar Bangladesh, A Tentative Report*, The Ford Foundation, 1 May 1973, p. 63, quoted as written.

seen as a major means to change the life of the community. Co-operatives can be used to provide inputs and the credit needed to purchase them, to inculcate habits of saving, to induce a readiness to accept new practices of cultivation and as an instrument for the education of farmers in improved agricultural practices through the model farmer system. Extensions of these activities can promote other objectives such as family planning and mass education. Altogether the co-operative is seen as a means of activating the community and giving it a sense of common purpose. The First Five Year Plan lays stress on such co-operative activity and regards it as an instrument for bringing together sections of the village community whose interests often diverge. The management committees of the co-operatives are to be elected in such a way that the landless, small independent farmers and larger farmers who employ labour and direct operations rather than participate directly in them, will be proportionally represented.

If the co-operatives are to succeed as instruments of social change there may be no half-way house. The uni-purpose co-operative existing for the provision of credit has not succeeded in Bangladesh. The strength of the Comilla approach depends on putting the co-operative in a dominant position. Advocates of it feel that the co-operative should be at the centre of village activities, that it should be the sole supplier of inputs of fertiliser and seeds as well as the marketing agency, that it should be the means through which decisions are taken about what crops to plant and how production should be organised, that it should assume responsibility for the purchase of consumer goods, and so on; in short, that it should control so many of the typical village activities as to submit most behaviour activity to the tests of communal will and common purpose.

This aspect of rural development in Bangladesh has now reached an impasse, and it is unlikely to get going without a substantial reorganisation of systems of local government and strong political leadership. There are signs of growing unrest in the villages and political forces at work resisting the traditional rural élite. With insecure government in the rural areas, development is bound to be held back, and it will be difficult to build up the institutions needed.

Part of the difficulty has been the failure to establish effective systems of local government. In 1973 it appeared to be the intention to establish local governments at various levels. Elections were held in December of that year for representatives at the Union level, i.e. the lowest governing level consisting of ten to fifteen villages. Subsequent elections for the establishment of local government at the *Thana* level were to have taken place, but were not in fact held. The *Thana* covers an area on the average of about 100 square miles and may include about 150,000–200,000 people. Also, no steps were taken to use the District, the major administrative unit of Bangladesh, as a further unit of local government.

Failure to proceed with the extension of local government to higher echelons beyond the Union was attributed largely to political forces, to the wish of members of parliament to be in sole control of the country and the geographical area constituting their respective constituencies. Political events in 1975 have led to some changes in the system of local government, but villagers continue to be without any real opportunity to make their views felt through a democratic process. Whatever system of political organisation is attempted, rural works and the creation of village initiatives cannot be done by central direction alone; local institutions are indispensable. The natural unit of administration is the *Thana*, provided that its activities can be supplemented by organised efforts at village self-help as intended by co-operative activity. The works schemes were based on the *Thana* in the 1960s and in many cases the organisation seemed to work well. The *Thana* can be used both as a co-ordinating centre for works put forward by the Union *Panchayats* and as a channel for the submission of proposals to higher levels of administration, for example the Districts. Thus it is possible to elaborate a chain of command for the control of rural works.

A number of problems have to be overcome if the administrative systems envisaged are to work effectively. The first is that of combining local initiatives with the degree of central control that those government departments most closely concerned with rural development are likely to wish to operate. In the First Five Year Plan it was envisaged that preparation of plans at the *Thana* level would be supervised by a committee consisting of representatives of various so-called nation building departments, presumably the ministries with involvement in rural development, and that all plans would have to conform to policies and principles laid down by the Planning Commission, although the Ministry of Local Government would guide, supervise, monitor and evaluate the rural works programme and allocate finance and technical assistance.[10] Clearly a very considerable degree of central control was intended.

For development at the local level to go ahead, finance will of course have to be made available. This must come largely out of the development budget of the Ministry of Finance, but could also include contributions made from local taxes and, as time went on, from beneficiaries of the schemes initiated. The sources made available could then be used to hire the services of extension workers,

[10] *The Plan*, p. 164.

to construct roads or bridges, finance tube-wells or promote tank reclamation and drainage and irrigation works. In some cases work could be directly organised using local labour and technical skills; in other cases it might be necessary to rely on the expertise of ministries. But in all cases the responsibility would be fairly and squarely with the *Thana* representatives to use their money in the best way open to them. Their activities would be supplementary to those of the ministries, not competitive with them; large schemes for flood control and drainage would be unaffected, as would other major construction projects and development activities covering a wide area and requiring centralised control.

There would, of course, be risks in devolving control over rural works to this degree. Money might be used for bad projects or diverted from development to other purposes; friends and relatives might be favoured and nests feathered in other ways. Central administration does not avoid these things either, but clearly some supervisory machinery must be devised. Corruption is endemic in Bangladesh at present. One of the needs is to establish a strong, élite and incorruptable inspectorate to act as a deterrent to mal-practice. This is as necessary for central government activities as it is for local activities, but it would help to provide rather necessary checks on the activities of persons with a local interest at stake.

A second problem is that of assembling an able team of administrators to operate at *Thana* level. Considerable pressures will have to be put on those employed in the civil service to ensure that able men are sent to organise and supervise local development works. Service outside the capital and large towns might be made a condition of promotion for most top level civil servants. Finally, it would be desirable to instil a sense of regional pride in the progress of development. It is here that the Minister of Local Government could exercise his influence, by relating grants of money to performance and by chiding or encouraging *Thanas* as they deserved.

6. *Education*

Education in Bangladesh may be classified into three levels, those of primary, secondary and higher education. Primary education consists of five years' instruction, secondary education of five to seven years, depending on whether the pupil proceeds from taking the Secondary School Certificate to taking the Higher Secondary School Certificate. There were about 11 million children registered in primary schools in 1972–3 according to official statistics, and about 2 million in secondary schools of various types.

Higher education colleges teach for pass degrees requiring two years' study. Standards are very variable. The six universities in Bangladesh teach for honours degrees which require three years of study and also undertake some postgraduate work. There are roughly 25,000 students at universities.

Education impinges on every aspect of development in Bangladesh. The present system of education is widely regarded as being unsuitable for the needs of a developing country. It still reflects the needs of a bygone age concerned more with colonial administration and academic content than with the information, mind-training and orientation needed for development. It is curious that inherited systems of education can change so slowly. Britain has introduced vast changes in her educational system since 1947 when India gained independence, but the British system of education seems to have rested largely immune to change in Bangladesh.

In some respects the aims of education remain the same. There can be little dispute that literacy is one of these and that any educational system must depend on its attainment. The proportion of people who can be regarded as literate in Bangladesh depends on how literacy is defined. Probably one-fifth to one-quarter of the population of Bangladesh should be regarded as literate. The proportion varies considerably from village to village. In the village studied by Ellen Sattar[11] the literacy rate of male Hindus aged five years and over was nearly 70 per cent; that for male Muslims was nearly 60 per cent; while for females the figures were approximately 40 and 35 per cent respectively. Clearly this was exceptionally good and it demonstrates that the educational system can function effectively given the right climate. For Bangladesh as a whole there is clearly a long way to go before it can be said that minimum standards have been attained.

In economic development education is not an end in itself, it is an end with a purpose in mind. It is necessary to design educational systems that can assist in attaining the purpose. The general complaint about education in Bangladesh is that it is too academic, too much oriented to the passing of examinations as a stepping-stone to ultimately getting a well-paid government job.

At the primary level of education, buildings and teaching materials will be rudimentary. This may not cause too much difficulty. In Bangladesh buildings can be simple and it is possible to teach the "three Rs" with little more than blackboards and slates. For those whose only formal education may be to spend a limited number of years in the village school, literacy, though exceptional as we have seen, is not likely to survive for long unless there are opportunities to use this basic skill, and there may be no other opportunity to

[11] Op. cit.

enlarge knowledge and educational experience. Somehow primary education must be directed to giving the kind of educational experience that will enable the child to be able to prepare itself for working life more effectively. Dumont considers that this could best be done by giving more attention to the teaching of agriculture in the schools, concentrating on major innovations in agricultural techniques and cultivating practices.[12] He goes further and considers that the schools should educate the pupils in a practical way by actual farming and by being ready to experiment with new crops and methods. The attachment of a farm to the school would also help to improve nutritional standards, as the output of the farm could be used to feed the children. The idea is attractive in many respects, even though such innovations have not been successful in other countries. It does raise the problem of obtaining staff who would be capable of giving the kind of practical instruction that would be needed. The village schoolmaster would not need to have the same extensive knowledge of new agricultural practices that would be required of an extension worker; and as we have argued previously) basic instruction in the new technology could be provided in a course lasting only a few weeks. Given the numbers involved, however, it would be difficult to develop training schemes that would enable the teachers, many of whom are not themselves farmers, to acquire the necessary knowledge and skills, unless a quite new approach were adopted, as we describe below. There would also be other allied problems such as securing the land needed for teaching farming. Inputs would also have to be acquired, but if successful, the teaching farms should be well able to cover the cost of such purchases.

In a country in which one-third of the population is of primary school age, the cost of primary education is bound to be quite considerable and in 1974–5 recurrent costs were estimated to be about Taka 40 crores. This was at a time when 50 per cent or less of children of primary school age were enrolled in schools. To provide education for all children of primary school age at that time would have cost about 12 per cent of total revenue expenditure, quite apart from the cost of other forms of education. If the size of classes were to be reduced (many of them have fifty or more children), costs would rise still further.

The cost of secondary education is less than that of primary education because only about two million pupils are enrolled for secondary education, but the cost is not negligible. The budgetary estimates provided Taka 14 crores for it in 1974–5. If secondary education were to be provided for all, the cost would be quintupled.

---

[12] In his *Second Tentative Report*, op. cit., p. 35.

When roughly 30 per cent of the population is of primary school age and no more than 40 per cent in the working age group, and roughly half of these, the women, mostly not employed outside the home, the cost of education is bound to take a high percentage of the GNP. Thus the aims of educationalists to educate all children to the age of fifteen will prove to be costly if put into execution.[13]

There can be little doubt that the educational effort should be concentrated on primary education. It will not be possible to ensure that all children receive a good grounding for some years. It might be a mistake to extend the educational net too rapidly. Better progress might be made if it were possible to ensure that those who started school finished it. Half of the boys enrolled in Class I drop out before reaching Class V.

Higher education is a totally different story. About 100,000 students are enrolled in colleges doing degree work and nearly 25,000 in universities. The total compares, in a very rough and ready way, with about 450,000 students in higher education in the United Kingdom; even allowing for the difference in population, the number of such students in Bangladesh is very high. There is pressure to expand higher education still further. The First Five Year Plan, for instance, proposed that enrolment in universities should be increased in five years by 60 per cent and in colleges by 50 per cent. It is hard to justify such increases. Pressures naturally build up from those engaged in the higher levels of education but they have to be resisted.

Studies of the employment of graduates do not suggest that the problem of graduate employment is as severe in Bangladesh as in India or some other countries. A study by the University of Dacca directed by M. Obaidullah[14] has shown that students graduating with honours in science and engineering do not have difficulty in getting jobs. For science and arts students graduating with pass degrees, about 25 per cent were out of work. It may be judged from this that the more academic the study undertaken, the less the chance of getting employment; closer examination of the figures for arts subjects bears this out, purely academic education is not in demand in the market place. These conclusions suggest that there is no case for an expansion of students reading for arts, but that there is probably

[13] There has been no shortage of ideas about how to keep the cost of education in bounds. The use of cheap student labour has frequently been seen as a means to reinforce teaching endeavours. One way in which this might be done would be to get all university graduates and qualified college students to teach for a year in their village as a return for their education.

[14] *A Study of Employment Survey of Graduates*, University of Dacca, 1971.

still a market for good-quality graduates in science and technology.

By the end of the century the young children of today and those to be born in the next five years will have grown to maturity. Many of them will be neither better educated nor better prepared for life than those of today. At the top of the scale, the proportion of them educated to first degree standard and beyond will certainly be much greater; it is not for nothing that the universities and colleges have increased the number of their students. The danger is that they will sit like a crust above an empty pie dish as the duality of education is increased still further. If Bangladesh is to keep on the narrow path we have prescribed, the real need is for a vast improvement in the quality and extensiveness of primary education and for the use of education as more effective participation is economic life and development, particularly in the villages. There is a long gestation period in changing educational systems. To pass from one conventionally organised to one directed to economic development involves working out new ideas, training teachers to put them into effect and retraining those already engaged in teaching. To do this by conventional means would take too long and make it impossible to transform the situation, as is needed, in the next twenty-five years. Technically there may be some ways in which this prolonged period of preparation can be shortened.

The most obvious way would be to make much more use of radio and preferably television as instruments of education. Universities of the air have demonstrated that it is possible to reach large numbers of people relatively economically. There is no reason why such methods should not be applied both to pupils and to the training of teachers to put the new ideas across. One of the great advantages of using mass methods of instruction is that it is economical to spend great time and effort on the preparation of teaching materials and the improvement of teaching methods. No isolated teacher can spend weeks preparing a single lesson, but teams of teachers knowing that what they devise is destined to reach a wide audience can economically and rewardingly devote such an effort to the preparation of their material. What is more, the teachers in the villages can be fully drawn into an education programme by the same means. It can be explained to them how to use the material prepared for transmission by radio or television. They are on the spot to provide the reinforcement that any form of impersonal system of instruction requires. Programmes need not be confined to purely instructional material. It will be far easier to keep children at school if it provides an opportunity for enjoyment as well as for instruction. There is no reason also why the curriculum should be narrowly confined in other ways. There is still no great sense of national identity in Bangladesh; political education could also form part of the programmes devised, and the objectives of development, and the way in which it is being attempted, explained. Such programmes will not cut the cost of education but rather increase outlays. There will be the need to prepare programmes, to provide the receivers that will be needed to get the programmes into the schools and to ensure that there is an efficient system for the maintenance of such equipment. Electronic equipment is much more reliable than it used to be, but it would be disastrous if an education programme based on material sent over the air were to be interrupted because of technical breakdown of the receiving equipment. The cost involved in realisation of this form of far-reaching instruction should not be too great, Television receivers could be installed for Takas 2,000 each; to equip 50,000 villages in this way would cost Taka 100 crores. This is not a small sum, but it is of the same order of magnitude as the amounts that it is planned to spend during the First Plan Period on expanding higher education where the economic and, even more, the social returns are likely to be much inferior.

The use of television as a means of instruction in the villages could extend far beyond the education of those of primary school age. It could be used for a whole host of other things; for education generally, for explanation of the objectives of economic development and the means taken to achieve it, for the dissemination of information about family planning and for nation building. Educationally it would have the great advantage not only of reaching many people but of making it possible to make changes in vital aspects of the educational system that otherwise would take years to accomplish. It is this above all that is the attraction of the system.

7. *Conclusions*

Employment presents great difficulties, and continuing population increase in Bangladesh can do nothing but aggravate a situation in which unlimited requirements press on the most limited factor available—land. It may be that if agricultural output increases as we hope, there will be a rise of accompanying employment in other occupations in rural areas. Some commentators have suggested that this will occur on a sufficient scale; we find this uncomfortably hard to believe, and feel that special programmes will be needed to expand employment. The key to this lies in the villagers themselves. There is plenty of work to be done; the problem is to activate people and convince them to work to common ends, even though there is little prospect that sufficient funds could be raised by conventional taxation methods to allow this to be done through government financed employment.

There is much that the villagers could do to help themselves but little mechanism to organise it. China appears to be doing much better in organising rural activity. Central direction is not the answer to the need for local activity, and there is a deadly gap in the Bangladesh system of leadership at this point. Somehow village initiative has got to be encouraged and given its place. Local government has been deliberately neglected under the pressure of political events. This cannot be allowed to continue; without it development will not succeed.

Village life would not remain so unchanged and traditional as it is, if education progressed. Few people in villages know what is going on. Communication is bad in every sense; education is largely ineffective and restricted. The favoured ones get the opportunity to be educated to the highest level, and educationalists in the top echelons will press for money to be spent at the top end of the educational scale. The need, however, is greatly to improve the education of villagers; unconventional measures are needed for this. Radio and television offer some hope in this process and will need to be mobilised as a force not only of conventional education but also as a means to bring home to all an awareness of life beyond the village, in the nation as a whole and even in the wider world. In education, mobilisation of initiative and leadership at the village level is needed from every point of view.[15]

[15] Since these passages were written it has been reported in the *Wireless World*, December 1975, p. 549, that the Applications Technology Satellite ATS-6 in orbit (then) over Lake Victoria was 'irradiating' India from a single source with instructional programmes transmitted by All India Radio. This experiment, unfortunately, is to last only a year, as the Satellite is due to be moved to a new position in the Western Hemisphere.

CHAPTER IX

INDUSTRY

1. *Structure and Growth Prospects of Manufacturing Industries*

Yearly censuses of manufacturing industry in Bangladesh give some impression of the structure of established industry although the information is very incomplete. The censuses do not cover factories employing less than ten workers, and it seems that the coverage of those included is defective; clearly care is needed in comparing the information given in successive censuses because of changes in coverage. In Table IX.1 information is given from the provisional results of the 1970–1 census. Since small-scale and cottage industries are not included in the census, the table probably covers only about two-thirds of industrial output.

The overwhelming importance of jute as a source of employment and value added in 1970–1 is immediately apparent. It accounts for about half the total fixed capital invested in industry and about the same proportion of employment, although it produces only one-third of the value added. Because jute was produced in Bangladesh, industrial development was rather lopsidedly directed to jute manufacture. The industry is now in a very insecure position, and it can no longer be regarded as a growth industry. Less jute in being produced in response to the scarcity of rice; the world market for jute manufactures is no longer expanding on any significant scale; very little has been done to improve jute cultivation, to develop alternative markets for new jute products or to improve efficiency in the mills. The prospect for jute manufacturing is rationalisation, not expansion. Since the industry is now nationalised, there is an opportunity to try to improve its structure. Studies have shown that units consisting of 400–600 looms have tended to be of optimum size and this might be borne in mind in trying to improve the efficiency of the industry.

It will thus be necessary to find a new growth point for Bangladesh industry. This might be found in a switch to the production of other types of textile goods and eventually in light engineering production. After jute, textile manufacture is next in importance in terms of employment and value added. There is no doubt about the availability of domestic markets for the products of the textile industries;

TABLE IX.1
CENSUS OF MANUFACTURING INDUSTRIES 1970–1
(PROVISIONAL)

	No. of Establish- ments	Fixed assets (million Taka)	Employment (thousands)	Value added (million Taka)
Food	216	228	22·5	234
Beverages	7	6	0·6	11
Tobacco	27	53	4·8	184
Textiles				
Jute	65	1,165	143·4	546
Other	461	381	46·5	203
Footwear and apparel	104	5	1·5	5
Furniture and fittings	31	4	0·5	2
Paper products	16	160	2·2	21
Printing and publishing	106	12	2·6	9
Leather products	98	9	2·2	14
Rubber products	—	—	—	—
Chemical products	263	94	15·9	133
Products of petroleum and coal	1	109	0·4	17
Non-metallic minerals	33	29	2·8	16
Basic metal industries	27	48	2·5	29
Metal products excluding machinery	114	13	3·9	18
Machinery except electrical machinery	54	8	1·9	8
Electrical products	16	12	1·4	16
Transport equipment	19	4	0·8	3
Total (including miscellaneous)	1,727	2,368	258·7	1,491

the real problem is the availability of raw material. Historically Bangladesh was a producer of cotton, and provided the raw material needed for the finest of muslins. The variety known as *ab-e-rawan* was so fine that it could hardly be perceived if thrown on running water; *sabnam* was supposed to be invisible when spread on the damp grass. So fine was the product that weaving had to be done in the early morning or afternoon, when the light was less dazzling to the eyes. Small wonder that Hindu women who spun the thread were unable to see well enough to do it after the age of thirty.[1] There is no

[1] See *The East Pakistan District Gazetteer (for Dacca)*, East Pakistan Government Press, Dacca, 1969, p. 194.

hope of resurrecting textile exports on the basis of such methods of manufacture. Output was very low and sufficient cotton was available only for small-scale luxury textile production. Cotton is still cultivated in Bangladesh, but agricultural conditions suggest that other crops are more rewarding. At one stage it was hoped that the production of synthetic fibres from the natural gas found in Bangladesh would provide an alternative material for the textile industry. The composition of the gas permits only the production of acrylics by a process involving the production of hydrocyanic acid—which, besides being potentially dangerous (particularly in conditions in which saboteurs may attack chemical plants, as happened to the urea factory at Ghorasal in 1974), is now outdated, and it is doubtful if it should be used in Bangladesh.

The prospects for producing synthetic fibres from indigenous sources of raw materials might change if gas were discovered with constituents that would enable polyesters to be produced; the present gas is 95 per cent methane and this limits what can be done economically with it. There are other routes by which the raw materials for synthetic fibres could be manufactured in Bangladesh. One such way would be to use the refinery, after suitable modification and enlargement, to produce naphtha and from that polyesters. Oil of course has to be imported, but there need be no adverse affect on the balance of payments. The domestic gas that might have been used for the production of synthetic fibres, had it been of a suitable composition, could equally well be exported to India either as a fuel if this were politically acceptable, or in the form of urea. If this were done, what was lost on the swings could be more than regained on the roundabouts.

Increased supplies of textile fibres would enable the handloom industry to continue to function but the development of the textile industry as a growth point should not be based on cottage manufacturing. A dynamic textile industry must do much more than meet indigenous needs, and if money is to be put into textile manufacturing, attempts will have to be made to export as well as to provide for the domestic market.

Chemical manufacturing is already comparatively well represented in Bangladesh; it could be expanded using natural gas, amongst other things, as a basis for production. More than enough gas is available for domestic needs in the foreseeable future and it should be possible to produce urea and export it to other countries, particularly India. But as a vehicle for industrial development the manufacture of urea is far from ideal. The capital costs are very heavy; the construction of a plant to produce $\frac{1}{2}$ million tons of urea would have cost about $250 million in 1975. The amount of direct employment given, moreover, is very small in relation to the capital expenditure involved and the generation of linkages is not high either. The production of other chemicals might be more advantageous in this respect, although efforts to see how the gas could be used for the development of other products for which linkage effects might be more considerable have not thrown up many attractive alternatives; its use for the production of acrylic fibres is not, as we have seen, promising. The production of PVC from the gas is possible, and the price might be competitive. PVC is used in Bangladesh for a variety of purposes such as pipes, sheets and shoes. Ureaformaldehyde might also be made which is used in the production of melamine, and caustic soda could be produced. Capital costs are, however, high for most chemical processes and this presents problems and enforces reliance on aid donors for the means to carry out such projects.

The paper industry in Bangladesh has had a chequered history, but at times overseas markets are good and there is a large and growing domestic demand for paper. The problem in expanding paper production is obtaining suitable materials. There are a number of possibilities. At present certain sources of suitable timber including bamboo are very inaccessible, for example in the Chittagong hill tracts where the quality of bamboo is so high as to justify transplanting it to other regions. Construction of roads could improve supplies substantially. Bagasse from the sugar mills is also another potential raw material as well as straw from rice, and jute sticks. If such supplies were to be used, pulp would have to be prepared in small mills able to draw on available supplies. Again, if suitable material could be provided, an increase in the production of rayon would improve the prospects for textile manufacturing. Rayon of good and exportable quality is already produced by the Kharnaphuli mill.

One of the factors curtailing Bangladesh's development effort has been supplies of cement. This could be manufactured in the country in greater quantities if adequate supplies of limestone could be made available. India is a supplier of limestone, but there may be some reluctance to depend entirely on this. An alternative source is the deposit of limestone in the Jamalganj-Jaipurhat area. This is about 25 m. thick and lies about 500 m. below the surface. The mineable deposit is thought to amount to 200 million tons and is far greater in amount than other deposits that have been found in Sylhet or at St. Martins Island near Chittagong, each of which amounts to only about 2 million tons. Mining limestone at the depth it has been discovered in the Jamalganj-Jaipurhat area is a major undertaking. Nevertheless, it is thought that it would be both technically feasible and economical. It would be possible to sink a shaft after first freezing the surrounding ground. The cost of mining investment would be

high, about Taka 200 crores (at 1974 prices), of which a large proportion would be in foreign exchange. Costs of production might be
little more than the cost of purchasing from other sources.

There are advantages in establishing the production of cement on
indigenous resources but the total cost involved, the high foreign
exchange content and the danger that unexpected technical snags
would be met raise some doubts about the desirability of the project.
Again the scale of the project is such that it could only be carried
through if external support were forthcoming. It might be surmised
that there might be better ways of using investment resources than
putting them into a project which is bound to have a very long
gestation period and perhaps doubtful returns.

The food industry in Bangladesh is the third largest industrial
sector after jute and other textiles. If agricultural production at least
keeps up with the increase in population, output of such products as
gur (a coarse domestically produced sugar) and refined sugar will
increase, so will the processing of rice, the production of edible oils
and the preservation of fruit, fish and vegetables and the local
manufacture of *bidi* (a domestically produced type of cigarette).
There are some ways in which food manufacturing can be boosted,
for example in long-term efforts to improve pisciculture.

At first sight, the production of refined sugar, for home use and
export, might seem also to present suitable opportunities for industrial expansion based in agricultural products. On detailed examination the possibilities are not very bright. Bangladesh does not have
any comparative advantage in the production of sugar in normal
circumstances. The crop takes a long time to mature and in most
cases it is possible to get two other crops in the time it takes for the
cane to grow. Yields are poor, largely becuase little research has been
done to ensure that good cane is planted, and the extraction rate is
also unsatisfactory because of the time taken to transport the cane
to the mills. Thus sugar refining, although it accounts for about one-
third of the value added by the food processing industries, cannot be
regarded as a major point of growth.

Among the remaining industries based on local materials is that of
leather manufactured in various ways. The leather industry is capable
of expansion if the number of animals can be increased, as would
be necessary to sustain the agricultural programme; there is also
scope for increased processing of hides and skins that are currently
exported largely in raw form. It might be possible to go beyond this
and to establish a number of leather-using industries making goods
of high quality for export markets if full advantage could be taken
of the potential linkages that could be developed from the availability
of this material.

It seems from the above that much of the industrial output of Bangladesh will unavoidably have to be based on imported materials. The question is which industries are likely to be the most promising for the future. A further question is should industrial expansion be sought in the expansion of cottage industry, small private industry or from the development of large-scale operations; should it be done in the private or the public sector of the economy?

Dr. A. R. Khan has attempted to work out social rates of return in various industries in Bangladesh using data from the 1962–3 census of manufacturing and accounting prices representing the real costs of resources of different kinds.[2] Some of the conclusions reached by Dr. Khan already appear curious, as might be expected as circumstances change. In the circumstances ruling in 1974, it might not have seemed such a good idea for Bangladesh to import sugar or paper as his calculations suggest should be done. In more normal circumstances, we have concluded, sugar is probably not a crop to be encouraged at the expense of other agricultural output; while in the longer run paper and certainly fertilisers might be regarded as something to export rather than import, contrary to the findings of the model used. Industrial efficiency turns on much more than relative costs as revealed by accounting prices, and it is a common-place that it varies greatly between firms and between countries in many ways similarly placed. In addition to knowing the appropriate prices to consider for costing purposes it is necessary to assess the opportunities to develop efficient and dynamic management, the extent to which round-the-clock working is feasible and acceptable and the possibility of finding markets. In industry, as in many other spheres in Bangladesh, the motto might well be "if it moves, push!".

If the assessment of industrial efficiency is so difficult and full of pitfalls, it is all the more important to examine the kind of framework in which industrial development might be fostered. In Chapter III we have discussed this from the point of view of government control of industry and management of nationalised industries; here only a few comments need be added.

The large sector of industry put under public control after Independence greatly reduced the size of the private sector of the economy Jute, the single largest industry, cotton textiles, sugar, substantial parts of chemical production and engineering operations as well as oil refining and steel production passed into the public sector. It is not certain how much industry remains actively in private hands, but as much as 80 per cent of industry covered in the censuses of manufacturing may have been taken over in this way.

---

[2] A. R. Khan, *The Economy of Bangladesh*, Macmillan, 1972.

Some comparisons have been made of the comparative performance of the public and private sectors in Indian industry. They are inconclusive because public enterprises were often given the most difficult sectors of the economy to deal with and this may explain their poor performance in some cases. Nevertheless, Jagdish N. Bhagwati and Padma Desai have called attention to many criticisms of the functioning of the public industrial sector in India. Rates of return are low by comparison with the private sector, though not always due to the fault of the industries concerned. A major factor in this has often been the action of government, sometimes by proceeding to establish projects that were inadequately prepared and costed, sometimes through political involvement contributing to overstaffing of unskilled labour and sometimes from laying the heavy hand of traditional administrative services on management policies in general. The effect of traditional civil service control was not merely general incompetence but also rapid turnover of people in important roles such as those of chairman, managing director and general manager. Probably rather over-cautiously, one supposes, the argument concludes: "The overall dissatisfaction with the public sector's performance so far is therefore not entirely unjustified, and the prospects of its future performance are fairly dim, unless the political intrusions into its working are removed."[3] This is also a danger for Bangladesh, and many of the comments made about India can be applied there also.

The opportunities for the private sector of the economy to invest were widened by measures taken in July 1974, although of course still confined to those approved within the industrial investment schedule and excluding investment in eighteen industries reserved for the public sector. Government obsession with the size of unit allowed to operate in the private sector is probably largely a reflection of fears that too much power will concentrate in the hands of a limited number of families, as occurred in Pakistan before separation, unless some checks are applied to keep this under control. The 1974 measures should serve as a considerable encouragement to private enterprise provided that conditions can be created in other ways that will enable it to operate efficiently.

2. The Potential of Small-scale Industry

It is large rather than small-scale and cottage industry that has made the running in Bangladesh. Information about small-scale industrial

[3] Jagdish N. Bhagwati and Padma Desai, *India Planning for Industrialisation*, Oxford University Press, 1970, pp. 165 and 167.

activity is very imperfect and rests mainly on surveys carried out by the then East Pakistan Small Industries Corporation in 1962–4 and on subsequent surveys, including one by the Central Statistical Office of the Government of Pakistan for 1969–70. In terms of employment in industrial occupations, it is cottage rather than small-scale or large-scale industries that contribute most. There are something like 400,000 family-based enterprises which operate largely in people's homes. About one-quarter of them may be located in towns. The use of hired labour is small, but in total about 1½ million people may find employment in this way. This is not negligible, as it accounts for about 6–7 per cent of the labour force, although it must be remembered that many of the workers were employed part time.

Nevertheless, the growth potential of cottage industries must not be overemphasised. In the main they are likely to expand as population increases largely in the direction of duplicating existing activities to take care of the needs of more consumers. They include domestic handloom weaving, a major occupation, and processing foodstuffs for local consumption, which together probably account for over half of cottage industry output, the rest being made up of a variety of village activities such as the manufacture of salt and wood products. In the past they have not received much encouragement, and government efforts were directed largely to the establishment of large-scale industry. For Pakistan as a whole the output of large-scale industry trebled between 1960–1 and 1970–1, but the recorded increase for small-scale industry was only one-third. This is not conclusive evidence of the limited scope for expansion of small-scale operations, but it is probably indicative of the need to appreciate that the seeds of industrial growth do not really lie in the country-side.

The government's policy in relation to the encouragement of small-scale (as opposed to cottage) industry has been subject to considerable change. Small-scale private industry was at first confined to enterprises which employed only Taka 1·5 million of fixed capital including land; subsequently this was raised to Taka 2·5 million in June 1973 (with an upper limit of Taka 3·5 million if profits were reinvested in the business), and in 1974 to Taka 30 million. Size of capital investment, however, is not the only restriction placed on small industry, the opportunities to expand and invest are also severely circumscribed by reason of the fact that investment is under the control of the government.

It would probably have been an impossible task to have brought all small industry into public ownership, but many writers have argued in favour of the advantages of small independent industrial concerns. It is frequently maintained that they are more economical of capital than larger concerns, that they give more employment per unit of capital, that because of personal management they are efficient and prepared to pioneer, and so on. Not all these arguments may be valid and there is something to be said on the other side. The argument that small industry is economical of capital in such countries as Pakistan or India appears to be in doubt. Cottage industries, it is true, do have a high output-to-capital ratio; some surveys have suggested that it may be as high as 2. In the case of industries employing twenty or more workers the limited amount of evidence available seems to suggest that larger firms may be at an advantage in this respect in a number of cases.[4] Large factories working more than one shift can increase the output–capital ratio quite considerably. In fact, in some of the factories in Bangladesh considerable excess labour is employed under pressure from the unions, and the effect of these social and political pressures might be to make large-scale industry both labour-intensive and output-productive in relation to the capital employed.

The view that small industry presents greater opportunities for the dispersal of industry is also sometimes advanced as a reason for encouraging the development of small industry in Bangladesh. Dispersal and the maintenance of a rural setting for most of the population is very desirable as a means to make high population densities more bearable. But it is also true that social advantage is gained in this respect to some extent at the cost of efficiency in industrial organisation, although the opportunity to combine industrial and agricultural activity might help to smooth out seasonal fluctuations in employment.

Other arguments for the support of small-scale industry are social in character and include widening the participation of the people in economic development and the need to develop managerial skills. The latter argument also counts against small industry, for it is very difficult to employ people of specialised skills in small enterprises. The extent of the drawback depends on the industry involved. Many small-scale operations require relatively little in the way of technical

[4] See, for example, data compiled by P. N. Dhar and H. F. Lydall in *The Role of Small Enterprises in Indian Economic Development*, Asia Publishing House, 1961. Similar data is presented by G. Ranis in his article "Production Functions, Market Imperfections and Economic Development", *Economic Journal*, June 1962, p. 345. Figures given by Dr. A. R. Khan for Bangladesh show large firms as having ratios of value-added to capital only one-third those of small and cottage industries (op. cit., p. 61). In fact, it may not be size so much as selection of appropriate technique and efficient management that matter. For an interesting discussion see Howard Park, "The Employment-Output Trade-Off in LDCs", *Oxford Economic Papers*, November 1974, p. 138.

skill and may not require much in the way of managerial flair or
management techniques. Large-scale industry, on the other hand,
always requires managerial skill of a high order and very frequently
makes heavy demands on special skills, and the need to provide these
may enforce a large scale of operation. In other areas also, economies
of scale may be important, notably in finding export markets.

The strongest arguments for fostering small industrial enterprises
lie not in the universal assumption that they are invariably more
efficient than large scale enterprises, but that there are cases in which
they are (just as in other cases it is abundantly clear that a large scale
of operation is unavoidable if costs are to be kept low). This is a valid
argument for fostering small industry.

3. *Conclusions*

While agriculture must in the next few years be the main growth point
for output in the economy, it is inconceivable that the Bangladesh
economy can expand production and employment without a fairly
rapid growth in industrial output. An increase in output of 10 per
cent per annum in the industrial sector would be in keeping with the
performance of other economies and something that it might be
hoped to attain. The opportunity to develop on the basis of locally
available materials is restricted. There is no real alternative to facing
the fact that it will be necessary to import industrial materials such as
ferrous and non-ferrous metals on a large scale and that this will
force the economy to orientate itself increasingly towards exports.
As is discussed in the next chapter, a start has already been made
in this respect through agreements with India which aim to allow
Bangladesh to pay for imported materials by exporting part of the
products made with these materials.

The form of industrial organisation adopted in the economy is
likely to affect its development quite considerably; in this respect the
adoption of a mixed economy is probably the best approach. The
very costly projects, that would make best use of indigenous materials,
are outside the compass and competence of private, local industrialists. Such projects, including the manufacture of urea, cement
and paper, require large amounts of capital which in Bangladesh
could not readily be provided outside the public sector. Of course,
none of these endeavours will succeed without good management
and there is a dearth of such skill throughout Bangladesh. In the
public corporations it could be possible to train managers through
well-organised programmes, including practical and theoretical
instruction, and to develop and promote those showing promise.

There are, however, many things in the industrial sector which can best be done by individual small-scale businesses. They could be more efficient, for example, at seeking out supplies of indigenous materials; they are almost certainly more efficient at providing small customer services than nationalised industries; they seem also to us to have greater potential to diversify the industrial base of the economy, both in producing for the home market and for export. Ask a set of government officials what products are likely to succeed in the world's markets ten years from now and they will not be able to answer. The chairmen and their advisers in the nationalised corporations will in all probability know much more about the prospects for their products. In the social and economic circumstances of Bangladesh, the possibilities for small and medium-sized industrial development over the next decade seem to us most likely to be discovered and exploited if there are a host of small businessmen striving to see how they can earn their living. There is really no lack of ingenuity and initiative among those engaged in manufacture, trade and commerce in Bangladesh. These talents can flourish, however, only if they are given opportunity. As has been stressed elsewhere in this book, this will necessitate a much increased flow of imports, and this in turn a large flow of aid. If the accepted role of the private sector of industry can be more clearly defined and firmly and consistently adhered to, the prospects of industrial growth will be greatly enhanced.

CHAPTER X

TRADE AND AID

1. *Import Requirements*

By the end of the century the *per capita* gross domestic product of Bangladesh as projected in Chapter V could perhaps reach $175 at 1974 prices. *Per capita* consumption may reach perhaps $150. Half of this will be consumed as food; the rest will be available for the purchase of services and manufactured goods. Inevitably it will be necessary to import a wide variety of raw materials which are not available in Bangladesh either in crude or manufactured form; also there will be a number of commodities that Bangladesh could not hope to be able to produce economically, for lack of production know-how, technical skills and access to large enough markets to make possible significant economies of scale. The fact that the market for many highly manufactured products will be small will also make it desirable for Bangladesh to specialise in the production of only some of them, relying on imports for the supplies of others. But within the general constraints of size of markets and economies of scale it will be possible to choose whether to try to balance trade at a high or low level after taking account of the aid that is made available. The extent to which this can be done will depend, among other things, on how far import substitution can go, as well as the possibilities for export promotion. It is quite possible that in the long term many things currently imported can be provided from Bangladesh's own production.

While we do not intend to indulge in wishful thinking, we recognise that oil may be discovered in the Bay of Bengal. If this were to be the case it would be no longer necessary to obtain imported supplies; this would ease the balance of payments of a burden which is already heavy and which will increase, as consumption of oil would inevitably increase with growth in population and increase in income per head. Used as a raw material, domestic oil would also make it possible to do with less imports; the way would become clear to produce synthetic fibres and to save on the import of cotton, as well as plastics and certain chemicals.

The most important single saving in import requirements would occur if imports of foodgrains were no longer necessary because of increased domestic production (saving say $300 million). Other imported foods could also be produced at home if agriculture improved its performance. An increase in the output of edible oils could make a major contribution to the balance of payments (saving $60 million spent in 1974–5) and would be all the more valuable as population increases. Diversification of agricultural output could also contribute substantially to the balance of payments. It is now clear from trial plantings that it is possible to produce coffee in Bangladesh of average quality; it may also be possible to grow rubber and reduce the need to purchase from other countries. Mining deposits of limestone, if proved feasible and economical, would also make it possible to reduce imports of cement. It should also be possible to make significant savings in imports of manufactures. Altogether, it might be possible for Bangladesh to replace in an economic manner as much as half the present value of its imports within ten years time from her own indigenous resources, if suitable policies were followed and all went well, particularly if oil were discovered.

Bangladesh's poverty and exposed economic situation may well lead it to seek safety in trying to do as much as possible for itself and to avoid some of the uncertainties of trade with other countries. Traditionally, Bangladesh has been largely self-sufficient, living off what it could produce, and this may be the way that those responsible for directing its affairs may wish to go. If so they will lose opportunities to benefit from world trade, particularly in the early stages of development. Smuggling may be a reprehensible activity, but if it does nothing else, it demonstrates the desire of consumers to trade the goods that they are able to produce, or purchase, for others that are available from other countries. This need is a powerful force not to be ignored as an expression of what people hope to get out of life.

2. *Exports*

Whatever can be done in the way of import substitution there is no escaping the fact that a large increase in exports is unavoidable if Bangladesh is to secure the foreign exchange needed to pay for increased quantities of imports. The composition of exports in 1973–4 is shown in the table below.

The export base is a most unpromising one from which to work. The heavy dependence on jute and manufactures is evident from the table; unfortunately this has no long-term promise. There have been many studies of the potential of jute as an export material. The conclusions of those studies are that the market for jute manufactures is declining in the developed areas of the world, with some exceptions,

TABLE X.1

EXPORTS IN 1973-4

Takas in crores

Raw jute	106
Jute manufactures	159
Leather	10
Fish	13
Tea	13
Other	17
	318

and expanding only in the developing areas and most particularly in the Indian sub-continent itself. There have been two powerful forces at work to bring this about. The first has been the movement to bulk transport which has tended to reduce the demand for packaging materials, and the second the use of synthetics to replace jute where packaging continues to be required, as well as in other uses such as carpet backing. The competitive position of the major synthetic substitute for jute, polypropylene, which is often produced from oil, has been adversely affected by the upward movement of oil prices, but the effect is much less marked than might have been anticipated from the fact that oil prices quadrupled in 1973. Before the increase in the price of oil, raw material costs amounted to only about one-sixteenth of the cost of producing polypropylene, while the cost of polypropylene itself accounted for only about one-quarter of the cost of producing many finished articles competing with jute products. In short, the oil content of synthetic substitutes for jute was very small so that the increase in oil prices could be expected to lead to an increase in the cost of synthetic fabrics of only some 10 per cent. The capacity of synthetic substitutes to compete with jute is quite strong in the short run, for profits have been abnormally high and there has been scope to absorb some cost increase out of profits; there are also some possibilities of cutting costs by variations in refinery and processing operations. Another factor is that a considerable proportion of the output of synthetics depends not on oil but on natural gas for its feedstock and the increase in the price of the latter may well be much less that the increase in the price of oil. Thus in the next few years it is likely that synthetic fibres will continue to be formidable competitors of jute. In the longer run, the competitive balance is less easy to predict. The cost of constructing synthetics plants may rise, and costs may be affected in an upward direction in other ways, while for jute, reductions in costs could be made if new methods of cultivation were introduced. It might also be possible through international co-operation to stabilise the price of jute and ensure a regular supply not subject to the fluctuations experienced in the past. Jute production and manufacture has received very little attention from research and there is undoubtedly scope to work considerable improvement. The development of new products and imaginative marketing might go a long way in maintaining jute's position as an export earner for Bangladesh. But "maintain" is probably the right description. Producers and users of synthetics do not rest on their laurels. The exclusive use of jute in one of its last strongholds, secondary carpet backing, is now threatened by the investment of Patchogue Plymouth of $5 million in equipment to produce secondary backing.

It is difficult to envisage much more than a defensive set of measures designed to keep jute exports up until other sources of export earnings can take their place. The most important single measure that has been considered to improve Bangladesh's performance from jute in the long term has been the suggestion, advocated in the First Five Year Plan, of getting India's agreement to a considerable increase in the export of jute from Bangladesh to India. On paper some understanding seems to have been reached in this respect. The 1973–4 trade agreement with India provided for an increase in exports of raw jute, and it was hoped in the Annual Plan for 1973–4 that 800,000 bales would be sold through official channels, and that the figure would increase in future years. The agreement was not fulfilled in 1973–4 and exports were very small. The reason is not far to seek: India had no real need of jute from Bangladesh in that year. Why this was so is uncertain. Although it was reported that India had an exceptionally good jute harvest and this was adequate to provide the domestic supplies needed, it may be suspected that Indian domestic supplies were supplemented by the unofficial import of jute smuggled from Bangladesh.

Renewed contacts between India and Bangladesh in 1974 again resulted in a reaffirmation of the importance of trade between the two countries, and made it reasonable to hope that an increased flow of official jute exports would materialise in future. Outside observers, however, might feel sceptical about the possibility of such an arrangement working. From time to time in the past, India has emerged as an exporter of jute and it may be that she is more permanently in balance than Bangladesh might wish to hope. India can become an exporter of raw jute as well as of jute manufactures, and Bangladesh has to guard against the possibility that its exports of raw jute to India will merely supplement a high level of domestic production in India which, directly or indirectly, will enable India to export raw jute at the expense of Bangladesh. Hence it does not seem that raw jute can lead any large increase in Bangladesh's exports.

The prospects are not good either for jute manufactures. Great problems have been experienced in getting the jute mills to function effectively. The introduction and marketing of new products should not be beyond the Jute Manufacturing Corporation if it were left to its own devices, but in practice, as we have described in Chapter III, the nationalised industries are not given freedom to do what they think is in the best interests of their industries, and in the past efforts to develop sales have been frustrated by regulations or instructions limiting the use of foreign exchange for sales promotion or for the development of market information networks necessary for the launching of new products. If these problems could be overcome, some diversification of ouput could be managed and revenues shored up or perhaps even increased by this device.

No great expansion of Bangladesh's traditional non-jute exports can be hoped for in the immediate future. There is an opportunity to increase exports of fish, and the market is wide open. The problem is supply. Bangladesh is protein-deficient, and the additional fish produced could well be eaten at home. Production will be increased by both the development of deep-sea fishing and eventually by improved use of inland waterways and tanks, but the process will be slow. It is certainly possible to improve the processing of skins and increase export earnings that way; it also ought to be possible to increase the output of goat skins with proper management, although the pressure on the land is a limiting factor. The expansion of exports of tea can only be slow. It takes time for infilling to be carried out, for fresh areas to be planted and for the bushes to mature. The best way to get an increase in earnings from tea would be to improve the quality of the tea. This is less difficult than may appear. It is true that the height of the tea gardens makes it more difficult to grow tea of good quality, but what is equally important is the picking sequence; more frequent picking of smaller leaves would effect a very worthwhile improvement in quality and so make it possible to get better prices for the tea at auction.

None of this adds up to any great prospect of a sizeable increase in either the volume or the value of existing exports. Diversification must be embarked upon. It is never easy to see how this can be accomplished, although there are a number of opportunities. One of the most promising in the public sector is the export of natural gas in the form of urea. Proposals have been made for the establishment of a plant capable of producing about ½ million tons of urea for export to India. Such a quantity could be sold for about $100 million or more, depending on the long-run level of prices, determined in particular by Middle East competitors. Provided financing could be made available on concessionary terms, this would be a useful contribution to export earnings. One such export-based plant alone would increase present export earnings by as much as one-third.

The prospect of Bangladesh becoming an oil producer has already been touched upon in relation to import substitution. A really rich strike of oil would open up export prospects also. At the moment this must be pure speculation, but it is something that would radically change export earnings if it came about and opened up a new prospect for development.

Many of the new range of export goods that are needed by Bangladesh are not likely to be developed by nationalised corporations, which are at present the mainstay of industrial activity. It is always difficult to assess market prospects for new goods, but from common observation there are opportunities to widen the export base if certain conditions can be met. To take but a few examples of minor items; it might be possible to develop a range of beautifully bound books, for bookbinding can be done well and cheaply in Bangladesh; it might be possible to develop an industry producing for export optical goods and simple spectacle lenses, which Bangladesh can manufacture in a day or two; it should be possible to develop a cut-glass industry if suitable labour could be trained. As the manufacture of cars spreads to South America and Spain and other countries where labour is cheap, so could it to Bangladesh. Clays exist for the manufacture of earthenware, and these might be exploitable for the production of export goods if quality could be ensured. There exists a market in the Middle East and other countries for military helmets of a type already produced in Bangladesh. Capacity might be developed for the production of electrical goods including electronic equipment, and these could find export markets. Markets might be found for high-quality textile goods and clothing.

The opportunities are there, but if the private sector of the economy is to be able to exploit them certain conditions will have to be met. The first of these is the provision of imported requirements for the production of exports and an assurance that such imports will not be subject to interruptions and to cuts. This is not an easy thing for governments to do when the balance of payments is subject to such a range of fluctuations as that to which the Bangladesh economy is prey. As one device to get over this it has been suggested that a free trade zone should be set up. It is difficult to regard such an arrangement as having much to commend itself in the normal course of events. Free trade zones enable manufacturing activities to proceed without the need to pay taxes on the inputs used; but this can be done by other means, and there is machinery in existence for it already which, while imperfect, could fairly easily be improved. The major argument for the establishment of a free trade zone lies not in tax exemption so much as in the opportunity that it would give for the free import of goods needed for the production of exports, and in the freedom to operate beyond the pales of government intervention. From this point of view there is much to commend the ideas of establishing a free trade zone, and the experiment is worth trying. It would be necessary to provide a "float" of foreign exchange if such a scheme were to be launched, but this might be provided by donor agencies or countries interested in trying to encourage the development of a private enterprise export-oriented sector within the Bangladesh economy. It would also be necessary to ensure that the system was not abused by evasion and smuggling. One suggestion is that security could best be ensured by establishing the free trade area on an island in order to facilitate surveillance.

One of the most serious obstacles to increasing the flow of exports produced by small private sector firms is the need to ensure the high quality of production and designs that ensures good sales prospects. Embroidered jeans are sold in the Paris fashion shops at high prices; they could be made very cheaply in Bangladesh, but the problem is to establish the vital link between production potential and marketability. Bangladesh is aware of this gap and has established a government export agency to help private exporters. This does not seem to be the right answer to the problem; the real need is for direct links to private firms which are capable both of promoting sales in overseas markets and of commissioning production. If overseas importing firms were to decide to purchase in Bangladesh and to provide assistance with production facilities and production methods, the situation would be transformed. At present the prospect of establishing such links is remote. This means that small enterprises will have to make the running themselves as best they can.

3. Trade Agreements

Bangladesh's export trade can expand at present only if production of exportable goods can be increased. Bangladesh has not so far found difficulty in selling her exports, largely because price policy has been flexible, and until devaluation took place, the government was ready to subsidise exports to allow jute manufacturing to operate at a loss. Exports of paper have been helped greatly by a world shortage of supply; good markets are available for fish, leather and most other minor exports. Real difficulty has been experienced only in selling some types of goods which were formerly exported to the Pakistan market. Ready availability of markets will not always be the case. As the quantity of goods available for export increases and becomes much less stereotyped, finding markets will be more difficult.

Bangladesh has already shown itself alive to the need to develop trading partnerships with a view both to securing imports and finding markets for exports. Much of its trade continues to be conducted with West European countries and with the United States, which are important consumers of raw jute and manufactures, but the geographical pattern of exports is markedly diverse. It is clearly desirable in the future to maintain a wide spread of trade with different countries in order to ensure maximum access to the world's markets.

This includes the need to make the best of opportunities to trade with East European countries. Trade with these countries is conducted through agreements providing generally for a rough balance between imports and exports after taking the flow of aid from them to Bangladesh into account. Such agreements are likely to continue to be part of the pattern of Bangladesh's trade. They are not easy to administer; and arrangements for the flow of goods can be cumbersome, particularly if there is difficulty in making available the goods outlined in the agreements. It is also possible that these agreements, which are basically barter, do not make the best use of available exports in terms of the supplies they secure, but the measure of diversification they give to trading patterns is helpful and likely to be advantageous if supplies of exportable goods can be increased in the longer run.

The nearest mass market that might be tapped by Bangladesh is that of India, and co-operation between the two countries could help Bangladesh to afford more imports. The importance of this appears to have been grasped in principle. On 17 May 1974 it was announced that India and Bangladesh had agreed to undertake four joint ventures, two concerned with the supply of cement-making materials to Bangladesh, another with the supply of iron from India to Bangladesh and the establishment of a sponge iron plant to utilise it, and a fourth concerned with the establishment of a plant to produce urea for export to India. The intention was that India would extend credits to Bangladesh to help pay for the plants and that she would guarantee to take exportable surpluses. Major developments of this nature could be of very great help to Bangladesh. What is also needed is arrangements to secure markets for a miscellany of small products. This is not the kind of thing that it is easy to arrange between governments. Frame agreements can be set up under which trade can proceed, but these guarantee neither that the goods to be exported are available nor that markets will be found for them even if they can be supplied.

Gradual extension of the arrangements made under the agreements with India could hold out the possibility of a further substantial increase in trade with that country. Bangladesh may have misgivings about her economy becoming too dependent on that of India. In some respects this is wise; Bangladesh would be exposed if her economy became an appendage of India's. There is also lingering political distrust between the two countries which is likely to have the effect of limiting economic co-operation efforts, in spite of the readiness that India has shown in trade agreements to advance credits to Bangladesh and the assistance that she has given in other ways.

Caution is bound to dictate the kind of trading relations that Bangladesh is in the process of developing. The present policy of trying to widen trading relationships seems to be right and one which will facilitate the large increase in exports that is needed in the next twenty-five years.

4. *Aid*

Bangladesh was treated with unparalleled generosity by donors after its liberation. From 17 December 1971 to 30 June 1973, over $1,600 million of all types of aid had been committed. In 1973–4 total aid commitments came to over $1,000 million, and this was maintained the following year. Disbursements, as is usually the case, have lagged behind commitments, and a substantial pipeline of aid has been built up.

Aid like trade has been widely spread over a number of contributors. In addition to the more traditional donors and established international organisations, developments in 1974 indicated that the Arab world would probably provide a large amount of assistance. About a score of countries have furnished aid or are in the course of doing so in addition to some international agencies.

There is no doubt about the long-term need for aid if Bangladesh is going to develop its economy at more than a snail's pace. In 1972–3 when the First Five Year Plan was drawn up, it seemed possible to the planners that Bangladesh would be able to make do with about $500 million of aid per year or even less, but price levels have changed greatly, and both the internal and external economic situations of Bangladesh have deteriorated. The need for aid in the scenario sketched in Chapter V was shown to be a continuous and increasing one, rising from about $1,000 million in 1980 (at 1974 prices) to over $1,500 million in the 1990s; since no provision is made for loan service in these estimates, additional assistance will be needed to cover this.

It will take considerable persuasion to convince donor-countries and agencies that they should support the Bangladesh economy on this scale for a quarter of a century. If they are to do so, there will have to be convincing signs that the efforts to develop the country are bearing fruit and that there is a readiness to reform the administration of the country and to enforce the discipline that is needed for a concerted development effort.

The relationship between donors and recipient-countries is seldom easy. Both have their own approaches, and sometimes conflicting objectives; recipient-countries would like aid without strings; donors wish to see that the aid they furnish is used in a way that they approve, for objectives they approve and in a manner consistent with their national interests. For the first two-and-a-half years of Bangladesh's existence, relationships between donor-countries and agencies and Bangladesh were impeded by the need to ensure that the debts previously contracted by Pakistan would be serviced. It was felt by donors that part of these should be serviced by Bangladesh since some of the aid furnished had gone to East Pakistan. International institutions and some national governments exercised considerable pressure to get Bangladesh to accept this point of view. Bangladesh took the view that such debts should not be settled in isolation but only as part of a general agreement involving a settlement between Bangladesh and Pakistan of the claims that Bangladesh felt entitled to make in respect of war-time damage, and of assets (such as reserves of gold and foreign currency) previously belonging to both countries but now in the hands of Pakistan. In the end, a compromise solution was reached in which Bangladesh has assumed responsibility for the servicing of certain debts in respect of physical assets located in Bangladesh, and corresponding relief has been given to Pakistan.

The way was then clear for a better and more constructive relationship to develop between the foreign community committed to assisting Bangladesh and Bangladesh itself. If this relationship is to flourish it will need to be handled with care. Emerging countries do not take kindly to interference in their internal affairs, and Bangladesh is no exception. It may be true that its affairs are badly managed, that the country is unstable, that corruption is prevalent and that its prospects are unpromising in present conditions. But these factors cannot be changed overnight or simply in response to the exhortations of outsiders or the reports of experts. If donors are going to bestow their aid effectively and contribute decisively to the development process, as indeed they must, they will have to exercise more than usual patience, understanding and humility in helping to get things moving.

Nevertheless, it would be quite wrong for Bangladesh to think that it will be given aid on the scale needed without being ready to respond in some measure to the needs of the situation as seen by donors. It is to be expected that donor-countries will seek to ensure that measures are taken to deal with corruption (their legislatures cannot for long be expected to approve diversion of aid to unapproved ends); it is right that they should seek to ensure that their aid is used for productive purposes, and they are bound to insist on administrative procedures that ensure all these things.

Frequently the administrative procedures of aid donors and recipients differ significantly. It is no easy task to get the mutual acceptance of arrangements which can meet both sets of requirements. Any bureaucratic organisation is in its nature an obstacle to getting things done quickly; two bureaucratic organisations using different systems and procedures can have the utmost difficulty in aligning their requirements effectively. Experience in Bangladesh has been that, with goodwill, minor frictions can be greatly diminished, if never quite eliminated. In the early stages it was extremely difficult to ensure speedy use of commodity aid. Each country furnishing such aid laid down conditions as to how it was to be used: the commodities to be purchased, methods of reimbursement of expenditures, or procedures to be followed in making purchases; moreover, donors frequently altered these conditions and procedures in midstream. Bangladesh likewise was hamstrung by procedures devised for the issue of import licences, for the opening of letters of credit and for the placing of orders. Gradually, the difficulties experienced are being overcome and suitable routines established to enable aid to be used quickly.

It is easy for donors and experts to preach, but in matters of economic cooperation and foreign assistance, preaching is not only useless—it is counterproductive. What is needed is a co-operative and mutually reinforcing relationship between Bangladesh and those furnishing aid. There must be consultations about ways and means, mutual concern for progress in the use of aid, and effective co-ordination between Bangladesh and donor-countries to ensure that waste of aid through bad administration by donors or by Bangladesh on badly designed programmes of assistance is kept to a minimum.

With the best will in the world there are bound to be frictions. Accountability in Bangladesh is at a low ebb and until it is improved, countries cannot follow what is happening to the aid they give. Statistical reporting is poor and it is more than usually difficult to get accurate (and undoctored) figures that allow countries to discern what is going on. The need for good reporting is mutual, and its absence is a source of disharmony.

Another bone of contention sometimes lies in the use of outside consultants who may not be fully familiar with Bangladesh's position. It is also often not appreciated that a constant flood of experts from donor-countries and agencies make such demands on the limited time of the relatively few able administrators in key positions in Bangladesh that the business of government is impeded. Joint working parties concerned with project preparation, drawing up reports and devising strategies can often be more productive than procedures based on the view that donors must constantly use experts to expose shortcomings of local proposals. In recent years there have been notable examples both of the success of such co-operation and of total waste and high cost to Bangladesh of policy prescription and report writing by outsiders.

Bangladesh's relations with other countries are in large measure conditioned by the fact that it occupies the bottom rung of the development ladder, that its population is already large and growing rapidly, that it has only a limited range of natural resources, that its economy is burdened by serious structural imbalances, that the food balance is at the best of times precarious, that its dependence on foreign assistance for basic essentials of consumpion, current production and development is high and growing, and that at times like the present its situation is desperate. In a hard world of nation-states and international bureaucracies, the sovereignty and dignity of the nation and people of Bangladesh are at real risk; a relationship of "superior-creditor, inferior-debtor" emerges in the minds of both Bangalees and foreigners and in the attitudes and practices of domestic and foreign administrators of development co-operation; "Partnership in Development"[1] is a very distant ideal. Bangladesh does need assistance, because without it revival of economic life appears wellnigh impossible. It will be all the more gratefully received if offered in a spirit of co-operation.

NOTE TO CHAPTER X: *Settlement of Assets and Liabilities of Old Pakistan*

Even in a case of amicable separation, equitable distribution of assets and sharing of liabilities is difficult; Bangladesh achieved its independence through war. Until a settlement is reached on these matters, they will trouble and may even poison relations between the two countries. There is no objectively "right" solution, the

[1] This is the title of the *Report of the Commission on International Development*, headed by Lester Pearson in 1968-9. The report was designed to represent a "grand assize" of development assistance.

problem and its resolution are matters for political compromise and statesmanship. Nevertheless, economic and statistical analysis may clarify the nature and magnitude of the issue.[2]

An equitable "divorce" settlement may be approached either from a study of resource creation and resource flow (inter-wing and with foreign countries) or from an assessment of assets and liabilities at the date of divorce. Most of the discussion in the past has concentrated on resource flows, and further work may well be called for in that direction. This short note ignores implications of uneven resource flows, and deals exclusively with the balance-sheet of assets and liabilities as of 1971.

It seems reasonable in this context to take into account only "man-made" assets, not natural resources or for that matter any kind of resources or assets that each party brought into the "marriage" in 1947. The assets that were created between 1947 and 1971, however, must be regarded as common property, brought about by the efforts of all. The location of these assets was a result of government policy with respect to use of export proceeds, foreign assistance, taxes, licensing, defence, administration, etc. It is the purpose of a resource flow analysis to study all these factors, qualitively and quantitatively; the purpose of this note is to seek to establish the balance-sheet that was the total result of these resource flows and to set out the volume and location of assets created.

The physical asset creation can, in principle, be determined by an inventory; for some physical assets, that may be the only course open. However, as far as economic assets are concerned, those that constitute productive capital and contribute to current production of goods and services, it is possible to determine the orders of magnitude by an indirect, general approach. This method concentrates on the determination of the increase in current output that has occured over the twenty-four-year period, introduces an approximate estimate of how much additional capital is required to lift the volume of current output by a given amount (the incremental capital-output ratio [ICOR]), and then derives the estimate of the addition to the capital stock that has occurred. This exercise is reproduced in Table X.2.[3]

---

[2] Similar comments may apply to any claim Bangladesh may raise with respect to physical war damage. This might well be of the order of $1,000 to $1,500 million, see for instance *A Survey of Damages and Repairs*, United Nations Relief Operations, Dacca, 1972.

[3] More accurate figures of GNP *per capita*, population and ICOR can no doubt be found. For the purposes of establishing orders of magnitude, however, the figures in the table may serve well enough.

TABLE X.2

CALCULATION OF INCREASE IN GROSS NATIONAL PRODUCT (GNP) 1947–71

	1947	1960	1971	Increase 1947 to 1971
GNP per capita				
(*in US$ at about 1971 prices*)				
Bangladesh	60	65	70	10
Pakistan (West)	65	90	130	65
Population				
(*in millions*)				
Bangladesh	41	54	72	31
Pakistan (West)	34	45	62	28
Total GNP				
(*in US$ million at about 1971 prices*)				
Bangladesh	2,460	3,510	5,040	2,580
Pakistan (West)	2,210	4,050	8,060	5,850
Total for both countries	4,670	7,560	13,100	8,430

The efficiency of capital accumulation in terms of current output for whole economies is a most complicated and controversial concept and quantity. For the purpose of this illustrative exercise, we have used an ICOR of 2·5 for both countries.[4] On this basis the value of net productive capital assets created in the twenty-four-year period would be of the order of US$6,450 million in Bangladesh and US$ 14,625 million in Pakistan.

Before proceeding with the argument, it should be noted (*a*) that Pakistan also had assets abroad, both physical and financial, private and public; (*b*) that Pakistan also had liabilities abroad, public and private (and for both assets and liabilities this includes foreign ownership or share of ownership in capital assets in Pakistan and vice versa); and (*c*) that there was also an assets and liabilities balance (public and private) between Bangladesh and Pakistan. With respect to (*a*) and (*b*) we include in our calculations only *public financial* assets and liabilities; with respect to (*c*) we ignore all assets and liabilities, partly because they have been "nationalised" anyhow, partly because it is the "equitable" net balance in this category which we are trying to estimate.

As for old Pakistan's debts to foreign creditors, the principle that formal, legal liability for all debts contracted up to 1971 remains

---

[4] See our discussion of this issue in Note A to Chapter V: "The Concept and Use of Capital Output Ratios".

with Pakistan until and unless another party (Bangladesh) actually assumes liability, appears to be generally accepted. Nevertheless, Bangladesh has in fact assumed such liability for some categories of these debts. Nothing similar has yet taken place with respect to the old Pakistan's public financial assets abroad.

The amount of public financial liabilities of Pakistan to foreign countries was of the order of US$4,000 million equivalents. As a result of negotiations with creditors, a good deal of these debts were in fact, if not in form, written off by creditors, and the two countries assumed separate financial liability for a debt burden which in real terms (allowing for grant elements) were of the order of, say, $150 million and $850 million for Bangladesh and Pakistan respectively.[5]

With respect to public financial assets of Pakistan in foreign countries, data are not readily available. These assets include, *inter alia*, foreign exchange reserves and contributions to international agencies. Besides the need to establish what amounts are involved, the respective claims of Pakistan and Bangladesh on these assets may be the subject of heated and difficult debate. However, in line with the general approach in this note, all that is needed is the order of magnitude of the total of these assets; for illustrative purposes only we have included in our calculations a figure of US$500 million equivalents. All of these assets are presently held by Pakistan, and no division of such assets has been initiated.

For a "divorce" settlement to be reached it is necessary to establish whether the net value of assets would be divided equally or on a

TABLE X.3

BALANCE-SHEET AS OF 1971

(in US$ million)

	Pakistan	Bangladesh	Total
Value of domestic productive capital assets	14,600	6,450	21,050
Public liabilities abroad	850	150	1,000
Public financial assets held abroad	500	—	500
Net Assets before "divorce" settlement	14,250	6,300	20,550
"Equitable" (equal) division of net assets	10,275	10,275	20,550
Net liability of Pakistan to Bangladesh	−3,975	+3,975	—

[5] We have little firm basis for these estimates and they may well need substantial revision; for our purpose of demonstrating a method of approach and deriving an idea only of orders of magnitude, our estimates may serve well enough.

population basis between the two countries. Given the uncertainties attaching to our estimates of the amounts involved, we have arbitrarily based the calculation on the assumption that Bangladesh agrees on equal shares to each country. A "divorce" settlement in 1971 on the above basis would then come out as shown in Table X3.

On the assumption made above, including assumptions with respect to internal capital creation, external debt settlement and retention by Pakistan of external financial assets, Bangladesh has a claim on Pakistan equivalent to nearly US$4,000 million. With some adjustments in the above assumptions (which may not be in themselves unreasonable) the case could be made for an even higher claim. But it may not be worth it; Pakistan's obligations as here calculated can hardly be honoured—economically, financial or politically.

CHAPTER XI

PROGRESS WITH POVERTY

For many people Bangladesh is a catalogue of woes: constant food shortage and recurrent famine, devastating floods and cyclones, disorder, violence and corruption, an uncontrollable population explosion, failure of government and administration, a malfunctioning economy beset with financial crisis and bankruptcy—a begging bowl to the rest of the world. With this background view it is difficult to see anything but permanent disaster for Bangladesh. This need not be the case. It is not too late to reverse adversity, to bring events under control and gradually to ameliorate conditions of life.

At the beginning of 1975 there was an atmosphere of desperation in Bangladesh and people were losing hope that economic conditions could be improved. This triggered off a succession of political reactions: the assumption of absolute power by Sheikh Mujibur Rahman in January, his assassination in a *coup* in August, further *coups* and counter-*coups* in November. The basic problem of establishing stable government remains. Without this, hopes for development in Bangladesh will remain illusory. The first need is to carry out the difficult and painstaking task of improving the machinery of administration, training people to operate it and giving the incentives, hope and leadership needed to do this well.

Some of the changes in policy and administration needed to improve the situation are outlined in Chapters III and IV. The list is a long one; none of it is easy, and all of it needs to be put through because isolated measures will not contribute very much while a package of measures will be mutually reinforcing. This means that coherent and consistent policies will have to be devised as part of a total plan to deal with the situation.

If this can be done, there is no reason why in the next twenty-five years there should not be improvements in living standards, an expanding development effort and the gradual emergence of a self-reliant economy. Development is possible. The technical means exist to increase output, particularly of food, very greatly, and to diversify economic activities and to develop a broader economic base. As we have said, the problem is essentially one of government, administration and leadership. It is too much to hope for any dramatic changes in economic welfare by the end of the century, but enough could be done to make people feel better off and for all to realise that Bangladesh was beginning to get control of its future with the prospect that living standards could continue to improve. Further than this it is difficult to see. Bangladesh's luck might turn. There are hopes that the search for oil might succeed, and while policies cannot be based on that expectation, discovery of oil could change the situation markedly.

The growth of population is a threat which, if allowed to continue unchecked, could eventually bring the economy back—even after initial improvements in living standards—to a Malthusian state. Even if population can be controlled, we feel sure that life in Bangladesh will have to be radically different from that of Western industrialised countries living mainly in towns. It is only by setting a new pattern of rural living that Bangladesh can make the best of its limited land and natural resources.

Behind any views on the future of Bangladesh lie assumptions about some of the social factors that govern economic development. How far does it depend on individual effort and motivation? How far can the state intervene in the course of events to set a development effort in process? Can foreign aid really contribute to the development process, or is it possible that it would impede it?

Historical guidance is of limited value in answering such questions. Western Europe entered the industrial revolution at a far higher state of development than that of Bangladesh today. The revolution was very much an individual affair. Government was not then regarded as an instrument of development; intervention took the form of trying to deal with the worst social evils that resulted from work in factories and mines rather than attempts to promote development. In Russia, embarking on a process of economic growth after the Revolution, the state, in complete contrast, was seen as the inevitable instrument of progress and development. Arguments for and against state intervention in the abstract are too many and too well-known to bear rehearsal at length. They are also too inconclusive. Economic development can take place under varying systems of economic organisation, and it would be very hard to decide which would be the best without some reference to the case in point.

Bangladesh is ostensibly a socialist state in its approach to economic development. It is difficult to regard it as such in fact. It is true that it has had a planned economy throughout its existence, either as part of Pakistan or as an independent country; it is also true that state agencies are powerful and active in their own right, and that large-scale industry has been nationalised as well as the banking system, with the exception of foreign banks. Efforts to limit remuneration in the public sector might seem to point in the same direction of socialist control. But none of this, either individually or in total, adds up to socialism. Bangladesh is really a mixed economy, as are so many others.

In many ways the economy is falling between two stools. The system of controls has worked very badly. Perhaps in Bangladesh's first three very troubled years, this could scarcely have been otherwise. Difficulties with the balance of payments and violent increases in prices at a time when new institutions had to be established made it very difficult to administer the economy and plan effectively, for all plans in some measure assume a degree of continuity which has been wholly lacking. But there is much more to it than this. The system of controls being operated at present is different in detail from that operated in Pakistani days, but it is the same in principle and operated by people with similar outlooks.

In the first few years of the existence of Bangladesh, planning and controls have failed. It is probably true that once the international effort to restore the economy after the War of Independence was withdrawn, the economic system would have operated better without state intervention than it operated in fact under the system of government direction in force. Nowhere was the failure of controls more evident than in relation to imports. This sector has a major influence on the economy, imports corresponding to nearly one-fifth of gross domestic product; food imports meet the needs of one out of every five or six men, women and children in Bangladesh and also provide almost all the food for the rationing system. In conditions of food shortage on the scale of that in Bangladesh, government cannot abdicate from the control of imports but failure to do it properly has very serious consequences.

By arranging for the import of foodgrains, the government was able to support the real incomes of those living in towns. But in these areas it supported both the rich and the poor, those with plenty in hand as well as those who were destitute. It failed to follow up these measures with others that would have controlled the use of domestically produced rice. Procurement was a complete failure for no reasons that can easily be explained in economic terms. It was an unpopular measure; it impinged on the interests of the richer farmers, those with surpluses over and above their requirements who had sufficient reources to be able to send their rice to India, to move their capital abroad or to import goods which were in short supply either for their own use or to sell to others at a large profit.

Import controls are always difficult to administer. Bangladesh also had initially to contend with inexperience. Those responsible for importing commodities were asked to take over at short notice because others more accustomed to importing goods had fled the country. It is not surprising that imports languished for a long period. Eventually improvements were made to the administrative arrangements but it may take some years before the state machinery for importation can attain the efficiency of merchants activated by the profit motive.

The administrative arrangements for the import of commodities were designed in part deliberately to favour certain sections of the community. In some respects this is understandable. It was natural to wish to recognise the actions of the "freedom fighters" of the war with Pakistan and those who at considerable personal cost had helped the regime to establish itself against oppression and in war. But to put them in favoured positions, whether in relation to the provision of import licences or even employment, was not really the way to do it. Privilege is never easy to justify. The government has laid itself open to charges of manipulating the economy for the benefit of a few.

Although import controls must continue, they may have to be modified in various ways. Their tightness and severity depend very much on the extent of the scarcity of foreign exchange. Aid has continued to be furnished in generous amounts, and the flow of imports has increased; devaluation by raising prices has also helped to bring the demand for imports more closely into line with availability. If imports could be increased still further, it would be possible to operate controls more flexibly. With greater market freedom this would allow the creative energies of industrialists and agriculturalists to be directed to increasing production and exports.

In other sectors of economic and social development there has been too little government intervention. Population control must be exercised. This will not come about in the required time span without the firmest of government plans and measures being applied. Determining the size of a family in a real sense is a matter for individuals; but in the circumstances of Bangladesh government action is also needed. In its measures to control population, as in so many other things, Bangladesh is a soft state. It is true that there are programmes for the reduction of the birth rate, and that there is no shortage of quantified targets, but so far all efforts at population planning have failed. Such reductions of the birth rate as appear to have come about owe virtually nothing to the actions of the state. The effort to disseminate the view that birth rates can be reduced is almost certainly much less than it was. There are social as well as private costs. The social cost of a population increasing at the rate it is doing in Bangladesh is very great, and state programmes to reduce birth rate are indispensable. In Chapter VI we have suggested a number of measures which would help to reduce the birthrate. The Chinese approach to family planning is of special interest and may have some applicability to Bangladesh. In China there has been a conscious effort to mould social views against high birth rates and exert great social pressure to get individuals to accept population control in practice. Social change is also necessary in Bangladesh— to reduce birth rates, improve the status of women and mobilise communal efforts in the villages.

Indeed, more and more of the government's planning efforts need to be directed to the villages and to what can be done to preserve them; to improve them physically and to enliven them and remove some of the drabness out of living. In the circumstances of Bangladesh, town living is to be avoided. The squalor of towns with populations of 10 millions must not be repeated, or life in Bangladesh for many on small incomes will become unendurable. It should be possible to avoid the slums of Calcutta, but only if determined policies to this end are adopted. The weight of the development effort must be put into the countryside, into food production, and into improving the welfare of those in the villages, particularly those who do not command the means of production.

To give leadership in village communities is especially difficult. Arrangements for rural development have hung fire while politicians attempted to resolve their differences. There is still no sign that the strong administrative structures needed can be built or that local government can be developed in such a way as to bring about development at the grass roots. In the 1960s the rural works programme worked moderately well; it ought to be possible to reactivate it. Local development extends beyond bricks and mortar, *kutcha* roads, or drainage and irrigation schemes. There is a need to build up a momentum towards development from within the village itself. The Comilla pattern of integrated rural development which is being pursued may do something to get this going on a more extended scale, but it seems unlikely to work fast enough. One of the problems is that too much is expected from the government.

If government control has suppressed village incentive in some ways, more intervention may be needed in others to reactivate village life. The need for a reorientation of village education discussed in Chapter VIII is one of these. Others concern land use. Land will become increasingly scarce as it has to meet the needs of more people. Town and country planning, at present rudimentary, will be increasingly necessary; so will be the more efficient use of land in agriculture. By the end of the century, if present systems are continued, the need for reorganisation of the distribution of the land will become more apparent. The chances are that at that date there will be millions more landless labourers than at present, whose only livelihood will be seasonal and casual employment with wealthy landowners who have been able to take advantage of the new techniques to farm their land more efficiently and in the process to buy up their neighbours' land. Far from the distribution of income becoming better as development proceeds, it is likely to become much worse unless remedial measures are taken. It will be surprising if this does not give rise to a demand to nationalise the land. There is no doubt that land reform will be one of the major political and economic issues of Bangladesh for a long time ahead.

Adequate supplies of imports cannot be financed unless foreign aid of the order indicated in Chapter V is made available. Aid approaching $1,500 million annually is needed for decades if Bangladesh is to have real hope of overcoming its difficulties. Without aid the position would indeed be desperate. Earnings from jute and the few other goods that Bangladesh exports would scarcely do more than buy the imported food required to prevent starvation. Without aid the economy would collapse, and misery and degradation on a massive scale would ensue. It is possible that out of such a situation some form of new social order, perhaps communism, would emerge, although the outcome is unpredictable. In any case the cost of a social transformation by the route of deprivation would be very high in human terms and in terms of the savings in effort and assistance of affluent countries.

There is a path, as we have argued, that Bangladesh could follow to reach the goal of a stable population and a standard of living offering little in luxury but enough in meeting the fundamental requirements of life to make existence more than bearable. The path is narrow. Deviation from it could bring ruin to the inhabitants of Bangladesh and compel most of them to eke out their days inadequately fed and cared for. This can be avoided through the joint endeavours of Bangladesh and the international community. If development can be made to succeed in Bangladesh, there can be little doubt that it can be made to succeed anywhere else. It is in this sense that Bangladesh is the test case for development.

INDEX